ANALYSIS
OF
THYRISTOR
POWER-CONDITIONED
MOTORS

ANALYSIS OF THYRISTOR POWER-CONDITIONED MOTORS

S K Pillai
Professor
Department of Electrical Engineering
Indian Institute of Technology
Bombay

Universities Press

Universities Press (India) Private Limited

Registered Office
3-6-747/1/A & 3-6-754/1, Himayatnagar,
Hyderabad 500 029 (A.P.), India
e-mail: info@universitiespress.com

Distributed by
Orient Blackswan Private Limited

Registered Office
3-6-752, Himayatnagar, Hyderabad 500 029 (A.P.), India

Other Offices
Bangalore / Bhopal / Bhubaneshwar / Chennai
Ernakulam / Guwahati / Hyderabad / Jaipur / Kolkata
Lucknow / Mumbai / New Delhi / Patna

First published 1995
Reprinted 2003, 2005, 2008, 2010, 2013

ISBN: 978 81 7371 014 8

Typeset by
Jayigee Enterprises, Chennai 600 006

Printed in India at
Orion Printers Private Limited
Hyderabad 500 004

Published by
Universities Press (India) Private Limited
3-6-747/1/A & 3-6-754/1, Himayatnagar
Hyderabad 500 029 (A.P), India

Contents

Preface

During the last decade, a number of technical institutions in India have been offering a masters course in electrical engineering with power electronics as one of the specializations. This, of course, is in keeping with the rapid advances taking place both in semiconductor and signal electronics. Apart from other important subjects like modern semiconductor devices, analysis of power converters, microprocessors and microcomputers and digital control, Analysis of Power-Conditioned Motors is fundamental in formulating a good course in power electronics, since solid-state power-controlled variable-speed drives constitute a major industrial application for the power electronics engineer.

Essentially, the term 'analysis' when used with respect to power-conditioned motors implies predetermination of speed/torque characteristics of the motor during steady state and of variations in speed caused by sudden changes in either an electrical input variable to the motor, or in the load torque applied on the shaft of the motor. There are a very large number of papers published in technical journals on this subject. Besides, depending on their aim and scope, several books on power electronics also include an analysis of converter-controlled motors. But, for the student the most difficult problem is to choose the right book which, by presenting the basic method of analysis involving adequate simplifying assumptions on the parameters of both the motor and the power converter, could lay the foundation for a systematic study of the subject. If such literature were studied first, students could not only understand and assimilate subsequent papers on the topic, but could even point out the fallacies of certain assumptions made in those or new approaches to the analysis of power-conditioned motors.

This book has been written keeping these problems in view, to serve as a textbook for a first course in the Analysis of Power-Conditioned Motors. Only the basic and most simple method of analysis (that incorporates a large number of justifiable assumptions) of each one of the most commonly used power converter-controlled motors is described. No specific method is indicated for solving the performance equations governing the transient processes, since most of them have to be solved using only numerical techniques, and individuals have their own preference for a particular method. In order to complete the study, students must collect necessary data on converter and motor parameters from published papers or from technical reports, solve the performance equations corresponding to both steady state and desired transient conditions of the different types of power-conditioned motors and obtain the important characteristics of the drive system.

This textbook is more than adequate for a single-semester course for masters level students of power electronics. Much of the material is based on a course 'Thyristor-Controlled Drives' taught at the Indian Institute of Technology, Bombay.

S. K. PILLAI

Acknowledgements

While the choice of topics as well as the sequence and style in which the subject matter has been presented are my own, no originality is claimed for the technical contents of the book. In fact, I have drawn heavily on the scholarship and work of so many that even the list of references at the end of the book can only make a partial and obviously inadequate acknowledgement.

I would like to express my gratitude to the authorities of the I.I.T., Bombay for granting me an year's sabbatical leave for preparing the manuscript of this book, and to the Curriculum Development Cell of I.I.T., Bombay for giving me the necessary financial assistance to bring out the first version of this book. Grateful acknowledgement is due to the Institution of Engineers (India) for granting permission to use certain figures contained in references 4, 27, 28 and 29 published in their Electrical Engineering Division's journal. Thanks are also due to Mr Kunju Kunju who has done an excellent job of typing the manuscript and to Mr R.S. Patwardhan for transforming my rough sketches into neat illustrations. I also wish to thank the editorial staff at Universities Press for their interest and cooperation in bringing out this book. Last but not least, I wish to recognize and record the continuing support I get from my wife Vijaya and sons Sivan and Kumar.

S. K. PILLAI

List of symbols

We have endeavoured to use only the commonly accepted symbols for various quantities. In certain sections, however, for the purpose of clarity a different symbol may have been used for some quantities. If in doubt, please note carefully the context and the dimensions.

a	ratio of stator turns per phase to rotor turns per phase
B	coefficient of viscous friction, Nm/(rad/s)
E	average induced e.m.f. of d.c. motor, V
E_1	R.M.S. value of stator induced e.m.f., V
E_2	R.M.S. value of induced e.m.f. in the rotor at standstill condition, V
$E_{2\,max}$	maximum value of induced e.m.f. in the rotor at standstill condition, V
E_d	average value of voltage that appears on the d.c. side of an inverter, V
E_m	amplitude of sinusoidal supply voltage, V
E_u	voltage drop due to overlap of armature currents, V
e	instantaneous induced e.m.f. in d.c. armature, V
e_1, e_2	instantaneous values of voltage from sources 1 and 2, V
e_A, e_B, e_C	instantaneous values of induced e.m.f.s across stator phases A, B and C, V
f	supply frequency, Hz
f_1	stator supply frequency, Hz
f_2	frequency of rotor induced e.m.f., Hz
H	inertia instant, s
$I_{a\,max}$	maximum value of armature current, A
I_{av}	average value of armature current, A
I_d	average rectified current, A
I_m	magnetizing current, A
I_1	stator phase current, A
I_2	rotor phase current, A
I_2	rotor phase current referred to stator, A
i_D	instantaneous *d*-axis damper winding current, A
i_Q	instantaneous *q*-axis damper winding current, A
i_a	instantaneous value of armature current of d.c. motor, A
i_{a1}, i_{a2}	initial and final values of armature current during on-period of chopper, A
i_{ar}, i_{br}, i_{cr}	instantaneous rotor phase currents in a, b and c phases of a 3-phase machine, A
i_{as}, i_{bs}, i_{cs}	instantaneous stator phase currents in a, b and c phases of a 3-phase machine, A

i_c	instantaneous value of circulating current, A
i_d	instantaneous rectified current during duty interval, A
i_f	current during freewheeling interval, A
i_{f_1}	field current of synchronous motor, A
i_k	instantaneous value of commutating current, A
i_m	instantaneous value of current in magnetizing inductance, A
i_{1m}, $i_{1\psi}$	torque and flux-producing component space vectors of stator current space vector
i_α, i_β	instantaneous currents in α and β phase coils, A
$i_{\alpha r}$, $i_{\beta r}$	currents in rotor along α and β axes, A
$i_{\alpha s}$, $i_{\beta s}$	currents in stator along α and β axes, A
J	moment of inertia of the rotating parts of motor-load combinations, kg m^2
K_e	armature induced e.m.f. constant, V/rad/s) and motor torque constant, Nm/A
L	mean effective inductance, H
L_a	armature inductance, H
L_d, L_q	d-axis and q-axis stator self inductance, H
L''_d, L''_q	d-axis and q-axis subtransient inductances, H
L_F	filter inductance, H
L_T	total inductance of d.c. armature circuit, H
L_o	maximum value of effective inductance due to saliency, H
L_f (L_{fr})	inductance of the field winding, H
L_m	magnetizing inductance/phase, H
L_{af} (M)	maximum value of mutual inductance between a stator phase and field winding, H
L_{dr}, L_{qr}	d-axis and q-axis self inductances of rotor/phase, H
L_{ls} (L_1), L_{lr} (L_2)	stator and rotor leakage inductance/phase, H
L_{md}	d-axis magnetizing inductance/phase and mutual inductance between field and d-axis damper winding, H
L_{mq}	q-axis magnetizing inductance/phase H
L_{rm}	mutual inductance between rotor phases, H
L_{sm}	mutual inductance between stator phases, H
L_{add}	maximum value of mutual inductance between a stator phase and d-axis damper winding, H
L_{aqd}	maximum value of mutual inductance between a stator phase and q-axis damper winding, H
M	mutual inductance between filter chokes, H
M_{af}	mutual inductance between armature and field of a.d.c. motor, H
m	number of phases
n	order of harmonic
P	number of poles
P_{mech}	mechanical power developed by the motor, W
P_{ph}	power per phase, W
p	$\frac{d}{dt}$ operator

R_F	resistance of filter, Ω
R_a	resistance of armature of d.c. motor, Ω
R_f (R_{fr})	resistance of field, Ω
R_r (R_2), R_s (R_1)	resistance of rotor and stator/phase, Ω
R_{dr}, R_{qr}	*d*-axis and *q*-axis rotor (damper) resistance, Ω
R_{ex}	external resistance, Ω
S.M.	synchronous motor
S.R.M.	switched-reluctance motor
S.R.I.M.	slip-ring induction motor
s	slip
s_0	no-load slip
s_n	slip corresponding to the rotating field created by *n*th harmonic currents
T_l	load torque, Nm
T_e	electromagnetic torque developed, Nm
t	time, s
t_1, t_2, t_3 and t_p	time for on-period, off-period, zero-current period and total period of chopper, s
t_{off}	turn-off time of SCR, s
V	voltage applied to the motor, V
V_I (V_{di})	input d.c. voltage to the inverter, V
V_R (V_d or V_{dr})	average rectified output d.c. voltage, V
V_{Lm}	maximum value of a.c. line-voltage, V
V_b	counter e.m.f. produced by the inverter, V
V_f	voltage across the field winding, V
V_m	maximum value of a.c. source phase voltage, V
V_t	terminal voltage, V
V_{tl}	fundamental terminal voltage, V
V_1, V_2	R.M.S. values of phase voltages of stator and rotor, V
V_{1m}, V_{2m}	maximum values of phase voltages of stator and rotor, V
V	instantaneous value of applied voltage, V
V_A (V_{as}), V_B (V_{bs}), V_C (V_{cs})	applied instantaneous phase voltages across stator phases A(a), B(b) and C(c), V
V_a	instantaneous value of voltage across the armature of a d.c. motor, V
$v_{\alpha s}$, $v_{\beta s}$	instantaneous stator phase voltages along α and β axes, V
$V_{\alpha r}$, $V_{\beta r}$	instantaneous rotor phase voltages along α and β axes, V
X_F	reactance of filter, Ω
X_M	magnetizing reactance/phase, Ω
X_a	reactance of the armature of the d.c. motor, Ω
X_{lr} (X_2), X_{ls} (X_1)	leakage reactance of rotor and stator/phase, Ω
X_{rr}, X_{ss}	self-reactances of rotor and stator/phase, Ω
X_d, X_q	*d*-axis and *q*-axis self-reactances of stator, Ω

X_{dr}, X_{qr}	d-axis and q-axis self-reactances of rotor, Ω
X_{fr}	self-reactance of field winding, Ω
X_{md}, X_{mq}	d-axis and q-axis magnetizing reactances, Ω
α	firing angle of converter/inverter, rad
α_N, α_P	firing angle of negative and positive converters of a dual converter, rad
α_1	angle between stator current space vector and stator flux-linkage space vector, rad
α_2	angle between stator current space vector and rotor flux-linkage space vector, rad
β	angle at which armature current becomes zero, angle between stator and rotor m.m.f.s, rad
γ	angle at which supply voltage becomes equal to the induced e.m.f. of d.c. motor, rad
γ_o	firing angle of the inverter, rad
δ	angle at which armature current reaches its maximum value, rad; torque angle, rad; duty cycle of chopper
θ	angle of rotor position, rad
θ_k	angle between real axes of a reference frame rotating at speed ω_k and stationary reference frame, rad
$\theta_n\ (\phi_n)$	phase angle corresponding to the nth harmonic, rad
μ	angle of commutation overlap, rad
σ_d, σ_q	direct and quadrature axis leakage coefficient
τ	time-constant, s
Φ	magnetic flux/pole, Wb
ψ_t	total flux-linkage associated with the field winding, Wb-Turn
ψ_l, ψ_m	flux-linkages due to leakage and mutual flux, Wb-Turn
ψ_t	component of flux spacor perpendicular to stator current space vector i_1
ψ_{dd}, ψ_{qd}	total flux-linkages of d-axis and q-axis damper windings, Wb-Turn
ψ_{ds}, ψ_{qs}	stator flux-linkages along d-axis and q-axis, Wb-Turn
ψ_{ddo}, ψ_{qdo}	flux-linkages of d-axis and q-axis damper windings due to armature currents and damper currents, Wb-Turn
ψ_1, ψ_2	total flux-linkages associated with the stator, rotor, Wb-Turn
Ω	speed of rotation, mech. rad/s
ω	angular frequency of supply voltage, rad/s
ω_b	base angular frequency, rad/s
ω_k	angular speed of an arbitrary reference frame, rad/s
$\omega_s\ (\omega_1)$	synchronous speed, rad/s
ω_r	rotor speed, rad/s

Note ′and ¯ marked above many electrical quantities indicate that they are rotor quantities referred to the stator, and quantities expressed in space vectors respectively.

1 Phase-controlled converter-fed d.c. motors

Single-phase and three-phase natural-commutated controlled rectifiers (converters) are used in variable-speed drive systems to supply an adjustable d.c. voltage either to the armature of the drive motor or its field, or both. In each of these types half-wave, full-wave but half-controlled (semi), full-wave fully-controlled and dual converters are used depending upon the amount of power handled and the application requirement (e.g., reversible or non-reversible regeneration, quick response). The single-phase, half-wave and the full-wave, half-controlled converters allow only a positive d.c. voltage and unidirectional motor current. Fully-controlled and dual converters can both facilitate regeneration, i.e. the polarity of the voltage across the motor may be reversed. However, the current of the full-wave, fully-controlled converter is unidirectional. It is possible to change the connection of the full-wave, fully-controlled converter to the motor and hence reverse the direction of current flow through the motor, but current flow in both directions may be easily obtained with a dual converter. Therefore, dual converters are widely used in variable-speed drives in which the motor is required to rotate in both directions, as in rolling mills or crane-type mechanisms. For applications requiring a motive power over 20 kW, three-phase converters are often used as power sources.

1.1 Single-Phase, Half-Wave Converter-Fed d.c. Motor

Figure 1.1 is a schematic diagram of a simple controlled rectifier operating with a separately-excited d.c. motor.

Figure 1.1 Schematic diagram of a converter-fed separately-excited d.c. motor.

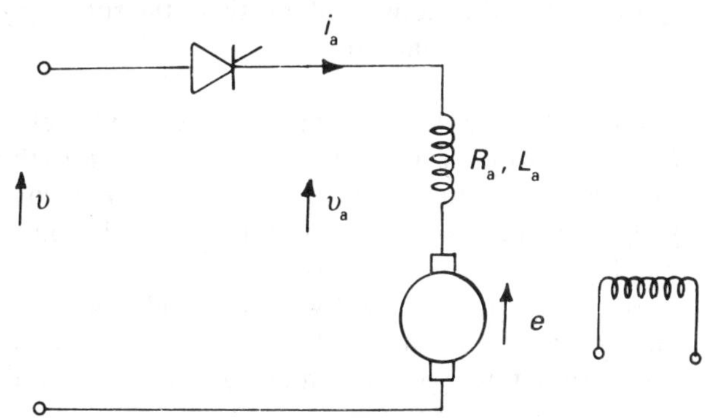

The following simplifying assumptions are made while analysing the steady-state performance of such a drive system.

(i) The silicon-controlled rectifier (SCR) is an ideal switch, that is, the voltage drop across the terminals is assumed to be zero when current flows through it, and its resistance infinite when there is no current passing through it.
(ii) The resistance and inductance of the motor armature are constant.
(iii) The field current is constant.
(iv) Effects of armature reaction, magnetic saturation and voltage drop at the brushes are negligible.
(v) The impedance of the single-phase a.c. source is trivial and, hence, commutation overlap is insignificant.

The equations that govern the performance of the drive system are as given below:

$$v_a = i_a R_a + L_a \frac{di_a}{dt} + e \qquad [1.1]$$

$$e = K_e \Phi \Omega \qquad [1.2]$$

$$T_e = K_e \Phi i_a \qquad [1.3]$$

$$T_e = J \frac{d\Omega}{dt} + T_L \qquad [1.4]$$

where v_a = the voltage across the armature of the motor,
i_a = the armature current,
R_a and L_a = the resistance and the inductance of the armature circuit including those of any filter inserted in series,
e = the emf induced,
K_e = the constant of proportionality for the e.m.f.,
Φ = the magnetic flux,
Ω = the angular speed of rotation (mechanical radians/second)
T_e = the electromagnetic torque developed by the motor,
T_L = the load torque, and
J = the moment of inertia of the rotating parts of the motor-load combination.

Figure 1.2 shows the variation of the supply voltage v (= $V_m \sin \omega t$), v_a, i_a, e and Ω with respect to time. α corresponds to the instant of firing of the SCR; β corresponds to the instant at which i_a becomes zero; γ corresponds to the instant at which the supply voltage becomes equal to the induced e.m.f. e; and δ corresponds to the instant when i_a reaches its maximum value[1].

Since we are concerned with a periodic process, it will be adequate to analyze the events during the interval $0 \leqslant \omega t \leqslant 2\pi$, which in turn will be divided into three parts depending on the period of conduction of the SCR[2].

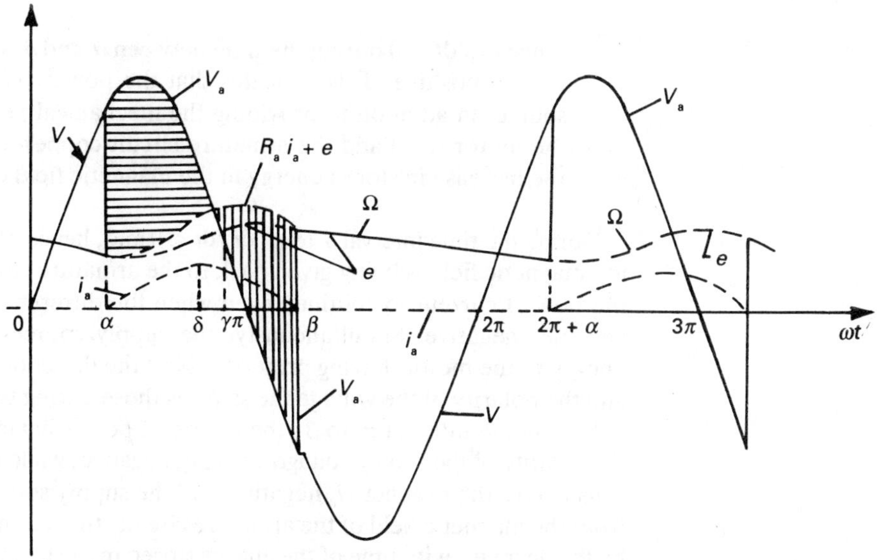

Figure 1.2 Variation of v, v_a, i_a, e and Ω with respect to time.

(1) **Time interval $0 \leqslant \omega t \leqslant \alpha$** The SCR can start conducting at α only when a firing pulse is applied to its gate. Hence, during this interval, the SCR is 'off' and $i_a = 0$. From eqn [1.1] it follows that $v_a = e$, which varies directly with Ω. Ω is not equal to zero due to the kinetic energy stored by the armature during the preceding running condition of the motor. Since $i_a = 0$, T_e is also equal to zero. Hence, Ω gradually decreases due to the braking effect caused by the load torque.

(2) **Time interval $\alpha \leqslant \omega t \leqslant \beta$** The SCR is triggered at α. If v is higher than e at this instant, current will start flowing in the SCR. v_a immediately becomes equal to v, but i_a cannot rise suddenly due to L_a. The current gradually increases, reaching a maximum value after which it starts decreasing, since v tends to zero at π and becomes negative in the interval $\pi \leqslant \omega t < 2\pi$. Although the difference between v and e becomes negative beyond γ, current will continue to flow through the motor armature because of the energy stored in the magnetic field of the armature winding. Let β, the time angle when i_a becomes zero and the SCR no longer conducts, be assumed to be greater than π. Between the instants α and δ, energy is stored in the magnetic field of the armature circuit. The fact that this energy obviously comes from the supply can be seen from the expression

$$v i_a = i_a^2 R_a + e i_a + \frac{d}{dt}\left(\tfrac{1}{2} L_a i_a^2\right) \qquad [1.5]$$

which is nothing but eqn [1.1] multiplied by i_a.

$$\frac{d}{dt}\left(\tfrac{1}{2} L_a i_a^2\right) = L_a i_a \frac{di_a}{dt} \qquad [1.6]$$

Since $di_a/dt > 0$ during the time between α and δ, the above quantity will be positive. This indicates that the power (vi_a) supplied by the source, in addition to providing the mechanical power developed by the motor ($e\ i_a$) and the armature circuit copper losses ($i_a^2\ R_a$), gives the increase in stored energy in the magnetic field of the armature.

During the time interval δ to π, $di_a/dt < 0$ and, hence, the stored energy in the magnetic field is being given back to the armature circuit, thus enabling the flow of current to continue even when the difference between v and e becomes negative. Simultaneously, the supply source continues to feed energy to the motor, having preserved both the direction of flow of current and the polarity of the voltage the same as those during the interval α to δ.

During the interval π to β, the nature of power balance changes again; the polarity of the supply voltage becomes negative, while i_a remains positive. This makes the product vi_a negative, i.e. the supply source receives energy from the magnetic field of the armature circuit. In fact, the power produced by the decrease with time of the energy stored in the magnetic field provides both the mechanical power developed by the motor and the copper losses in the armature circuit, until the current decreases to zero.

Let us now observe the effect of integrating eqn [1.1] over intervals α to δ and then δ to β.

$$\int_{\alpha}^{\delta} [v - (R_a i_a + e)]\,d(\omega t) = \omega \int_{0}^{Ia\ max} L_a di_a = \omega L_a I_{a\ max} \qquad [1.7]$$

$$\int_{\delta}^{\beta} [v - (R_a i_a + e)]\,d(\omega t) = \omega \int_{Ia\ max}^{0} L_a di_a = -\omega L_a I_{a\ max} \qquad [1.8]$$

(Note that i_a has decreased from $I_{a\ max}$ to zero during the interval δ to β).

The integral on the left-hand side of eqn [1.7] represents the area of the surface horizontally shaded in Fig. 1.2. Its upper boundary is the variation of v with respect to ωt and the lower boundary is that of ($R_a\ i_a + e$) with respect to ωt during the interval α to δ. The similar integral in eqn [1.8] represents the vertically shaded area. As indicated by the right-hand side terms of eqns [1.7] and [1.8], the two areas are equal and proportional to the maximum value of the current attained by the armature circuit at the instant δ.

The electromagnetic torque developed by the motor during the interval $\alpha \leqslant \omega t \leqslant \beta$ is positive since i_a is positive. When $T_e > T_L$, the armature speed increases, building up kinetic energy in the rotating parts of the motor and the load. This energy will be consumed when $T_e < T_L$.

(3) **Time interval $\beta \leqslant \omega t < 2\pi$** During this period, the SCR is 'off'; i_a and, hence, T_e is zero. v_a is equal to e, which gradually decreases since it is directly proportional to Ω. The situation is similar to that existing during the time interval $0 \leqslant \omega t \leqslant \alpha$.

1.1.1 *Predetermination of Speed/Torque Characteristics*

The steady-state speed/torque curve of the drive can be determined by considering the average values of v_a, i_a and T_e over a whole period of the a.c. source voltage . Equation [1.1] when integrated over a full period, with all terms divided by 2π, becomes

$$\frac{1}{2\pi}\int_{\alpha}^{\beta} v_a \, d(\omega t) = \frac{R_a}{2\pi}\int_{\alpha}^{\beta} i_a \, d(\omega t) + \frac{\omega L_a}{2\pi}\int_{\alpha}^{\beta} di_a + \frac{1}{2\pi}\int_{0}^{2\pi} e \, d(\omega t) \quad [1.9]$$

Each term of eqn [1.9] except the inductance term, which becomes zero because the values of the current at the limits of integration remain the same, may be interpreted as average values leading to the expression

$$V_{av} = I_{av} R_a + E_{av} \quad [1.10]$$

where

$$E_{av} = K_e \Phi \, \Omega_{av} \text{ or } K\Omega_{av}$$

Equation [1.3] averaged over a whole period will become

$$T_{e\,av} = K_e \Phi \, I_{av} \text{ or } KI_{av} \quad [1.11]$$

Equations [1.10] and [1.11] indicate that the relationship between the average speed and average torque is given in terms of average motor voltage and average current, just as for a d.c. motor operated from a conventional, fixed direct-voltage source. However, it is not as simple to predict the speed/torque curve as in the case of the latter, since V_{av} is not an independent variable. It depends both on α and β and even for a given firing angle, β, the angle at which the SCR stops conducting, can be found only by trial and error after solving the differential equation

$$V_m \sin\omega t = R_a i_a + L_a \frac{di_a}{dt} + K_e \Phi \, \Omega_{av} \quad \text{for } i_a$$

taking the initial condition (that is, the value of current $\omega t = \alpha$) to be zero.

1.1.2 *Influence of a Freewheeling Diode Across Motor Armature*

As seen earlier, during the interval π to β, a portion of the energy stored in the magnetic field is fed back into the a.c. source. If this energy were to be used in the armature circuit so as to extend the flow of i_a beyond β instead of returning to the network, it would be possible to make $I_{a\,max}$ smaller for the same load current or average current. This would result in a lower root-mean-square (r.m.s.) value and, hence, the form-factor of the armature current. A simple method to achieve the above objective is to connect a freewheeling diode across the armature circuit as shown in Fig. 1.3. Until v is positive and the SCR is 'on', the diode remains 'off' and the polarity of

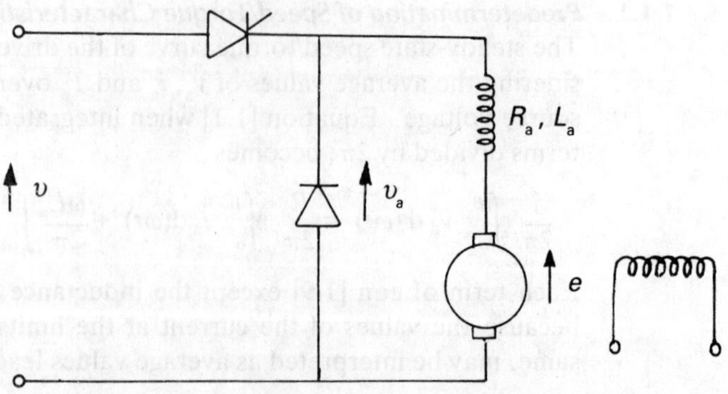

Figure 1.3 Freewheeling diode connected across armature of d.c. motor.

the voltage across it is opposite to that required for conduction. At $\omega t = \pi$, v changes its polarity and the diode starts conducting. Thus, it offers a path for the flow of current i_a, which no longer passes through the SCR, thereby switching it off. The current continues to take this path till the energy stored in the magnetic field is consumed.

Figure 1.4 shows the nature of variation of v, v_a, i_a, e and Ω with respect to time during steady-state operation. α, δ and β still satisfy the condition of equal areas stipulated by eqns. [1.7] and [1.8].

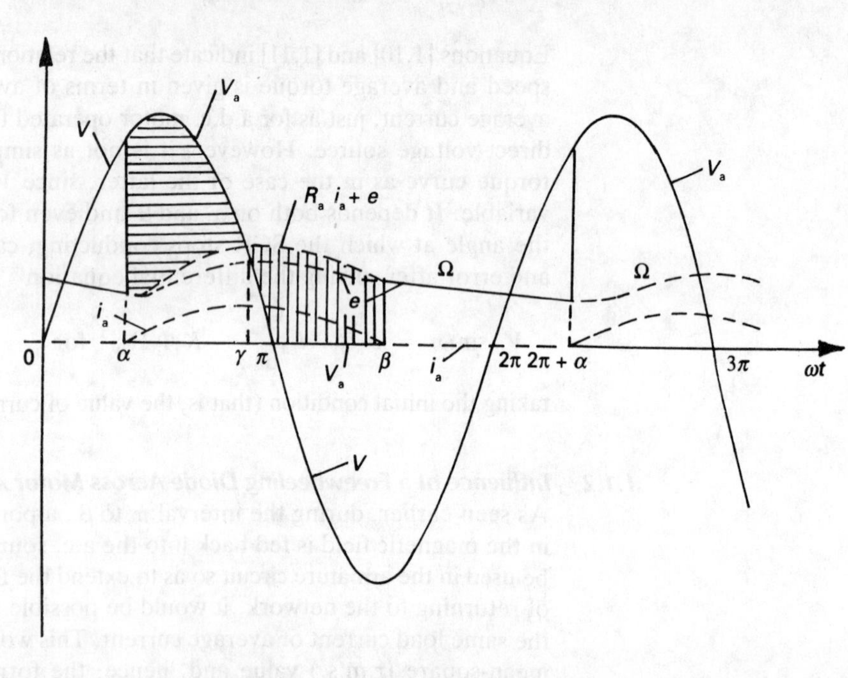

Figure 1.4 Variation of v, v_a, i_a, e, and Ω with respect to time during operation with freewheeling diode.

It can be seen that the current flowing in the armature winding of the motor is zero during the interval β to $(2\pi + \alpha)$ in both the above-mentioned schemes. The circuit is said to have discontinuous conduction. The conduction is termed continuous when there is no zero-current interval present. Continuous conduction does not normally occur in single-phase, half-wave rectification. It can take place only when the motor is subjected to a heavy load torque and an inductor of large value is inserted in the armature circuit.

In spite of their simplicity and low cost, single-phase, half-wave converters are rarely used due to the disadvantages listed below.

(i) The form-factor of the armature current is quite high. Hence, for the same load torque (average current) the armature copper losses in the motor would be large.
(ii) The secondary winding of the transformer, introduced between the supply and the motor to adjust the rectified voltage of the motor to the rated voltage, will carry a pulsating current consisting of a significant d.c. component that saturates the magnetic circuit.
(iii) The oscillations in speed of rotation of the armature are considerable, since energy is fed in one pulse per period only. The motor operation can even be jerky at low speeds with heavy load torques.

1.2 Single-Phase, Full-Wave Bridge Converter-Fed d.c. Motor

The full-wave, phase-controlled converter, obviously, has a better form-factor for the load current than its half-wave counterpart. Between the two basic configurations used for full-wave converters, the bridge-type is preferred since, for the same voltage output, the centre-tapped converter has to block twice the a.c. supply voltage. These bridge converters can either be half-controlled or fully-controlled. While the former can operate only as a rectifier as the firing angle changes from zero to $\pi/2$ radians, the latter can function also in the inverting mode, when the firing angle is varied from $\pi/2$ to π radians. Consequently, the half-controlled converter is known as a single-quadrant converter and the fully-controlled one is called a two-quadrant converter. Both these types of full-wave converters are widely used in industry for controlling the speed of d.c. separately-excited motors, which have comparatively low armature inductance. Moreover, the motor back-e.m.f. is independent of load current and discontinous armature-current conduction, invariably, occurs at high-speed and light-load conditions. Hence, the load current, in general, can be either continuous or discontinuous. In the case of continuous current conduction, the load-voltage waveform comprises only portions of the a.c. source-voltage waveform and, hence, the average value of the voltage across the motor armature is dependent only upon the converter firing angles and can easily be obtained. The determination of the speed/torque characteristic is quite simple in this case. But, in the case of discontinuous conduction, the load-voltage waveform and, hence, its mean value depends upon the firing angles, motor back-e.m.f. and the phase angle of the impedance of the armature circuit. Various types of load-voltage waveforms arise depending upon the firing angle and the parameters of the motor circuit. These are known as modes of operation. The voltage/current relationships required to determine the performance of the motor are different for different modes of operation. Hence, in order to predetermine the speed/torque characterisitics of the full-wave bridge converter-fed motor, a prior knowledge of the different modes of operation is essential.

1.2.1 Steady-State Performance

Figure 1.5 shows the basic circuit of a full-wave converter-controlled separately-excited d.c. motor. While the scheme as shown is for fully-controlled operation, half-controlled operation can be achieved simply by connecting a freewheeling diode across the motor armature terminals.

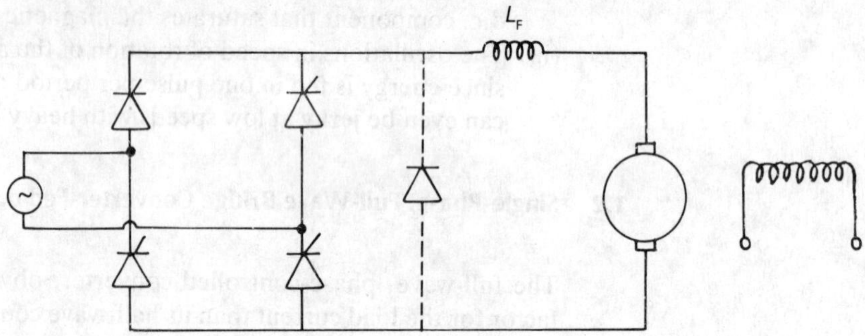

Figure 1.5 Basic circuit of a full-wave, converter-controlled separately-excited d.c. motor.

For the purpose of steady-state analysis, in addition to the assumptions listed in Section 1.1, it is assumed that

(i) the diode is also an ideal switch,
(ii) the motor speed is constant during steady state, and
(iii) the firing circuit for the SCRs provides a continuous string of pulses from α to π.

Both fully-controlled and half-controlled converter-fed d.c. motors have four different modes of operation depending upon the instants of firing and extinction of the SCRs. Typical waveforms of v, v_a, E and i_a corresponding to different modes[3,4] are shown in Figs. 1.6 and 1.7.

Mode 1

The load current is continuous. Hence the SCRs can be triggered at any angle α irrespective of whether it is less than or greater than the angle γ at which the instantaneous value of the source voltage is equal to the motor back-e.m.f. E. Figures 1.6a and 1.7a represent this mode for fully-controlled and half-controlled converter operation respectively.

Mode 2

In this mode (Figs. 1.6b and 1.7b), the armature current falls to zero before

Figure 1.6 Waveforms of v, v_a, E and i_a corresponding to four modes of operation of a fully-controlled converter-fed motor.

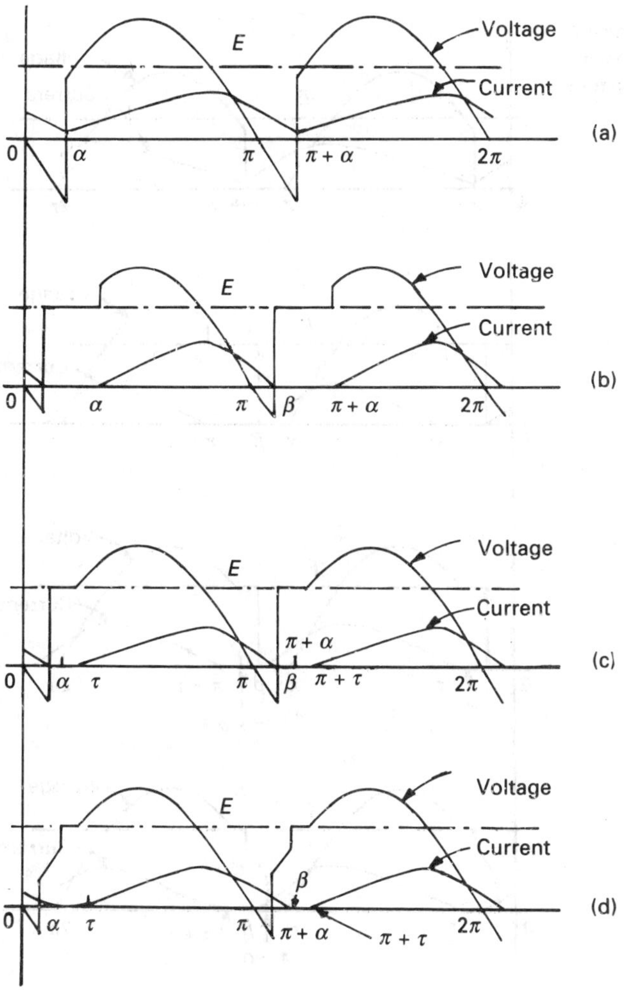

the next SCR is gated, i.e. the current is discontinuous in nature. The back-e.m.f. acts as a reverse bias on the SCR to be triggered and, hence, the earliest instant at which the SCR can be gated is γ. Thus, the firing angle α will be $> \gamma$.

Mode 3

During this mode, the firing angle $\alpha < \gamma$. The load current is discontinuous and has become zero before α, i.e. β, the angle at which the current becomes zero, will be less than $(\pi + \alpha)$. Therefore, the SCRs start conducting only at γ (Figs. 1.6c and 1.7c).

Mode 4

In this mode also, the firing angle $\alpha < \gamma$ and the load current is discontinuous; but it has not yet become zero at α. The motor back-e.m.f.

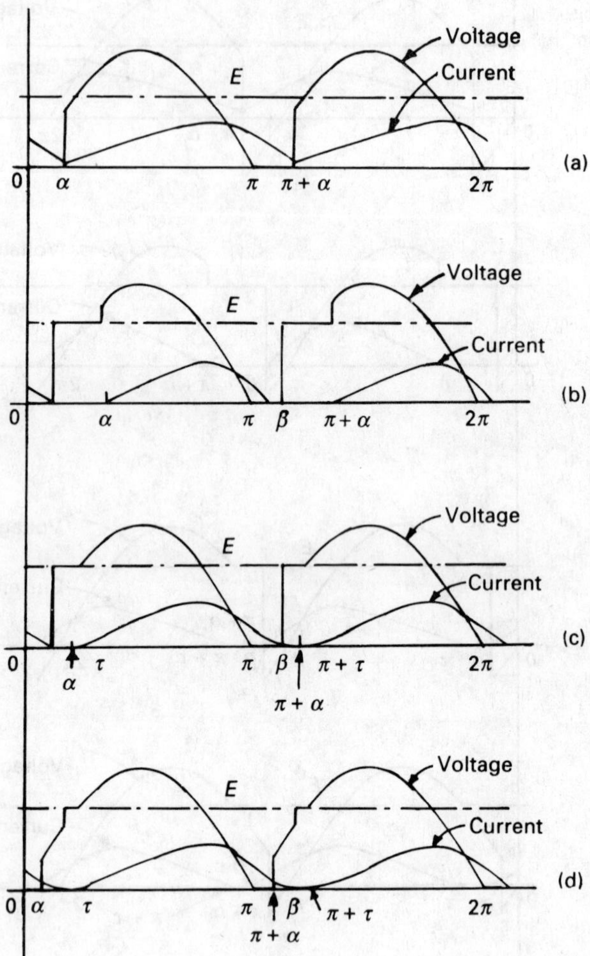

Figure 1.7 Waveforms of v, v_a, E and i_a corresponding to four modes of operation of a half-controlled converter-fed motor.

does not act as a reverse bias on the SCR to be triggered, as long as a current is flowing in the armature circuit. Therefore, the SCRs which are triggered at α start conducting. But, since the instantaneous supply voltage is less than the motor back-e.m.f., the armature current reduces and becomes zero at $\beta < \gamma$. At γ, the SCRs start conducting again and the armature current builds up (Figs. 1.6d and 1.7d).

The converter will operate satisfactorily in modes 2, 3 and 4 only if the triggering circuit for SCRs were to provide either a string of pulses from α to π or a wide pulse of adequate duration.

1.2.1.1 *Voltage/current relationships in different modes*

The generalized voltage/current relationship is expressed in the form

$$bV_m \sin \omega t = L_a \frac{di_a}{dt} + R_a i_a + E \qquad [1.12]$$

where variable b may assume the values 1, 0 or -1 depending on the mode of operation of fully-controlled or half-controlled converters.

1.2.1.2 Predetermination of speed/torque curve of fully-controlled converter-fed motor

Mode 1

$b = +1$ for $\alpha \leqslant \omega t \leqslant (\pi + \alpha)$

Taking the average over the half-cycle and bearing in mind that the average voltage across L_a will be zero, the average value of the armature current is given by

$$I_{av} = \frac{2/\pi V_m \cos \alpha - K\Omega_{av}}{R_a} \qquad [1.13]$$

At a given speed (Ω_{av}), for a particular firing angle (α), I_{av} is calculated from eqn [1.13], and $T_{e\,av}$ is obtained from eqn [1.11]. The instantaneous current variation is obtained by solving eqn [1.12] with $b = +1$ for $\alpha \leqslant \omega t \leqslant (\pi + \alpha)$ and is expressed as

$$i_a(\omega t) = I_m [\sin(\omega t - \psi) - \frac{2 \sin(\alpha - \psi) \exp\{-\cot \psi\,(\omega t - \alpha)\}}{1 - \exp(-\cot \psi)(\pi)}] - I \qquad [1.14]$$

where

$\psi = \tan^{-1}(\omega L_a/R_a)$ and
$I = E/R_a$

Mode 2

$b = +1$ for $\alpha \leqslant \omega t \leqslant \beta$, where $\beta \leqslant (\pi + \alpha)$

Taking the average value over the half-cycle and noting that

(i) the induced e.m.f. acts as the voltage applied across the motor terminals from β to $(\pi + \alpha)$ and
(ii) the average voltage across L_a is zero, we have

$$\frac{1}{\pi} \int_a^{\beta} V_m \sin \omega t \, d(\omega t) + \frac{E}{\pi}[(\pi + \alpha) - \beta] = E + R_a I_{av}$$

i.e.

$$\frac{V_m}{\pi}(\cos \alpha - \cos \beta) = E\frac{(\beta - \alpha)}{\pi} + R_a I_{av}$$

Therefore

$$I_{av} = \frac{V_m(\cos \alpha - \cos \beta) - E(\beta - \alpha)}{\pi R_a} \qquad [1.15]$$

I_{av} can be calculated if β were known. β can be determined as given below.

The solution of eqn [1.12] taking the initial condition to be zero (due to the discontinuous nature of current conduction, the initial value of current during this mode is zero) is expressed as

$$i_a(\omega t) = I_m [\sin(\omega t - \psi) - \sin(\alpha - \psi) \exp(x)] - I [1 - \exp(x)] \qquad [1.16]$$

where

$$I_m = \frac{V_m}{\sqrt{R_a^2 + \omega^2 L_a^2}}$$

$$x = -\cot \psi \, (\omega t - \alpha).$$

β can be calculated from eqn [1.16] by trial and error so as to satisfy the condition of the current falling to zero at β. Once β is known, I_{av} can be obtained from eqn [1.15]. $T_{e\,av}$, then, can be found from eqn [1.11].

Mode 3

$b = +1$ for $\gamma \leqslant \omega t \leqslant \beta$, where $\beta \leqslant (\pi + \alpha)$.

Since the SCRs start conducting only at γ, and the armature current is zero before and remains zero upto γ, the expression for I_{av} is the same as eqn [1.15], with γ replacing α.

Taking the initial condition to be zero owing to discontinuity, the solution of eqn [1.12] yields

$$\begin{aligned} i_a(\omega t) = I_m & [\sin(\omega t - \psi) - \sin(\gamma - \psi) \exp\{-\cot \psi \, (\omega t - \gamma)\}] \\ & - I [1 - \exp\{-\cot \psi \, (\omega t - \gamma)\}] \end{aligned} \qquad [1.17]$$

β can be found by trial and error using eqn [1.17] and, therefore, I_{av} and T_{av} can be determined.

Mode 4

$b = +1$ for $\gamma \leqslant \omega t \leqslant (\pi + \alpha)$

$b = -1$ for $(\pi + \alpha) \leqslant \omega t \leqslant \beta$

Taking the average value over the half-cycle and noting that

(i) during the period between $(\pi + \gamma)$ and β the induced e.m.f. acts as the voltage applied across the motor terminals, and
(ii) the average voltage across L_a is zero, we get

$$\frac{1}{\pi}\left[\int_{\gamma}^{(\pi+\alpha)} V_m \sin \omega t \, d(\omega t) + \int_{(\pi+\alpha)}^{\beta} - V_m \sin \omega t \, d(\omega t)\right]$$

$$+ \frac{E}{\pi}(\pi + \gamma - \beta) = E + I_{av} \cdot R_a$$

i.e.

$$\frac{V_m}{\pi}(2\cos\alpha + \cos\gamma + \cos\beta) = \frac{\beta-\gamma}{\pi}E + I_{av}\cdot R_a \quad [1.18]$$

I_{av} can be found if β were known. In order to determine β, the time-angle at which the armature current becomes zero, it is necessary to know the solution of i_a for the generalized voltage/current relationship when $b = -1$. This solution is of the form

$$\begin{aligned} i_a(\omega t) = I_m\,[&-2\sin(\alpha-\psi)\exp\{-\cot\psi\,(\omega t-\pi-\alpha)\} \\ &-\sin(\gamma-\psi)\exp\{-\cot\psi\,(\omega t-\gamma)\} \\ &-\sin(\omega t-\psi)] - I\,[1-\exp\{-\cot\psi\,(\omega t-\gamma)\}] \end{aligned} \quad [1.19]$$

1.2.1.3 Speed/torque curve of half-controlled converter-fed d.c. motor

Mode 1

The current is continuous in nature.

$$b = +1 \text{ for } \alpha \leqslant \omega t \leqslant \pi$$

and

$$b = 0 \text{ for } \pi \leqslant \omega t \leqslant (\pi+\alpha)$$

Taking the average over the half-cycle and keeping in mind that the average voltage across L_a is zero, we have

$$\frac{1}{\pi}\int_{\alpha}^{\pi} V_m \sin\omega t\, d(\omega t) = E + I_{av} R_a$$

i.e.

$$\frac{V_m}{\pi}(1+\cos\alpha) = E + I_{av}\cdot R_a$$

Therefore

$$I_{av} = \frac{(V_m/\pi)(1+\cos\alpha) - E}{R_a} \quad [1.20]$$

Hence, T_{av} for a particular firing angle and speed of rotation can be calculated easily.

In case one is interested in knowing the instantaneous variation of current during this mode, the solutions of the differential equation governing the voltage/current relationship corresponding to the two different intervals of operation must be found. They are of the form given below.

For the condition $b = +1$ $(\alpha \leqslant \omega t \leqslant \pi)$,

$$\begin{aligned} i_a(\omega t) = I_m\,[&\sin(\omega t-\psi) + \{\sin\psi\exp(-\cot\psi\cdot\alpha) \\ &-\sin(\alpha-\psi)\}\exp\{-\cot\psi\,(\omega t-\alpha)\}/ \\ &\{1-\exp(-\cot\psi\cdot\pi)\}] - I \end{aligned} \quad [1.21]$$

For the condition $b = 0$ $(\pi \leqslant \omega t \leqslant \pi + \alpha)$,

$$i_a(\omega t) = I_m [\sin\psi - \sin(\alpha-\psi)\exp\{-\cot\psi\cdot(\pi-\alpha)\}] \exp\{-\cot\psi\,(\omega t-\pi)\}/\{1-\exp(-\cot\psi\,.\,\pi)\} - I \qquad [1.22]$$

Mode 2

The conduction is discontinuous in nature.

$b = +1$ for $\alpha \leqslant \omega t \leqslant \pi$
$b = 0$ for $\pi \leqslant \omega t \leqslant \beta$

where $\pi < \beta < (\pi + \alpha)$

Taking the average over the half-cycle and noting that

(i) the induced e.m.f. acts as the voltage across the motor terminals during the time-interval β to $(\pi + \alpha)$, and
(ii) the average voltage across L_a is zero, we get

$$\frac{1}{\pi}\int_{\alpha}^{\pi} V_m \sin\omega t\, d(\omega t) + \frac{E}{\pi}[(\pi+\alpha)-\beta] = E + I_{av}R_a$$

i.e.

$$\frac{V_m}{\pi}(1+\cos\alpha) = E\cdot\frac{(\beta-\alpha)}{\pi} + I_{av}\cdot R_a$$

Hence

$$I_{av} = \frac{V_m/\pi\,(1+\cos\alpha) - E\cdot\dfrac{(\beta-\alpha)}{\pi}}{R_a} \qquad [1.23]$$

I_{av} can be calculated if β were to be known. β can be determined as given below.

Taking the initial condition to be zero owing to discontinuity of load current, the solution of eqn [1.12] for $b = +1$ $(\alpha \leqslant \omega t \leqslant \pi)$ is given by eqn [1.16]. The initial value of the current during the time-interval π to β is found by substituting $\omega t = \pi$ in eqn [1.16]. With this as the initial condition, the solution of eqn [1.12] for $b = 0$ is obtained as

$$i_a(\omega t) = I_m[\sin\psi\exp\{-\cot\psi\,(\omega t-\pi)\} - \sin(\alpha-\psi)\exp\{-\cot\psi\,(\omega t-\alpha)\}] - I[1-\exp\{-\cot\psi\,(\omega t-\alpha)\}] \qquad [1.24]$$

where $\pi \leqslant \omega t \leqslant \beta$. The value of β can now be determined by calculating the time, angle ωt which would give a zero value for the right-hand side of eqn [1.24].

Mode 3

$b = +1$ for $\gamma \leqslant \omega t \leqslant \pi$
$b = 0$ for $\pi \leqslant \omega t \leqslant \beta$

I_{av} can be calculated in a manner almost similar to that indicated for mode 2, bearing in mind that in this mode the SCRs start conducting only at γ, although they are triggered earlier at α. The load current has become zero even before α.

$$I_{av} = \frac{V_m/\pi\,(1+\cos\gamma) - E\cdot(\overline{\beta-\gamma}/\pi)}{R_a} \qquad [1.25]$$

The solution of eqn [1.12] for the condition $b = +1$ ($\gamma \leqslant \omega t \leqslant \pi$) is given by eqn [1.17]. For the condition $b = 0$ ($\pi \leqslant \omega t \leqslant \beta$), the solution is given by

$$\begin{aligned} i_a(\omega t) = I_m\,[&\sin\psi \exp\{-\cot\psi\,(\omega t - \pi)\} - \sin(\gamma - \psi) \\ &\exp\{-\cot\psi\,(\omega t - \gamma)\}] \\ &- I\,[1 - \exp\{-\cot\psi\,(\omega t - \gamma)\}] \end{aligned} \qquad [1.26]$$

β can be found by trial and error using eqn [1.26].

Mode 4

$b = +1$ for $\gamma \leqslant \omega t \leqslant \pi$
$b = 0$ for $\pi \leqslant \omega t \leqslant (\pi + \alpha)$
$b = -1$ for $(\pi + \alpha) \leqslant \omega t \leqslant \beta$

Noting these conditions and the fact that the counter e.m.f. acts as applied voltage during the interval from β to $(\pi + \gamma)$, we have

$$\frac{1}{\pi}\left[\int_{\gamma}^{\pi} V_m \sin\omega t\, d(\omega t) + \int_{(\pi+\alpha)}^{\beta} - V_m \sin\omega t\, d(\omega t)\right] + \frac{E}{\pi}\,(\overline{\pi + \gamma - \beta}) = E + I_{av}\cdot R_a$$

i.e.

$$\frac{V_m}{\pi}\,(1+\cos\alpha + \cos\gamma + \cos\beta) = E\,\frac{\beta-\gamma}{\pi} + I_{av}\cdot R_a$$

Hence

$$I_{av} = \frac{V_m\,(1+\cos\alpha + \cos\gamma + \cos\beta) - E\,(\beta-\gamma)}{\pi R_a} \qquad [1.27]$$

Here also, I_{av} is calculated by determining β from the appropriate current expression which itself has to be found first by using the solutions of eqn [1.12] for $b = +1$ and $b = 0$ in order to determine the initial condition, while solving eqn [1.12] with $b = -1$. This is found to be

$$\begin{aligned} i_a(\omega t) = I_m[&\sin\psi \exp\{-\cot\psi\,(\omega t-\pi)\} \\ &-\sin(\alpha-\psi)\exp\{-\cot\psi\,(\omega t-\pi-\alpha)\} \\ &-\sin(\gamma-\psi)\exp\{-\cot\psi\,(\omega t-\gamma)\} \\ &-\sin(\omega t-\psi)] - I\,[1-\exp\{-\cot\psi\,(\omega t-\gamma)\}] \end{aligned} \qquad [1.28]$$

From the foregoing analysis, it is clear that the determination of the motor-performance characteristics is quite complex and cumbersome, since E, γ and β for a specified value of firing angle are all unknown and are dependent upon the type of current conduction. A digital computer solution employing an iterative method becomes a necessity.

The first step in the analysis is to determine whether, for a particular firing angle and chosen speed of rotation of the motor, the armature current is continuous or not. This can be done by evaluating the critical speed of the motor at which the current is just continuous. It is found by assuming the armature current to be continuous and by determining the condition when current momentarily becomes zero.

In the case of a fully-controlled converter, eqn [1.14] gives the instantaneous value of the continuous load current for the interval $\alpha \leqslant \omega t \leqslant (\pi + \alpha)$. The instant at which this current becomes a minimum is determined by differentiating and using numerical techniques. The value of the motor speed which makes this current zero is the critical speed. Thus, if the load current is minimum at $\omega t = \phi$, then from eqn [1.14] the critical speed is given by

$$\Omega_{cr} = \frac{I_m \cdot R_a}{K}\left[\sin(\phi - \psi) - \frac{2\sin(\alpha - \psi)\exp\{-\cot\psi(\phi - \alpha)\}}{\{1 - \exp(-\pi \cot\psi)\}}\right] \qquad [1.29]$$

For all speeds below this value the conduction of current is continuous, and for those above this value, it would be discontinuous. It must be borne in mind that the critical speed varies with the firing angle and ψ, which depends on the electrical time-constant of the armature circuit.

Having determined the nature of current conduction, it is necessary to identify the three modes of operation in which the current remains discontinuous. For a specified firing angle and a chosen speed above the critical value, determine E and hence γ, the angle at which E becomes equal to the voltage applied to the motor. If $\alpha \geqslant \gamma$, the current discontinuity occurs in mode 2. In case $\alpha < \gamma$, evaluate β, the instant at which the current becomes zero using eqn [1.17]. If $\beta \leqslant (\pi + \alpha)$, the current discontinuity takes place in mode 3. Otherwise, it occurs in mode 4.

Once the modes of operation are clearly distinguished, the family of speed/torque curves for various values of α, both during continuous and discontinuous conduction, can be determined by calculating the average developed torque corresponding to a motor speed as explained earlier.

The same procedure is adopted to determine the performance curves of a half-controlled converter-fed d.c. motor. The expression for critical speed is obtained, using eqn [1.21], as

$$\Omega_{cr} = \frac{I_m \cdot R_a}{K}[\sin(\phi - \psi) + \{\sin\psi \exp(-\cot\psi \cdot \alpha) - \sin(\alpha - \psi)\}$$

$$\exp\{-\cot\psi(\phi - \alpha)\}/\{1 - \exp(-\cot\psi \cdot \pi)\}] \qquad [1.30]$$

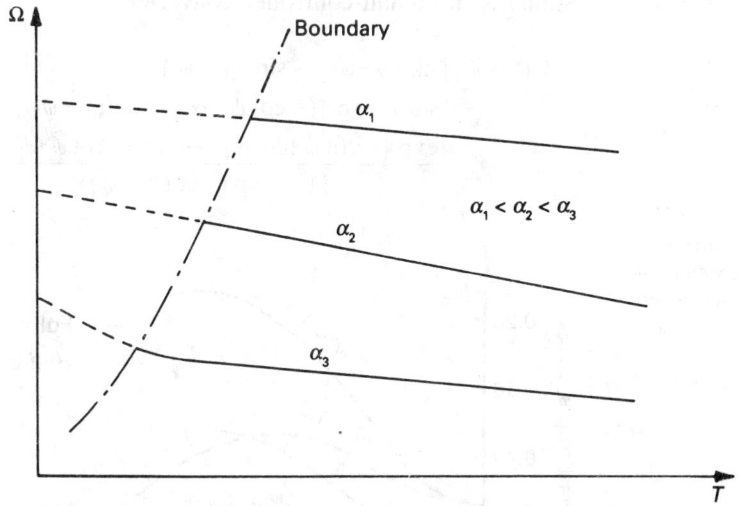

Figure 1.8 Speed/torque curves of a converter-fed separately-excited d.c. motor for different firing angles.

The nature of speed/torque curves of a converter-fed separately-excited d.c. motor is shown in Fig. 1.8 for various values of firing angles. The continuous-conduction zone is indicated by continuous lines and the discontinuos-conduction zone by dotted lines.

1.2.1.4 *Armature current ripple*

With converter control, the armature current, irrespective of the type of conduction, is not a smooth ideal d.c., but has an a.c. ripple superimposed on the d.c. component. This current ripple (CR) is defined by the expression

$$\text{CR} = \frac{i_{max} - i_{min}}{2} \qquad [1.31]$$

As long as the current is continuous, the current ripple is independent of the variation in the motor back-e.m.f., that is, the speed of the motor. The change in back-e.m.f. affects only the average value of the armature current.

For specific values of ψ and α, the points at which the current is minimum and maximum are determined by differentiating armature current expressions (eqn [1.14] for a fully-controlled converter and eqn [1.21] for a half-controlled converter) and employing numerical techniques. If the minimum occurs at $\omega t = \phi$ and the maximum at $\omega t = \phi'$, then for a fully-controlled converter,

$$\text{CR} = I_m \Big[\sin(\phi - \psi) - \sin(\phi' - \psi) \frac{2\sin(\alpha - \psi)\exp\{-\cot\psi\,(\phi - \alpha)\} - \exp\{-\cot\psi\,(\phi' - \alpha)\}}{\{1 - \exp(-\cot\psi \cdot \pi)\}}\Big] \qquad [1.32]$$

Similarly, for a half-controlled converter,

$$\mathrm{CR} = I_m [\sin(\phi-\psi) - \sin(\phi'-\psi) + \{\sin\psi \exp\{(-\cot\psi\cdot\alpha) - \sin(\alpha-\psi)\} \frac{[\exp\{-\cot\psi(\phi-\alpha)\} - \exp\{-\cot\psi(\phi'-\alpha)\}]}{\{1-\exp(-\cot\psi\cdot\pi)\}} \qquad [1.33]$$

Figure 1.9 Variation of current ripple with firing angle for various values of ψ.

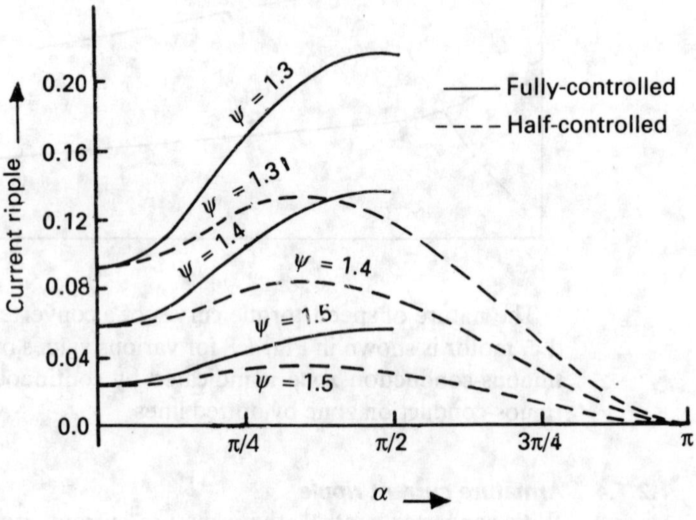

Figure 1.9 shows the variation of current ripple with firing angle α for various values of ψ. I_m has been normalized by taking $2V_m/\pi R_a$ as the base value of the current. It is obvious from Fig. 1.9 that for the same value of ψ, a half-controlled converter-fed motor has much less maximum current ripple than a fully-controlled converter-fed motor. Also, for the same value of α, current ripple of motors fed from both types of converters significantly reduces with increase in ψ.

The phenomena of discontinuous conduction and a.c. ripple are both undesirable features as they adversely affect the commutation in the machine and increase the losses leading to reduction in efficiency and, hence, derating of the motor. Further, discontinuous conduction results in poor speed regulation and reduces the transient response of the drive.

Discontinuous conduction can be eliminated and a.c. ripple reduced by increasing ψ (or, in other words, the electrical time-constant) of the motor by introducing an external inductance in series with the armature circuit. It has an additional beneficial effect on the speed drop under impact-load conditions. However, the addition of a series inductor in the armature circuit results in an increase in cost, weight, size and noise, reduction in efficiency due to losses in the inductor and deterioration of transient response.

1.2.1.5 *Choice of external series inductor*

It has been seen earlier that there exists a critical speed which enables us to demarcate the boundary between continuous and discontinuous conduction for each value of the firing angle α and ψ. For a specified value of ψ, different values of critical speeds can be found corresponding to various values of the firing angle. Equation [1.29] for critical speed, when normalized against a base value of current equal to $2\,V_m/\pi\,R_a$, is given as

$$\Omega_{cr\cdot N} = \frac{\pi}{2}\cos\psi\left[\sin(\phi-\psi) - \frac{2\sin(\alpha-\psi)\exp\{-\cot\psi(\phi-\alpha)\}}{\{1-\exp(-\pi\cot\psi)\}}\right] \quad [1.34]$$

Since the current is continuous at this speed, the average load current is given by

$$I_{av} = \frac{2/\pi\, V_m \cos\alpha - E}{R_a} \quad [1.35]$$

Normalizing eqn [1.35], the torque corresponding to $\Omega_{cr\cdot N}$, known as critical torque, is expressed as

$$T_{cr\cdot N} = \cos\alpha - \Omega_{cr\cdot N} \quad [1.36]$$

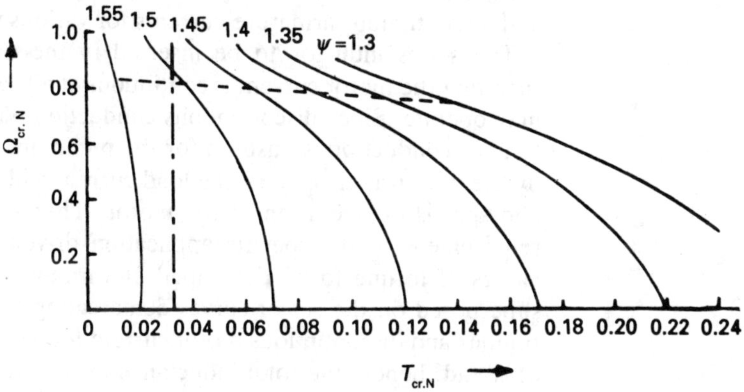

Figure 1.10 Family of critical speed/critical torque curves for various values of ψ for a fully-controlled converter-fed d.c. motor.

Using eqn [1.36], a plot of $\Omega_{cr\cdot N}$ against $T_{cr\cdot N}$ for various values of α can be obtained. Repeating the same procedure for various values of ψ, a family of critical speed/critical torque curves can be plotted as shown in Fig. 1.10.

A similar set of curves (Fig. 1.11) in the case of a half-controlled converter-fed d.c. motor can be obtained by using appropriate expressions for $\Omega_{cr\cdot N}$ and $T_{cr\cdot N}$ as indicated below.

$$\Omega_{cr\cdot N} = \frac{\pi}{2}\cos\psi\Big[\sin(\phi-\psi) + \frac{\{\sin\psi\exp(-\cot\psi\cdot\alpha) - \sin(\alpha-\psi)\exp\{-\cot\psi(\phi-\alpha)\}}{\{1-\exp(-\cot\psi\cdot\pi)\}}\Big] \quad [1.37]$$

$$T_{cr \cdot N} = (1 + \cos \alpha) - \Omega_{cr \cdot N} \tag{1.38}$$

Figure 1.11 Family of critical speed/critical torque curves for various values of ψ for a half-controlled converter-fed d.c. motor.

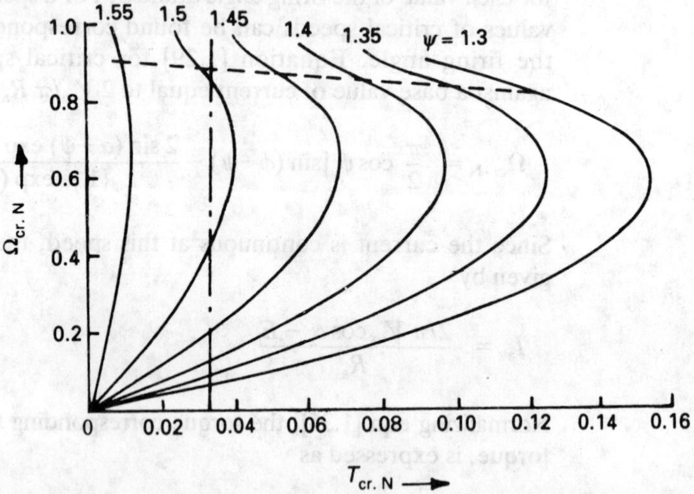

This family of curves actually indicates the boundaries between continuous and discontinuous armature currents for various values of ψ.

The series inductor to be inserted in the armature circuit is chosen such that the motor current is continuous at all speeds and loads at which it may operate. Since discontinuous conduction occurs at light loads, if continuous conduction is ensured for the minimum load torque to be catered by the motor at all speeds, the load current will be continuous at all loads and speeds of operation of the motor. Therefore, from the load torque requirement of the specific application driven by the motor, minimum values of torque to be developed at various speeds are determined and superposed on the set of curves demarcating the boundary between continuous and discontinuous motor current for various values of ψ. The value of ψ and, hence, the total inductance in the armature circuit is so chosen that the boundary between continuous and discontinuous conduction falls to the left of the desired load torque characteristics. In case the motor is likely to operate on no-load, viscous and coulomb friction will provide the minimum load torque. Once the continuity of motor current is assured, the current ripple can be calculated as described earlier. If it is not within the specified permissible limit, a larger value of inductance is selected. The external inductance to be inserted can be determined by subtracting the value of the armature inductance from the chosen value of the total inductance.

1.2.2 *Transient Performance*

Let us assume continuous conduction of motor current and confine the transient behaviour to the determination of the temporal variation of the average values rather than the instantaneous values of current and speed for any given disturbance. The current being unidirectional, the average voltage across the inductance of the motor will be zero over a half-cycle.

For a fully-controlled converter-fed d.c. motor, the average armature current can be expressed as

$$i_{av} = \frac{2/\pi\, V_m \cos\alpha - K\,\Omega_{av}}{R_a} \qquad [1.39]$$

The equation of motion is given by

$$J\,\frac{d\Omega_{av}}{dt} = K\,i_{av} - B\,\Omega_{av} - T_L \qquad [1.40]$$

assuming T_L, the load torque, to be independent of speed.

Substituting eqn [1.39] into eqn [1.40] and rearranging the terms we get

$$\frac{d\Omega_{av}}{dt} + \frac{(K^2 + BR_a)}{JR_a}\,\Omega_{av} = \frac{2K\,(V_m/\pi)\cos\alpha - R_a\,T_L}{JR_a} \qquad [1.41]$$

For a given α, eqn [1.41] is a first-order linear differential equation with constant coefficients and can be solved for Ω_{av} as a function of time.

The variation of i_{av} with respect to time, then, can be obtained using eqn [1.39].

1.2.3 Analysis of d.c. Series Motor Fed From Full-Wave Converter

Direct-current series motors have their field winding connected in series with the armature. Hence, the total circuit inductance will be high and the armature current will invariably be continuous. Further, the probability of discontinuous armature current flowing in the armature is low with d.c. series motors, since the back-e.m.f. of the motor is proportional to the armature current at a constant speed. Hence, while analysing the performance of such motors fed from converters, continuous conduction alone need be considered.

The differential equation describing the performance of a d.c. series motor fed from a single-phase, full-wave, *fully-controlled converter* is given as

$$V_m \sin\omega t = (R_a + R_f)\,i + (L_a + L_f)\,\frac{di}{dt} + M_{af}\,i\,\Omega_{av} \qquad [1.42]$$

during the interval α to $(\pi + \alpha)$.

R_f denotes the resistance of the series field, L_f the inductance of the field and M_{af} the mutual inductance between the field and the armature.

Assuming that all the motor parameters remain constant and do not vary with the armature current, and taking the average for the terms on both sides of eqn [1.41] for the period $\alpha \leqslant \omega t \leqslant (\pi + \alpha)$, we get

$$\frac{2V_m}{\pi} \cos\alpha = (R_a + R_f)\, I_{av} + M_{af}\, I_{av}\, \Omega_{av}. \tag{1.43}$$

Therefore

$$I_{av} = \frac{2V_m \cos\alpha}{\pi\,[(R_a + R_f) + M_{af}\,\Omega_{av}]} \tag{1.44}$$

For a particular value of α and chosen speed Ω_{av}, I_{av} can be calculated from eqn [1.44].

$$T_{e\,av} = M_{af}\, I_{av}^2 \tag{1.45}$$

Speed/torque curves can be plotted for various values of α using eqns [1.44] and [1.45].

In case a *half-controlled converter* is used, the average voltage across the motor terminals is given by $(V_m/\pi)(1 + \cos\alpha)$ instead of $(2/\pi)V_m \cos\alpha$ and, therefore, eqns [1.43] and [1.44] should be modified accordingly. Typical speed/torque curves of converter-fed series motors are shown in Fig. 1.12 for various values of firing angles.

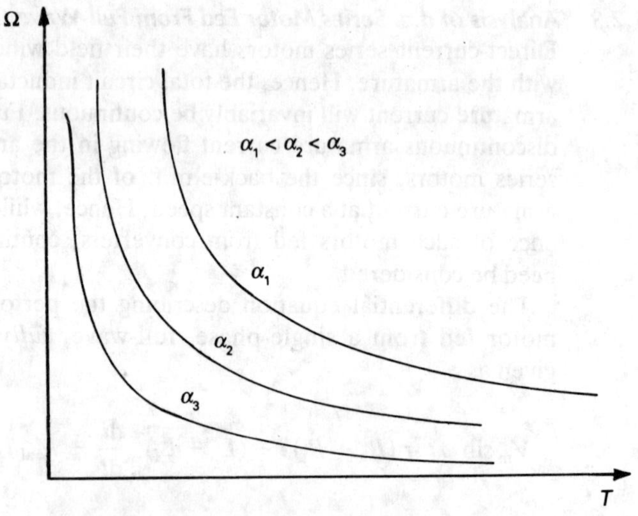

Figure 1.12 Speed/torque curves of converter-fed d.c. series motor for various firing angles.

The *transient analysis* can again be performed by confining ourselves to the determination of the variation of the average values rather than the instantaneous values of current and speed.

Considering the case of a half-controlled converter-fed d.c. series motor, the relationship governing the average value of the current and speed is given by

$$i_{av} = \frac{V_m (1 + \cos\alpha)}{\pi\,[(R_a + R_f) + M_{af}\,\Omega_{av}]} \qquad [1.46]$$

The equation of motion for a constant load torque T_L acting on the shaft of the motor is expressed as

$$J \cdot \frac{d\,\Omega_{av}}{dt} = M_{af}\,i_{av}^2 - B\,\Omega_{av} - T_L \qquad [1.47]$$

Solving eqns [1.46] and [1.47] by numerical methods, Ω_{av} against time and i_{av} against time can be obtained. The transient response can be found for perturbations in load torque or firing angle.

1.3 Dual Converter-Fed d.c. Motor

Dual converters are commonly used as power sources for reversible electrical drives which demand uninterrupted operation of the driving motor in all the four quadrants of the speed/torque plane. They consist of two fully-controlled three-phase, six-pulse bridge converters connected in antiparallel across the motor as shown in Fig. 1.13. In addition to providing voltage of either polarity, this scheme enables flow of current in either direction, 'positive' load current being given by the 'positive' converter and 'negative' current by the 'negative' converter. There are two modes of operation, known as circulating current-free mode and circulating-current mode.

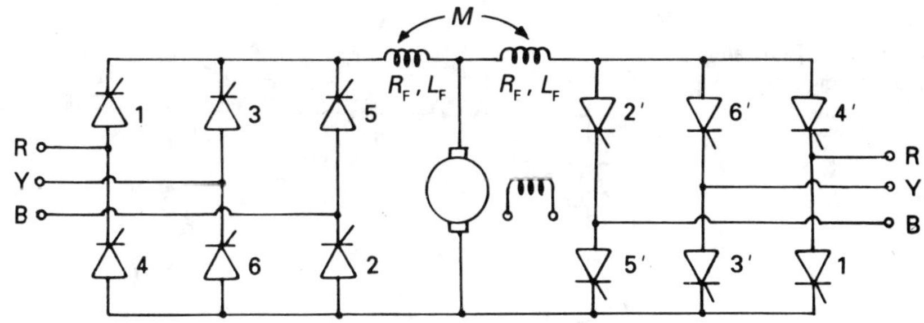

Figure 1.13 Basic scheme of dual converter-fed separately-excited d.c. motor.

In the circulating current-free mode of operation, only one rectifier bridge conducts at any particular instant. The gating pulses to the other are completely blocked during steady-state operation of the drive. When it is desired to reverse the speed setting, the conducting converter is made to operate with firing angles greater than 90°. Soon the d.c. circuit inductance discharges its stored energy into the motor, the a.c. source and circuit resistance till the current comes down to zero. At the instant when current becomes zero, a logic circuit withdraws the gating pulses from the converter for an interval of time called 'dead time' to ensure the turn-off of the conducting SCRs. After this period of time, the other converter is gated with firing angle greater than 90°.

In the circulating-current mode of operation, both converters function simultaneously—one operating as a rectifier and the other as an inverter so that they produce voltage of similar polarity across the motor. Firing angles of individual converters are adjusted such that each converter produces the same average d.c. voltage at the output terminals. This would happen when the sum of the firing angles of the positive and negative converter would be equal to 180°. However, since the instantaneous values of d.c. terminal voltages of the two converters are different, chokes are inserted in between the d.c. terminals to limit the circulating current caused by the difference in the instantaneous values of the d.c. output voltages. The circulating current acts as a base load on the converters, thus keeping them virtually in continuous conduction over the whole range of control.

1.3.1 *Steady-State Analysis*

The analysis of a dual-converter system feeding a separately-excited d.c. motor is done under the following assumptions:

(i) Power sources and SCRs are ideal.
(ii) SCRs are triggered continuously by recurring pulses for a duration of 120°.
(iii) Motor parameters are constant.
(iv) During steady state, the motor speed is invariant.
(v) Both chokes (Fig. 1.13) have equal values of L_F and R_F.
(vi) Saturation in the magnetic circuits of the motor and chokes is ignored.

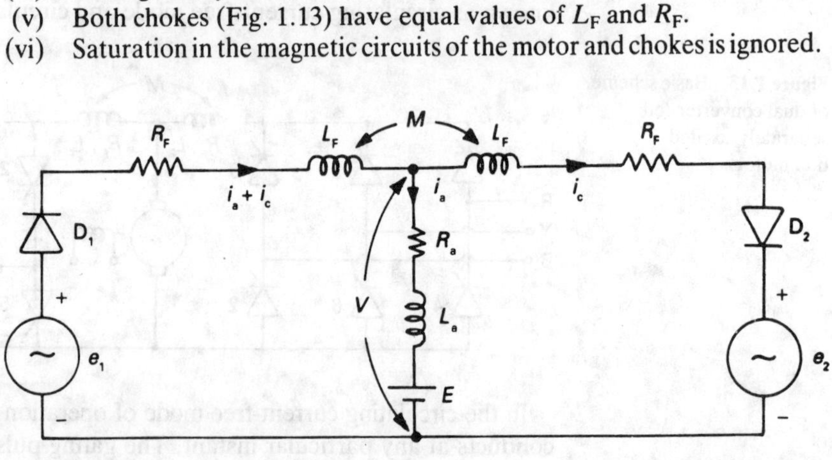

Figure 1.14 Equivalent circuit during circulating-current mode.

The circulating-current mode of operation can be represented by an equivalent circuit as shown in Fig. 1.14. Both the converters are represented by a voltage source in series with a diode. The waveform of the voltage source will be the same as the output waveform of the corresponding converter. The diodes take care of the reverse-current-blocking property of the SCR converters. The motor load is represented by a R-L-E load. Figure 1.15 represents the dual-converter system feeding the separately-excited motor when operated in the circulating current-free mode.

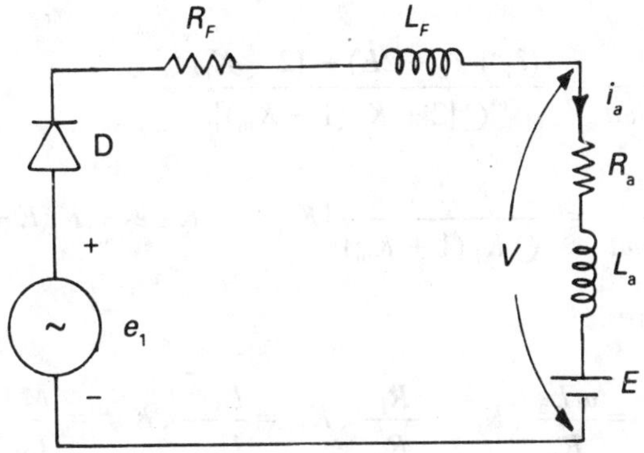

Figure 1.15 Equivalent circuit during circulating current-free mode.

Let us first consider the circulating-current mode of operation. From Fig. 1.14, it is obvious that three different types of operation are possible.

(1) Continuous conduction in both the converters.
(2) Discontinuous conduction in the negative converter.
(3) Discontinuous conduction in the positive converter.

The system may have any or all of these types during a complete cycle. The circuit equations corresponding to these cases are given below.

Continuous conduction

$$e_1 - V = R_F(i_a + i_c) + L_F \frac{d}{dt}(i_a + i_c) + M\frac{di_c}{dt} \qquad [1.48]$$

$$V - e_2 = R_F i_c + L_F \frac{di_c}{dt} + M\frac{d}{dt}(i_a + i_c) \qquad [1.49]$$

$$V = R_a i_a + L_a \frac{di_a}{dt} + E \qquad [1.50]$$

Normalizing the voltages and currents using base voltage E_m and base current E_m/R_a and representing the normalized quantities with a cap above, we have

$$\left.\begin{aligned} \hat{e}_1 &= \frac{e_1}{E_m},\ \hat{e}_2 = \frac{e_2}{E_m},\ \hat{E} = \frac{E}{E_m} \\ \hat{i}_a &= \frac{i_a R_a}{E_m} \text{ and } \hat{i}_c = \frac{i_c R_a}{E_m} \end{aligned}\right\} \quad [1.51]$$

From eqns (1.48) to (1.51) we get

$$\frac{d\hat{i}_a}{d\,\omega t} = \frac{(\hat{e}_1 + \hat{e}_2 - 2\hat{E}) - (2 + K_r)\,\hat{i}_a}{Q\,[2 + K_1\,(1 - K_m)]} \quad [1.52]$$

$$\frac{d\hat{i}_c}{d\omega t} = \frac{1}{Q\,K_1\,(1 + K_m)}\,[K_{e_1}\,\hat{e}_1 - K_{e_2}\,\hat{e}_2 + K_e\,\hat{E} + K_i\,\hat{i}_a - K_r\,\hat{i}_c] \quad [1.53]$$

where

$$\left.\begin{aligned} Q &= \frac{\omega L_a}{R_a},\ K_r = \frac{R_F}{R_a},\ K_1 = \frac{L_F}{L_a},\ K_m = \frac{M}{L_F} \\ K_{e_1} &= \frac{1 - K_m K_1}{2 + K_1 - K_m K_1},\ K_{e_2} = \frac{1 + K_1}{2 + K_1 - K_m K_1} \\ K_e &= \frac{K_1\,(1 + K_m)}{2 + K_1 - K_m K_1},\ K_i = \frac{K_1\,(1 + K_m) - K_r\,(1 - K_m K_1)}{2 + K_1 - K_m K_1} \end{aligned}\right\} \quad [1.54]$$

Discontinuous conduction in negative converter

$$\frac{d\hat{i}_a}{d\,\omega t} = \frac{1}{Q\,(1 + K_1)}\,[\hat{e}_1 - \hat{E} - (1 + K_r)\,\hat{i}_a] \quad [1.55]$$

and

$$i_c = 0 \quad [1.56]$$

Equations [1.55] and [1.56] are satisfied if

$$V - M \cdot \frac{di_a}{dt} - e_2 < 0$$

i.e. in terms of normalized quantities, if

$$Q \cdot \frac{d\hat{i}_a}{d\omega t}\,(1 - K_m K_1) + \hat{i}_a + \hat{E} - \hat{e}_2 < 0 \quad [1.57]$$

Discontinuous conduction in positive converter

$$\frac{d\hat{i}_c}{d\,\omega t} = \frac{1}{Q\,(1 + K_1)}\,[\hat{E} - \hat{e}_2 - \hat{i}_c\,(1 + K_r)] \qquad [1.58]$$

and

$$i_c = -i_a \qquad [1.59]$$

Equations [1.58] and [1.59] are satisfied if

$$e_1 < M\,\frac{di_c}{dt} - i_c\,R_a - L_a\,\frac{di_c}{dt} + E$$

i.e.

$$\hat{e}_1 - \bar{E} + \hat{i}_c + Q\,(1 + K_1\,K_m)\,\frac{d\hat{i}_c}{d\,\omega t} < 0 \qquad [1.60]$$

In the case of the circulating current-free mode the equations can be written as (refer Fig. 1.16)

$$e_1 - V = R_F\,i_a + L_F\,\frac{di_a}{dt} \qquad [1.61]$$

$$V = R_a\,i_a + L_a\,\frac{di_a}{dt} + E \qquad [1.62]$$

From eqns [1.61] and [1.62], using normalized quantities we get

$$\frac{d\hat{i}_a}{d\,\omega t} = \frac{1}{Q\,(1 + K_1)}\,[\hat{e}_1 - \hat{E} - (1 + K_r)\,\hat{i}_a] \qquad [1.63]$$

If at any instant i_a tries to reverse, the diode D forces it to zero until $e_1 \geqslant E$.

In the above equations $\hat{e}_1 = \sin(\omega t + \phi_1)$ and $\hat{e}_2 = \sin(\omega t + \phi_2)$, where ϕ_1 and ϕ_2 are functions of time and will change at the switching instants of the converter thyristors. Figure 1.16 shows the waveforms of e_1 and e_2 for a given α_p and α_N, indicating how ϕ_1 and ϕ_2 change.

A digital solution of eqns [1.52], [1.53], [1.57] and [1.60] starting from known values of α, Q, K_1, K_m, K_r and E (or speed) would enable us to obtain i_a and i_c. The solution can begin with setting initial values of i_a and i_c to be zero so as to determine the values of ϕ_1 and ϕ_2 at $\omega t = 0$. When steady-state conditions are reached, the average armature current $\bar{I}_a$ and average value of circulating current $\bar{I}_c$ in per-unit values can be calculated.

In the case of the circulating current-free mode of operation, the solution of eqn [1.63] would give the value of i_a and, hence, $\bar{I}_a$.

Figure 1.16 Waveforms of e_1 and e_2 for a given α_P and α_N.

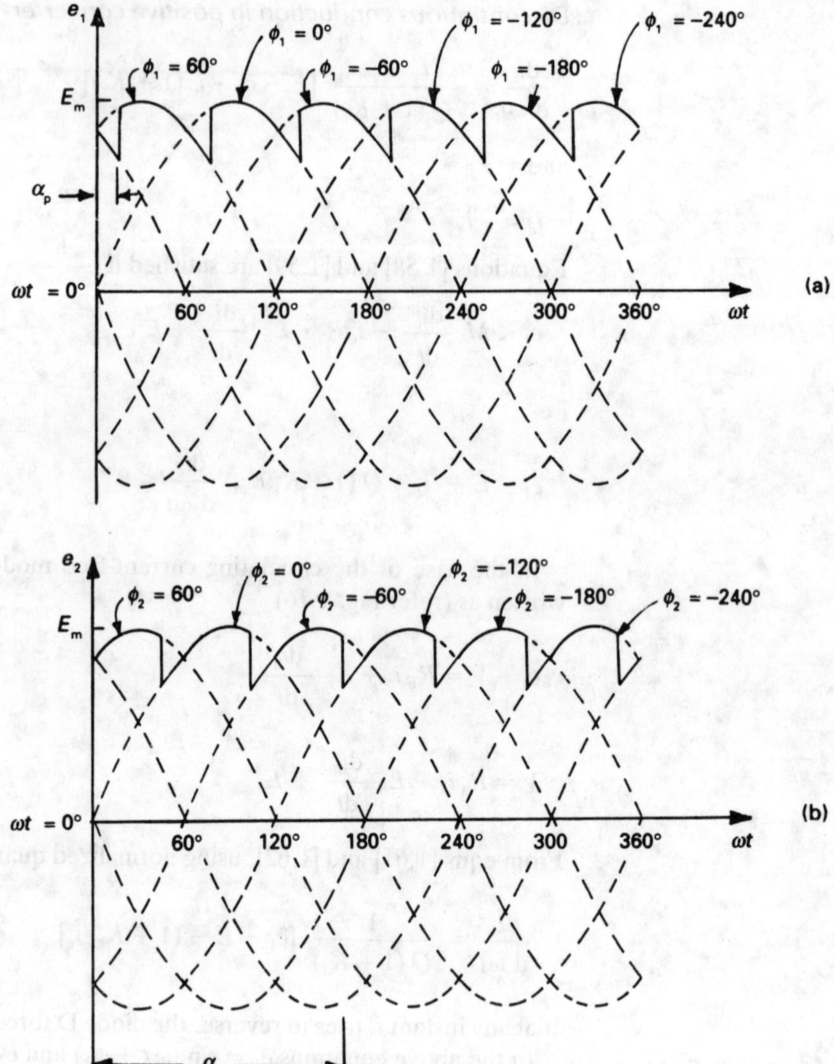

Thus, it is possible to obtain the speed/torque characteristics (back-e.m.f. vs. armature current characteristics) for various values of α and chosen values of K_1 and K_m for both modes of operation, as illustrated in Fig. 1.17. It is found that in the circulating-current mode, continuous conduction is maintained even at low values of armature current and that the speed/torque curves for different values of K_1 merge together. K_m has practically no effect on the speed/torque characteristics. However, in the circulating current-free mode, discontinuous conduction occurs at low values of armature current, thereby increasing the droop in the speed/torque curves.

The performance of the system improves with increase of K_1, and a suitable value of K_1 can be determined from Fig. 1.17 for continuous conduction over the desired range of armature current[5].

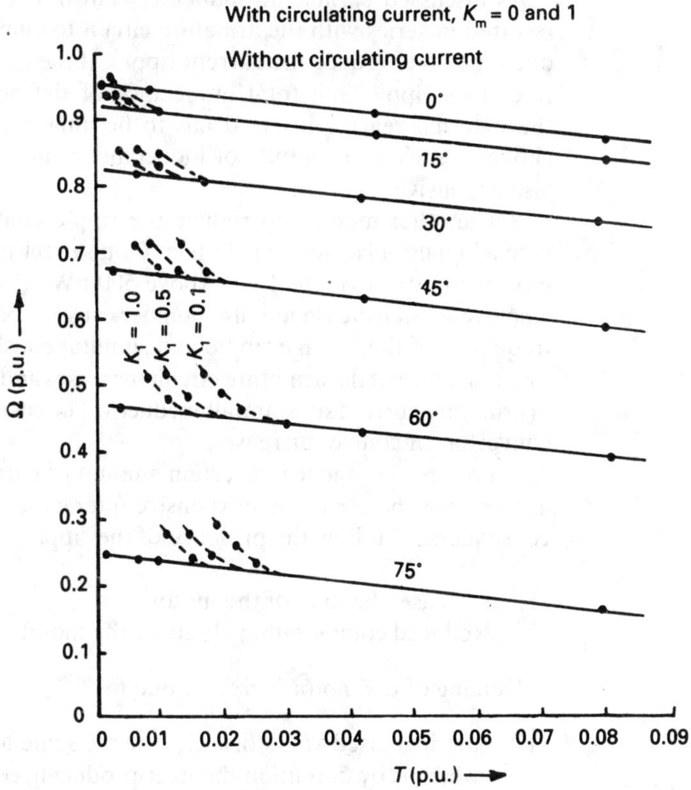

Figure 1.17 Speed/torque characteristics for various values of α.

The *transient performance*, namely the variation of armature current and speed with respect to time for sudden changes in firing angle or load torque can be obtained by including the equation of motion of the drive

$$J \frac{d\Omega}{dt} = T_e - B\Omega - T_L$$

for a digital solution.

1.4 Effect of Static Rectified Power on the Performance of d.c. Motors

It is well known that static a.c/d.c. converters supply only voltages containing ripple to d.c. motors connected to them. The electrical time-constant of the armature circuit (comprising the armature, interpole and compensating windings) is relatively low, so that the ripples of the armature current are quite significant in comparison with the average value of the current. Furthermore, at light loads (the average value of the armature current is low) the phenomenon of discontinuous conduction arises, causing even higher ripples.

As discussed earlier, an inductor, known as filter choke or reactor, is inserted in series with the armature circuit to eliminate discontinuous conduction and to reduce the current ripple. If the current has to be practically free from ripple, the total inductance of the armature circuit including the external reactor inserted has to be almost close to infinity. A filter choke of such a magnitude of inductance is not only rather unwieldy but also expensive.

Yet another method to reduce the ripple content is to use converters with a higher pulse number. In fact, 6-pulse rectifiers are normally used for motors rated above 100 kW. Above 500 kW, 12-pulse rectifiers are often employed. An increase in pulse number causes a proportional increase in the frequency of the voltage ripple and simultaneously reduces its magnitude. The reactance of the armature circuit increases and hence, the ripple content in armature current substantially reduces. The cost of the high pulse-number converter, of course, increases.

Therefore, in practice, a certain amount of current ripple is tolerated so as to permit the use of an inexpensive filter choke or converter. Two major consequences[6] follow the presence of the ripple.

(1) Increased heating of the motor.
(2) Reduced commutating ability of the motor.

Heating of the motor increases due to

(i) the increased value of $I_{r.m.s}$ (for the same average value of current), which is by definition the heat-producing component,
(ii) the increase in resistance of the armature circuit because of skin effect, and
(iii) the extra iron losses generated by the pulsating flux in the armature, interpole and yoke. It is noteworthy that unlike the armature winding, the interpole winding, situated in a stationary part of the motor, lacks the self-cooling effect provided by rotation and hence will have higher temperature rise unless countermeasures like laminating the interpole core are taken.

Commutating ability of the motor deteriorates because

(i) it primarily depends on the maximum value of the current, which is higher for the same average value of current, and
(ii) the pulsating interpole flux produces eddy currents in the solid-iron frame, which damp the interpolar flux and make it phase-displaced in time after the armature current, so that the reactance voltage in the commutating coil is not cancelled.

The two adverse effects described above become more predominant when the static converter-fed d.c. motor operates near one-half of the rated speed, since the percentage ripple content reaches its maximum at approximately half of the rated speed. The increase in current and the decrease in self-ventilation at reduced speeds quite often necessitates either derating of the motor or the use of forced ventilation for continuous operation at rated torque below and near half-speed.

2 Chopper-controlled d.c. motors

Direct-current choppers have long been used as sources of variable-voltage d.c. supplying traction motors on electric vehicles of all types, both battery- and mains-operated. Since recent times, they are also being employed as sources of variable-voltage d.c. for industrial drives. They have a number of advantages over their well-established competitor, the controlled rectifier, in spite of the complexity in control arising out of the introduction of forced commutation. The use of a constant-voltage d.c. supply input allows improved power factor and waveforms on the a.c. side. Also, the relatively high chopping frequency employed permits reduced ripple content, which ensures better motor performance as well as reduced time lag in the system response due to the lower value of filter inductance required. However, energy is lost at each commutation and the efficiency of the chopper decreases as the chopping frequency is increased.

The mean output d.c. voltage of the chopper is varied by varying its duty cycle δ (ratio of on-time to period). Two different techniques—time-ratio control (TRC) and current-limit control (CLC)—are often used to vary the δ of the chopper feeding a d.c. motor. While in TRC the chopping period is fixed and the on-time is varied to control the duty cycle, in CLC δ is varied indirectly by controlling the motor current between certain specified maximum and minimum values. In effect, this type of control is a variable-frequency control, variable on-time and off-time.

2.1 TRC Chopper-Fed Separately-Excited d.c. Motor

Figure 2.1 shows the circuit of a basic chopper supplying power at variable voltage v_a to a separately-excited d.c. motor from a source of fixed d.c. voltage V. T_1 is the SCR placed in series with the d.c. supply and is rapidly switched on and off to give an output voltage consisting of a series of rectangular

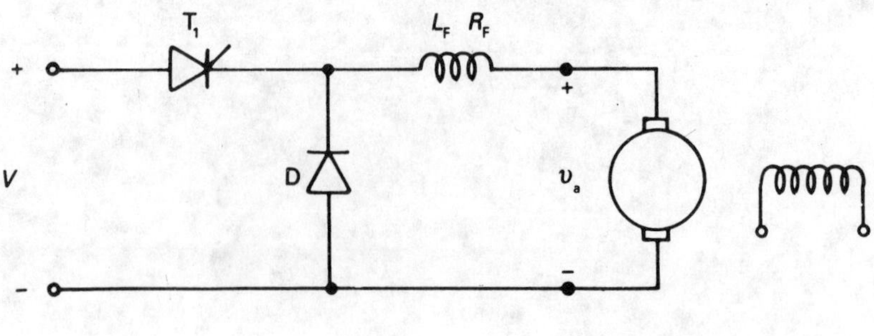

Figure 2.1 Basic chopper circuit feeding a d.c. motor.

pulses. CC is the commutating circuit used to switch off T_1. D is the free-wheeling diode and L_F is the filtering choke having a small resistance R_F.

The d.c. motor is assumed to be a load consisting of the armature resistance R_a, its inductance L_a and the counter e.m.f. E (mean value). Let the on-time, off-time and period of the chopper be denoted by t_1, t_2 and t_p respectively. During t_1 the supply voltage is driving the current into the armature against its e.m.f. so that the current is increasing. The SCR is commutated 'off' at the end of this period and the armature current circulates through the freewheeling diode for the period t_2. Energy to maintain this current flow is drawn from the circuit inductance and the current, therefore, decreases gradually. If the on-period t_1 is sufficiently long to store adequate energy in the inductance of the armature circuit so that the armature current never becomes zero during the freewheeling period, the current conduction is said to be continuous and the period of the chopper is the sum of t_1 and t_2. If the on-time is shorter, the energy stored in the circuit inductance may be inadequate to sustain the current flow until the end of the cycle. Conduction is, then, discontinuous and there is a period $t_3 = t_p - (t_1 + t_2)$ during which the load current is zero and the diode is reverse-biased by the armature induced e.m.f. (E). Typical armature voltage and current waveforms for both types of current conduction are shown in Figs. 2.2 and 2.3.

From the foregoing discussion, it is clear that the mode of current conduction in the armature of a TRC chopper-fed separately-excited d.c. motor depends on V, E, t_1, t_p and the electrical time-constant of the armature circuit τ. Hence, for a fixed input d.c. voltage and chosen value of chopping frequency, it is dependent on the values of E, t_1 and τ. Therefore, it is possible to fix the boundary between continuous and discontinuous modes

Figure 2.2 Armature voltage and current waveforms during continuous conduction.

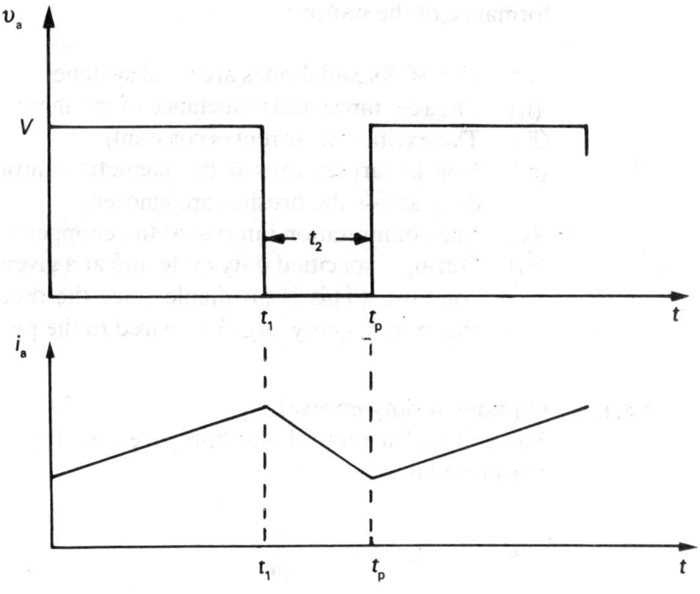

of current conduction either in terms of a critical on-time or critical speed of the motor, since the induced e.m.f. of a separately-excited d.c. motor depends only on the speed for a specified excitation current.

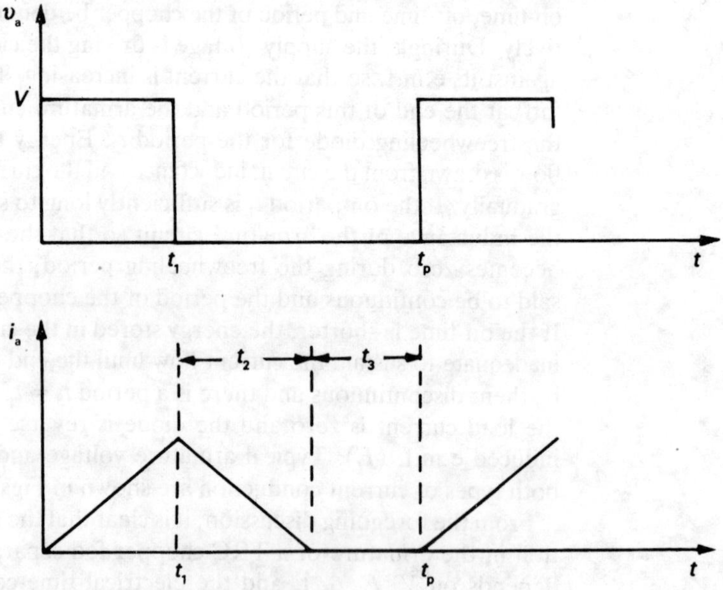

Figure 2.3 Armature voltage and current waveforms during discontinuous conduction.

2.1.1 *Steady-State Analysis*

The following simplifying assumptions are made for analysing the performance of the motor.

(i) The SCRs and diodes are ideal switches.
(ii) The resistance and inductance of the motor armature are constant.
(iii) The excitation current is constant.
(iv) Non-linearities caused by magnetic saturation and by the voltage drop across the brushes are ignored.
(v) The commutation interval of the chopper is negligible.
(vi) During a specified duty cycle and at a given load, the motor speed is constant. (This is justifiable since the mechanical time-constant of the motor is very large compared to the period of the chopper).

2.1.1.1 *On-time or duty interval*

The voltage/current relationship governing the motor performance during this period is

$$V = E + i_a R_T + L_T \frac{di_a}{dt} \qquad [2.1]$$

where

$$R_T = R_a + R_F$$

and

$$L_T = L_a + L_F$$

The solution to eqn [2.1] is

$$i_a(t) = \frac{V}{R_T} - \frac{E}{R_T} + A\, e^{-(t/\tau)} \qquad [2.2]$$

where $\tau = \dfrac{L_T}{R_T}$ and A is a constant depending on the boundary conditions.

At the beginning of the duty interval the current is

$$i_a(t)\big|_{t=0} = \frac{V}{R_T} - \frac{E}{R_T} + A \qquad [2.3]$$

At the end of the on-time state the current is

$$i_a(t)\big|_{t=t_1} = \frac{V}{R_T} - \frac{E}{R_T} + A \cdot K_1 \qquad [2.4]$$

where

$$K_1 = e^{-(t_1/\tau)}$$

2.1.1.2 *Off-time or freewheeling interval*

The voltage equation becomes

$$O = E + R_T\, i_a + L_T \frac{di_a}{dt} \qquad [2.5]$$

The solution is

$$i_a(t) = -\frac{E}{R_T} + Be^{-(t/\tau)} \qquad [2.6]$$

where B is a constant depending on the boundary conditions. At the beginning of the off-time state

$$i_a(t)\big|_{t=t_1} = -\frac{E}{R_T} + B\, e^{-(t_1/\tau)} \qquad [2.7]$$

In order to provide for current continuity at the changeover from the duty interval to the freewheeling interval, this current must be the same as that at the end of the duty interval. Therefore,

$$-\frac{E}{R_T} + B\,K_1 = \frac{V}{R_T} - \frac{E}{R_T} + AK_1$$

Hence

$$B = \frac{1}{K_1}\ \frac{V}{R_T} + A$$

Therefore

$$i_a(t) = -\frac{E}{R_T} + \left(\frac{V}{R_T}\ \frac{1}{K_1} + A\right)\ e^{-(t/\tau)} \qquad [2.8]$$

At the end of the freewheeling state

$$i_a(t)\big|_{t=(t_1+t_2)} = -\frac{E}{R_T} + \left(\frac{V}{R_T}\ \frac{1}{K_1} + A\right)\ e^{-(t_1+t_2)/\tau)} \qquad [2.9]$$

$$= -\frac{E}{R_T} + \left(\frac{V}{R_T}\ \frac{1}{K_1} + A\right)\ K_1\,K_2 \qquad [2.10]$$

where

$$K_2 = e^{-(t_2/\tau)}$$

For *continuous conduction*, the current-continuity condition demands that the currents given by eqns [2.3] and [2.10] be equal, i.e.,

$$A = -\frac{V}{R_T}\ \frac{(1 - K_2)}{(1 - K_p)} \qquad [2.11]$$

where

$$K_p = K_1\,K_2 = e^{-(t_p/\tau)}$$

Substitution of this value of A into eqns [2.2] and [2.8] gives expressions for the current waveforms during continuous conduction.

2.1.1.3 *Critical on-time*

The boundary between the continuous and discontinuous-conduction modes occurs when the currents expressed by eqns [2.3] and [2.10] are zero[7], i.e. when

$$A = -\frac{V}{R_T} + \frac{E}{R_T} = -\frac{1}{K_1}\frac{V}{R_T} + \frac{1}{K_p}\frac{E}{R_T} \qquad [2.12]$$

From this, we get

$$\frac{1}{K_1} = 1 + \frac{E}{V}\left(\frac{1}{K_p} - 1\right) \qquad [2.13]$$

so that

$$t_{1\,crit} = \tau \ln\left[1 + \frac{E}{V}\left(\frac{1}{K_p} - 1\right)\right] \qquad [2.14]$$

It can be seen that the critical on-time depends on τ, E, V and t_p. When the actual on-time is less than $t_{1\,crit}$, conduction is discontinuous.

2.1.1.4 *Critical speed*

Equation [2.13] can be written as

$$E = K_e\Phi\Omega = V\frac{(1/K_1 - 1)}{(1/K_p - 1)} \qquad [2.15]$$

Hence

$$\Omega_{crit} = \frac{V}{K_e\Phi}\frac{(1/K_1 - 1)}{(1/K_p - 1)} \qquad [2.16]$$

It is obvious that the critical speed that demarcates the boundary between continuous and discontinuous conduction depends on V, t_1, t_p, τ, the e.m.f.-constant of the motor and the flux per pole created by the excitation current.

If the speed of the motor were above the critical speed, the conduction would be discontinuous in nature. For discontinuous conduction, the on-time begins with the armature current at zero. From eqn [2.2] we have

$$A = -\frac{V}{R_T} + \frac{E}{R_T} \qquad [2.17]$$

Substituting this into eqn [2.8], the current during the off-state is given as

$$i_a(t) = -\frac{E}{R_T} + \left(\frac{1}{K_1}\frac{V}{R_T} - \frac{V}{R_T} + \frac{E}{R_T}\right)e^{-(t/\tau)} \qquad [2.18]$$

The off-period ends at a time $t = (t_1 + t_2)$ and the armature current is again zero at that instant. Therefore

$$i_a(t)|_{t=(t_1+t_2)} = 0 = -\frac{E}{R_T} + \left(\frac{1}{K_1}\frac{V}{R_T} - \frac{V}{R_T} + \frac{E}{R_T}\right) e^{-(t_1+t_2)/\tau}$$

i.e.

$$\frac{E}{R_T} = \left(\frac{1}{K_1}\frac{V}{R_T} - \frac{V}{R_T} + \frac{E}{R_T}\right) e^{-(t_1+t_2)/\tau} \quad [2.19]$$

From eqn [2.19] we get

$$t_2 = \tau \ln \left[K_1 + \frac{V}{E}(1 - K_1)\right] \quad [2.20]$$

The armature current is then zero for the remainder of the period $t_3 = t_p - (t_1 + t_2)$.

The current waveforms during the discontinuous-conduction mode are given as

$$i_a(t) = \frac{V}{R_T} - \frac{E}{R_T} + \left(-\frac{V}{R_T} + \frac{E}{R_T}\right) e^{-(t/\tau)} \quad [2.21]$$

during the on-state,

$$i_a(t) = -\frac{E}{R_T} + \left[\frac{V}{R_T}\frac{1}{K_1} - \frac{V}{R_T} + \frac{E}{R_T}\right] e^{-(t/\tau)} \quad [2.22]$$

during the off-state, and

$$i_a(t) = 0 \quad [2.23]$$

during the zero-current interval of time t_3.

2.1.1.5 *Determination of speed/torque characteristics*

For a specified speed of operation of the motor of known parameters and excitation current, first it is necessary to check whether the chosen value of duty cycle δ of the chopper of period t_p provides an on-time greater or less than the critical on-time. If it is greater, the current conduction is continuous in nature.

For continuous conduction, the average value of the motor current is straightaway given as

$$I_{av} = \frac{\delta V - E}{R_T} \quad [2.24]$$

$$T_{av} = K_e \Phi I_{av} = K I_{av} \quad [2.25]$$

For discontinuous conduction, the mean value of the armature current is found by integration of the current waveform given in eqn [2.21] over the period zero to t_1, followed by the integration of eqn [2.22] over the period t_1 to $(t_1 + t_2)$. The whole integral is averaged over the chopper period t_p. The result gives the average armature current as

$$I_{av} = \frac{V}{R_T}\frac{t_1}{t_p} - \frac{V}{R_T}\frac{\tau}{t_p}K_2(1-K_1) - \frac{E}{R_T}\frac{(t_1+t_2)}{t_p} + \frac{E}{R_T}\frac{\tau}{t_p}(1-K_1K_2) \qquad [2.26]$$

Having calculated I_{av} for the chosen values of δ and speed, the torque developed by the motor can be found from $T_{av} = K\,I_{av}$.

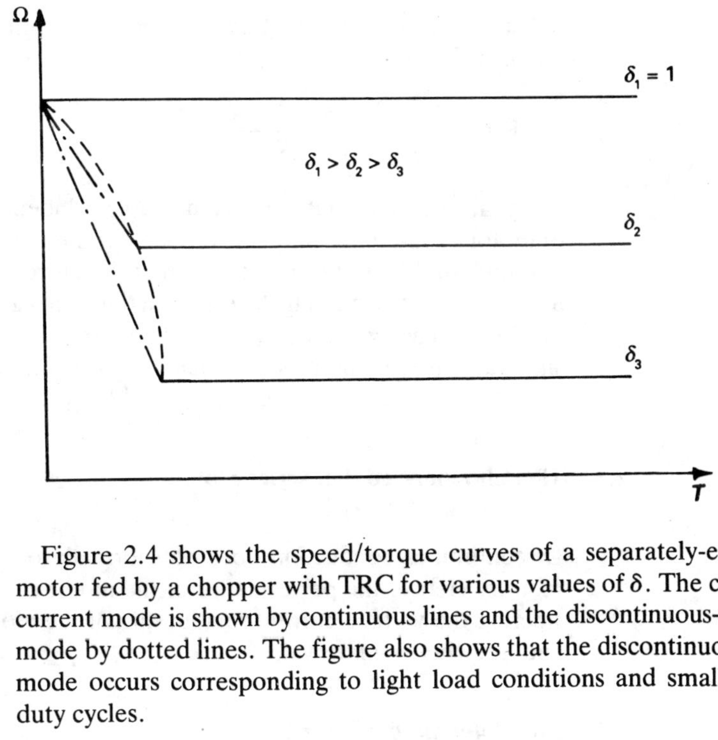

Figure 2.4 Speed/torque curves of a TRC chopper-fed separately-excited d.c. motor.

Figure 2.4 shows the speed/torque curves of a separately-excited d.c. motor fed by a chopper with TRC for various values of δ. The continuous-current mode is shown by continuous lines and the discontinuous-conduction mode by dotted lines. The figure also shows that the discontinuous-current mode occurs corresponding to light load conditions and small values of duty cycles.

2.1.1.6 *Armature current ripple*

As in the case of the controlled rectifier-fed d.c. motor, the motor current ripple is defined as

$$\mathrm{CR} = \frac{i_{max} - i_{min}}{2} \qquad [2.27]$$

For continuous conduction, i_{max} and i_{min} correspond to the values of current at the end and start of the on-period of the chopper respectively. Hence, from eqns [2.4] and [2.3] we get

$$i_{max} = \frac{V}{R_T} - \frac{E}{R_T} + AK_1$$

and

$$i_{min} = \frac{V}{R_T} - \frac{E}{R_T} + A$$

Therefore

$$CR = \frac{A(K_1 - 1)}{2} \qquad [2.28]$$

Substituting the value of A corresponding to continuous conduction from eqn [2.11], we have

$$CR = \frac{V}{2R_T} \frac{(1 - K_1)(1 - K_2)}{(1 - K_p)} \qquad [2.29]$$

Again, it is seen that the current ripple is independent of the magnitude of motor back-e.m.f. and, hence, speed of the motor.

From eqn [2.29] it can be found that the current ripple can be considerably reduced by increasing the electrical time-constant of the armature circuit, i.e. by increasing the inductance of the armature circuit. This technique simultaneously eliminates or at least reduces the possibility of occurrence of discontinuous conduction (refer eqn [2.16]).

2.2 TRC Chopper-Fed d.c. Series Motor

Discontinuous conduction does not normally occur in the case of series motors. Hence, the performance of the motor can be determined by considering the voltage/current relationship of the motor during duty interval and freewheeling interval.

2.2.1 *Duty Interval ($0 < t < t_1$)*

$$V = R_T i_d + L_T \frac{di_d}{dt} + E[= K(i_d)\Omega] \qquad [2.30]$$

where

$$R_T = R_a + R_f + R_F$$

and

$$L_T = L_a + L_f + L_F$$

R_f and L_f denote the resistance and inductance of the series field winding. Equation [2.30] can be written (in a form convenient for numerical solution) as

$$\frac{di_d}{dt} = \frac{1}{L_T}\,[V - R_T\, i_d - K\,(i_d)\,\Omega] \qquad [2.31]$$

2.2.2 *Freewheeling Interval* ($t_1 < t < \overline{t_1 + t_2}$)

The operation is described by the equation

$$O = R_T\, i_f + L_T\,\frac{di_f}{dt} + K(i_f)\Omega \qquad [2.32]$$

i.e.

$$\frac{di_f}{dt} = \frac{1}{L_T}\,[-\, R_T\, i_f - K\,(i_f)\Omega] \qquad [2.33]$$

In eqns [2.31] and [2.33] the terms $K\,(i_d)$ and $K\,(i_f)$ denote that K is a function of armature current.

Since K is a non-linear function of armature current, eqns [2.31] and [2.33] are non-linear differential equations which can be solved by using any of the numerical methods.

For a given duty cycle δ and a chosen value of speed Ω (which is assumed to be constant during the chopping period), an initial value of the armature current is assumed for the duty interval. By piecewise linearized approximation, using the final condition of the preceding mode as the initial state for each succeeding mode, the average current through the motor at every chopper cycle is calculated. The iterations are carried out until the difference between the average motor-current values between two consecutive chopper cycles is less than the permissible value. This method of determining I_{av} obviously requires considerable computational effort and time.

Once I_{av} is calculated, T_{av} for the given value of δ and chosen speed can be found as

$$T_{av} = K\,(I_{av}) \cdot I_{av} \qquad [2.34]$$

Or, using the value of I_{av}, the average value of the induced e.m.f. corresponding to the flux created by I_{av} and speed of rotation of the motor can be found and, then, the motor torque can be calculated from the relationship

$$T_{av} = \frac{I_{av} \times E_{av}}{\Omega} \qquad [2.35]$$

In order to save time and computation effort, the motor constant K can be assumed as a function of the average value of the armature current instead of its instantaneous value as in eqns [2.31] and [2.33].

Since during a given duty cycle and chosen speed of operation of the motor I_{av} is constant, K is also constant. K for a particular value of I_{av} can be obtained from the magnetization characteristic of the motor.

Taking the average for the terms on both sides of eqns [2.30] and [2.32] and noting that the average voltage across the inductance must be zero, we get

$$\delta V = I_{av} R_T + K\Omega$$

Hence

$$I_{av} = \frac{\delta V - K\Omega}{R_T} \qquad [2.36]$$

or

$$\Omega = \frac{\delta V - I_{av} \cdot R_T}{K} \qquad [2.37]$$

Therefore, the performance of the motor for a given duty cycle δ can now be calculated analytically by using the following sequence of steps.

(i) Assume a value of I_{av}. Obtain K from the magnetization characteristic.
(ii) Calculate T_{av} from the expression $T_{av} = K \cdot I_{av}$ and Ω from eqn [2.37].

The speed/torque characteristics of a d.c. series motor fed by a chopper with TRC[8] for various values of δ are shown in Fig. 2.5.

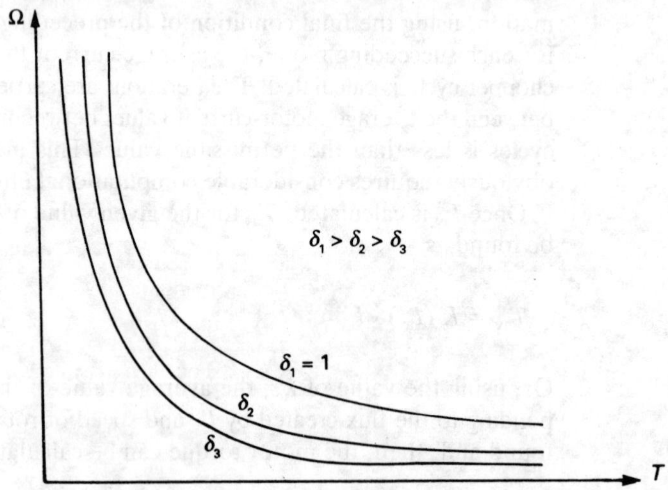

Figure 2.5 Speed/torque curves of a TRC chopper-fed d.c. series motor.

2.3 CLC Chopper-Fed Separately-Excited d.c. Motor

In the CLC technique the motor current variation takes place between a prescribed maximum value i_{a_2} and a minimum value i_{a_1}. Hence, there is no question of discontinuous conduction. The voltage/current relationships for duty interval and freewheeling interval are the same as eqns [2.1] and [2.5], namely

$$V = E + i_a R_T + L_T \frac{di_a}{dt} \qquad [2.38]$$

and

$$O = E + i_a R_T + L_T \frac{di_a}{dt} \qquad [2.39]$$

Solving eqn [2.38] for i_a and assuming its initial value to be i_{a_1}, the value of the current at the end of the on-period is given as

$$i_{a_2} = (\frac{V-E}{R_T})\ (1 - e^{-t_1/\tau}) + i_{a_1} e^{-t_1/\tau} \qquad [2.40]$$

Similarly, the solution of eqn [2.39] with i_{a_2} as the initial value would give the value of the current at the end of the off-period as

$$i_{a_1} = \ - \frac{E}{R_T}\ (1 - e^{-t_2/\tau}) + i_{a_2} e^{-t_2/\tau} \qquad [2.41]$$

From eqn [2.40] we get

$$t_1 = \tau \ln\ (\frac{V - E - R_T i_{a_1}}{V - E - R_T i_{a_2}}) \qquad [2.42]$$

and from eqn [2.41] we obtain

$$t_2 = \tau \ln\ (\frac{E + R_T i_{a_2}}{E + R_T i_{a_1}}) \qquad [2.43]$$

Adding eqns [2.42] and [2.43] we get the chopping period as

$$t_p = \tau \ln\ [\frac{(V - E - R_T i_{a_1})(E + R_T i_{a_2})}{(V - E - R_T i_{a_2})(E + R_T i_{a_1})}] \qquad [2.44]$$

Since the on-time $t_1 = \delta\ t_p$, we get the duty cycle δ by dividing eqn [2.42] by eqn [2.44].

$$\delta = \frac{\tau}{t_p} \ln \left(\frac{V - E - R_T i_{a_1}}{V - E - R_T i_{a_2}}\right) \tag{2.45}$$

Having determined δ for specified values of motor current i_{a_1} and i_{a_2} at a chosen speed Ω, I_{av} can be obtained from

$$I_{av} = \frac{\delta V - K\Omega}{R_T} \tag{2.46}$$

and

$$T_{av} = K \cdot I_{av} \tag{2.47}$$

The speed/torque characteristics shown in Fig. 2.6 indicate that for specified values of i_{a_1} and i_{a_2}, the motor developed torque remains constant at all speeds[8,9]. Thus, the CLC technique changes the fairly constant-speed characteristic of the separately-excited motor to constant-torque characteristic. This is an undesirable feature for most types of load torques leading to instability of operation, unless an additional closed loop is incorporated to control the motor speed.

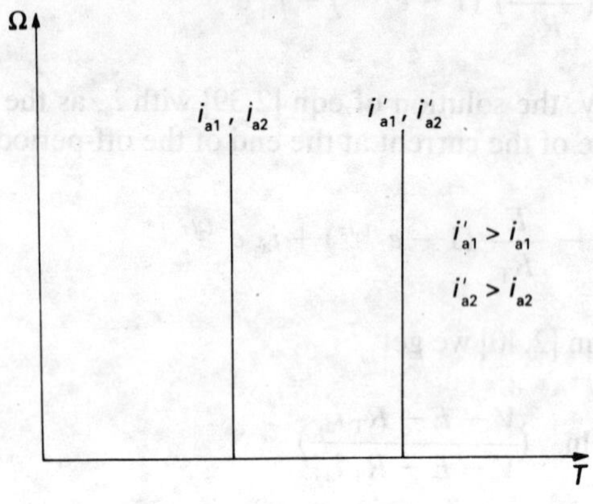

Figure 2.6 Speed/torque curves of a CLC chopper-fed separately-excited d.c. motor.

2.4 CLC Chopper-Fed d.c. Series Motor

The voltage/current equations governing the performance of the motor are the same as eqns [2.30] and [2.32]. They can be rewritten, for convenience of solving them numerically, as

$$(dt)_d = \frac{L_T \, di_d}{V - R_T i_d - K(i_d)\Omega} \tag{2.48}$$

and

$$(\mathrm{d}t)_\mathrm{f} = -\frac{L_\mathrm{T}\,\mathrm{d}i_\mathrm{f}}{R_\mathrm{T}\,i_\mathrm{f} + K\,(i_\mathrm{f})\Omega} \qquad [2.49]$$

Both on-period and off-period are determined as given below.

During the duty interval the current varies between i_{a_1} and i_{a_2} and during the freewheeling interval it varies between i_{a_2} and i_{a_1}. These ranges of current are divided into a suitable number of equal incremental-current intervals, say n. This determines the values of $\mathrm{d}i_\mathrm{d}$ and $\mathrm{d}i_\mathrm{f}$. The initial values of i_d and i_f for any incremental-current interval are calculated from the preceding interval. Values of $K(i_\mathrm{d})$ and $K(i_\mathrm{f})$ are assumed to be constant for each incremental-current interval and equal to their values at the initial value of the current in that interval. For the chosen value of the speed of the motor, $\mathrm{d}t$ corresponding to an incremental-current interval is calculated using eqn [2.48] for duty interval and eqn [2.49] for freewheeling interval

$$t_1 = \sum_{r=1}^{n} (\mathrm{d}t)_\mathrm{d} \qquad [2.50]$$

$$t_2 = \sum_{r=1}^{n} (\mathrm{d}t)_\mathrm{f} \qquad [2.51]$$

Therefore

$$t_\mathrm{p} = t_1 + t_2 = \sum_{r=1}^{n} (\mathrm{d}t)_\mathrm{d} + \sum_{r=1}^{n} (\mathrm{d}t)_\mathrm{f} \qquad [2.52]$$

$$\delta = \frac{t_1}{t_\mathrm{p}} \qquad [2.53]$$

The average value of current for any chopping period is determined from the equation

$$I_\mathrm{av} = \frac{\sum_{r=1}^{n} i_\mathrm{d}\cdot\mathrm{d}t + \sum_{r=1}^{n} i_\mathrm{f}\cdot\mathrm{d}t}{\sum_{r=1}^{2n} \mathrm{d}t} \qquad [2.54]$$

The torque developed by the motor can be found as

$$T_\mathrm{av} = K\,(I_\mathrm{av})\cdot I_\mathrm{av} \qquad [2.55]$$

The above approach obviously needs considerable computational time. A simple method of determining I_av would be to assume that the variation of current between prescribed limits both during on and off-periods takes place linearly. Then,

$$I_{av} = \frac{i_{a_1} + i_{a_2}}{2} \quad [2.56]$$

and

$$T_{av} = K\,(I_{av}) \cdot I_{av} \quad [2.57]$$

In case on-time and period of chopper are required to be calculated for a given speed of rotation of the motor, it can be done by using eqns [2.42] and [2.44].

It is obvious that the nature of the speed/torque characteristics of the series motor is the same as that of the separately-excited motor.[8,9]

2.5 Transient Analysis of Chopper-Controlled Separately-Excited d.c. Motor

Assuming that the SCRs and diodes are ideal switches and that the resistance and inductance of the motor armature are constant, the performance of the TRC chopper-fed motor during the different intervals of a chopper cycle is described by the following equations.

2.5.1 *On-Time* ($0 < t < t_1$)

The voltage equation of the motor

$$V = E + i_a R_T + L_T \frac{di_a}{dt} \quad [2.58]$$

can be rewritten as

$$L_T \frac{di_a}{dt} = V - R_T\, i_a - K\Omega \quad [2.59]$$

From the dynamics of the motor-load combination we get

$$\frac{J\,d\Omega}{dt} = K\, i_a - B\Omega - T_L \quad [2.60]$$

From eqns [2.59] and [2.60], by eliminating the variables, we obtain

$$\tau \frac{d^2\Omega}{dt^2} + \left(1 + \frac{\tau}{\tau_{m_1}}\right) \frac{d\Omega}{dt} + \frac{1}{\tau_{m_2}}\Omega = \frac{K_1}{\tau_{m_2}} \quad [2.61]$$

$$\tau \frac{d^2 i_a}{dt^2} + \left(1 + \frac{\tau}{\tau_{m_1}}\right) \frac{di_a}{dt} + \frac{1}{\tau_{m_2}} i_a = \frac{K_2}{\tau_{m_2}} \quad [2.62]$$

where

$$\tau_{m_1} = J/B$$

$$\tau_{m_2} = JR_T/(BR_T + K^2)$$

$$K_1 = \tau_{m_2}(KV - R_T T_L)/JR_T$$

$$K_2 = \tau_{m_2}(BV + KT_L)/JR_T$$

2.5.2 *Freewheeling Time ($t_1 < t < \gamma t_p$)*

If the conduction of motor current is continuous, there are only two modes in a chopping cycle and $\gamma = 1$. $\gamma < 1$ for discontinuous conduction. The voltage/current relationship becomes

$$L_T \frac{di_a}{dt} = -R_T i_a - K\Omega \quad [2.63]$$

The equation of motion remains as

$$J \frac{d\Omega}{dt} = Ki_a - B\Omega - T_L \quad [2.64]$$

Elimination of variables gives

$$\tau \frac{d^2\Omega}{dt^2} + \left(1 + \frac{\tau}{\tau_{m_1}}\right)\frac{d\Omega}{dt} + \frac{1}{\tau_{m_2}}\Omega = \frac{K_3}{\tau_{m_2}} \quad [2.65]$$

$$\tau \frac{d^2 i_a}{dt^2} + \left(1 + \frac{\tau}{\tau_{m_1}}\right)\frac{di_a}{dt} + \frac{1}{\tau_{m_2}}i_a = \frac{K_4}{\tau_{m_2}} \quad [2.66]$$

where

$$K_3 = -\frac{\tau_{m_2}T_L}{J}$$

and

$$K_4 = \frac{\tau_{m_2} K T_L}{J R_T}$$

2.5.3 *Zero-Current Interval ($\gamma\, t_p < t < t_p$)*

The equations governing the performance are

$$i_a = 0 \quad [2.67]$$

and

$$J \frac{d\Omega}{dt} = -B\Omega - T_L \quad [2.68]$$

The transient response of the drive system can be determined by solving eqns [2.61], [2.62], and [2.65] to [2.68] sequentially for each interval in a chopping cycle.[10] Of course, the time required for computation is quite large, particularly for systems with slow transient response or in which discontinuous conduction takes place. Further, this method of solution cannot be used for derivation of transfer function.

In the case of the CLC chopper-fed motor[11], discontinuous conduction does not occur and, therefore, the transient response can be obtained by solving eqns [2.61], [2.62], [2.65] and [2.66] (with $\gamma = 1$) sequentially for duty and freewheeling intervals. As the on- and off-periods are variable, the solution of these equations demands considerable computational time.

2.6 Transient Analysis of Chopper-Controlled d.c. Series Motor

In the case of a series motor, discontinuous conduction does not normally take place. The transient performance of a TRC chopper-fed motor is described by the following equations.

2.6.1 *Duty Interval ($0 < t < t_1$)*

$$L_T \frac{di_d}{dt} = V - R_T i_d - K(i_d)\,\Omega \qquad [2.69]$$

$$J \frac{d\Omega}{dt} = K(i_d)\, i_d - B\Omega - T_L \qquad [2.70]$$

2.6.2 *Freewheeling Interval ($t_1 < t < t_p$)*

$$L_T \frac{di_f}{dt} = -R_T i_f - K(i_f)\,\Omega \qquad [2.71]$$

$$J \frac{d\Omega}{dt} = K(i_f)\, i_f - B\Omega - T_L \qquad [2.72]$$

In eqns [2.69] to [2.72], $K(i_d)$ and $K(i_f)$ denote that K is a function of instantaneous value of armature current. Since K is a non-linear function of armature current owing to the non-linearity of the magnetization characteristic, eqns [2.69] to [2.72] are non-linear differential equations and they have to be solved with the help of numerical techniques. The correct method of calculating the transient response is to solve eqns [2.69] to [2.72] numerically for each interval of chopping cycle by using the final conditions of the previous interval as the initial conditions for each successive chopping interval.[12] The computation time taken is necessarily large.

The CLC chopper-fed series motor operates within the specified maximum and minimum current limits i_{a_2} and i_{a_1}. Then, the duty interval will consist of an unknown duration in which the current changes from i_{a_1} to i_{a_2} and the performance will be described by the non-linear differential equations [2.69] and [2.70]. The freewheeling interval again is of unknown duration in which the current changes from i_{a_2} to i_{a_1} and the performance will be described by eqns [2.71] and [2.72].

The exact calculation of transient response can be done by solving eqns [2.69] to [2.72] numerically for each interval of the chopping cycle, using the final conditions of the preceding interval as the initial conditions for each succeeding chopping interval.

From eqns [2.69] and [2.70], we have for the duty interval

$$dt = \frac{L_T \, di_d}{V - R_T i_d - K(i_d)\,\Omega} \qquad [2.73]$$

$$d\Omega = \frac{K(i_d)\, i_d - B\Omega - T_L}{J} . dt \qquad [2.74]$$

During a duty interval, the current varies from i_{a_1} to i_{a_2}. This current variation is divided into a suitable number of equal incremental currents, say n, which fixes the value of di_d. Initial values of i_d and Ω for any incremental-current interval are known from the calculations of the preceding incremental-current interval. The value of $K(i_d)$ is assumed to be constant for each incremental-current interval, equal to its value at initial value i_d of that interval. For any incremental-current interval, dt is calculated from eqn [2.73] and, then, $d\Omega$ is found using eqn [2.74]. Values of Ω, i_d and t at the end of this incremental-current interval are then found and used as the initial values for the next incremental-current interval.

The same technique is employed for the solution of the corresponding equations

$$dt = -\frac{L_T \, di_f}{R_T i_f + K(i_f)\,\Omega} \qquad [2.75]$$

$$d\Omega = \frac{K(i_f)\, i_f - B\Omega - T_L}{J} \cdot dt \qquad [2.76]$$

of the freewheeling interval.

Average values of speed and current during any chopping cycle may simultaneously be calculated from the following equations:

$$I_{av} = \sum_{r=1}^{2n} i_d \cdot dt / \sum_{r=1}^{2n} dt \qquad [2.77]$$

$$\Omega_{av} = \sum_{r=1}^{2n} \Omega \, dt \Big/ \sum_{r=1}^{2n} dt \qquad [2.78]$$

Since the calculations are to be done numerically—step-by-step in each interval of chopping cycle and sequentially between different intervals of chopping cycles—the computation time required is quite large, especially for systems with slow transient response.

'.7 Effect of Power Pulses Provided by Choppers on the Performance of d.c. Motors

Adverse effects of current ripple on motor performance described in Section 1.4 are equally applicable to chopper-fed d.c. motors. From equations derived earlier for armature current of chopper-fed d.c. motors, it is obvious that the current ripple can be reduced by increasing the ratio of armature time-constant to chopping period. Hence, this can be achieved by operating the chopper at higher frequency in addition to inserting an inductance in series with the armature.

The operation of the chopper at high frequency generates harmonics of higher frequencies at the input side and, hence, requires a relatively small and cheap filter to keep the amount of harmonics in the supply lines below a permissible value. But the high chopping frequency introduces two main problems.

(1) With a given chopper circuit the available ranges of the duty cycle reduce, since all practical chopper circuits will require a small interval of time for commutating the main thyristor.

(2) The switching losses in the SCR and commutation circuit increase, thereby reducing the efficiency of the chopper.

3 Stator voltage-controlled induction motors

Stator voltage-control, which does not need any variable-frequency source, is a simple and cheap method of varying the speed of an induction motor. However, it has to be selectively used, depending on the nature of the load connected to the shaft of the motor.

It is well known that the torque developed by the induction motor fed from a fixed-frequency supply, at a given speed, varies approximately as the square of the applied voltage, and steady-state operation occurs when the motor torque balances the load torque. Therefore, the rotor speed is determined by the load torque and the applied voltage. Figure 3.1 shows a family of speed/torque characteristics of the motor for various applied voltages as well as a constant load torque curve and a variable load torque curve superposed on them. It is obvious that the range of speed control is quite limited in the case of constant torque load and is substantially wide with the variable load torque. Of course, the range can be extended in the former case by making the operation at points such as P and Q stable with

Figure 3.1 Speed/torque curves of induction motor for different stator voltages.

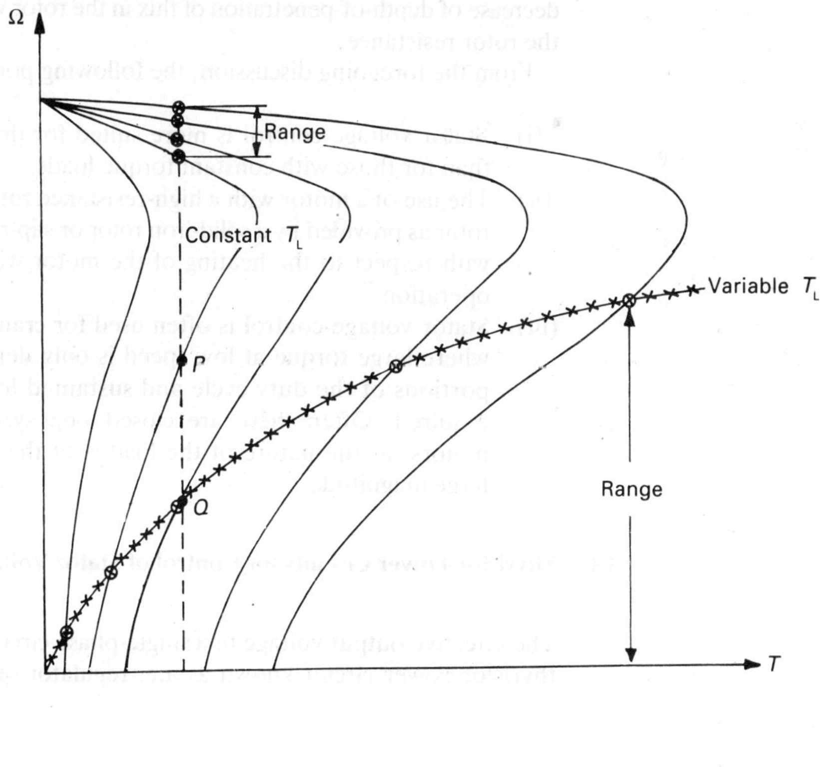

the help of a feedback loop which continuously adjusts the motor voltage so as to maintain the required output speed.

It must also be borne in mind that this type of speed control is necessarily associated with I^2R losses in the rotor. At any speed of operation ω_r, the rotor loss is equal to $T(\omega_s - \omega_r)$, where ω_s indicates the synchronous speed and T the motor torque, which must also be equal to the load torque at steady state. It follows, therefore, that the rotor loss and, hence, the heat generated within the rotor increases as the speed of rotation decreases, when the motor is subjected to constant torque loads. The efficiency becomes poor and derating is essential at low speeds to avoid overheating due to excessive losses and reduced ventilation. However, the rotor loss would not be continuously increasing with decrease in speed if the load torque were to decrease rapidly with decreasing speed, as in the case of fan or pump loads. In fact, at speeds less than two-thirds of the synchronous speed, the speed/torque characteristic of the fan is such as to reduce the amount of heat generated below the peak value. This result is independent of motor size and rotor design. The rotor design, however, affects the I^2R losses in the stator. The ratio of stator loss to rotor loss is approximately 1.1 times the ratio of stator resistance to rotor resistance referred to stator. Hence, the problem of heating of stator winding is less severe in motors with comparatively high rotor resistance. Such motors can be of cage-or slip-ring or, better still, of solid-rotor type. The latter is favoured in small-power drives since, in this motor, the very act of reducing the speed by decreasing the stator voltage brings about a reduction of the induced e.m.f. and thus a decrease of depth-of-penetration of flux in the rotor which, in effect, increases the rotor resistance.

From the foregoing discussion, the following points emerge.

(i) Stator voltage-control is more suited for drives with fan-type loads than for those with constant torque loads.

(ii) The use of a motor with a high-resistance rotor or variable-resistance rotor as provided by a solid-iron rotor or slip-ring rotor is advantageous with respect to the heating of the motor windings at low speeds of operation.

(iii) Stator voltage-control is often used for crane and hoist applications where large torque at low speed is only demanded for intermittent portions of the duty cycle and sustained low-speed running is not required. Often these are closed-loop systems involving slip-ring motors, as the nature of the load is of the constant-torque type of large magnitude.

3.1 Thyristor-Power Circuits for Control of Stator Voltage

The effective output voltage in a single-phase circuit can be controlled by a thyristor-power circuit known as a.c. regulator or chopper. It consists of two thyristors connected in inverse parallel or back-to-back and fired symmetrically at identical points in their anode-to-cathode voltage cycles. By controlling the conduction periods of the thyristors, the effective voltage delivered to the load can be varied from zero to the full supply voltage.

Several three-phase versions of a.c. regulators are possible[13]. They may be introduced in the three supply lines of a star-or delta-connected motor, as shown in Fig. 3.2 (a) and (b). In the circuit shown in (c), each pair of

Figure 3.2(a) Basic scheme of a.c. regulator-fed star-connected induction motor.

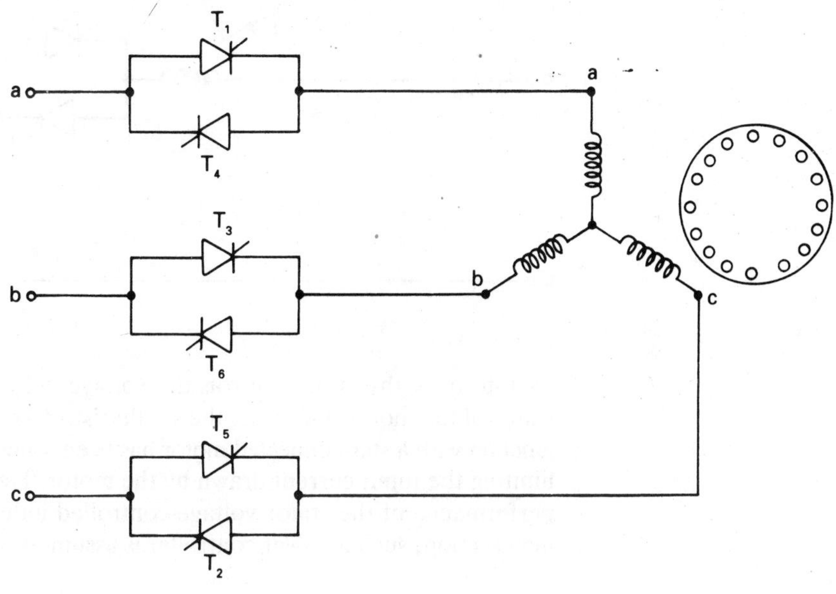

Figure 3.2(b) Basic scheme of a.c. regulator-fed delta-connected induction motor.

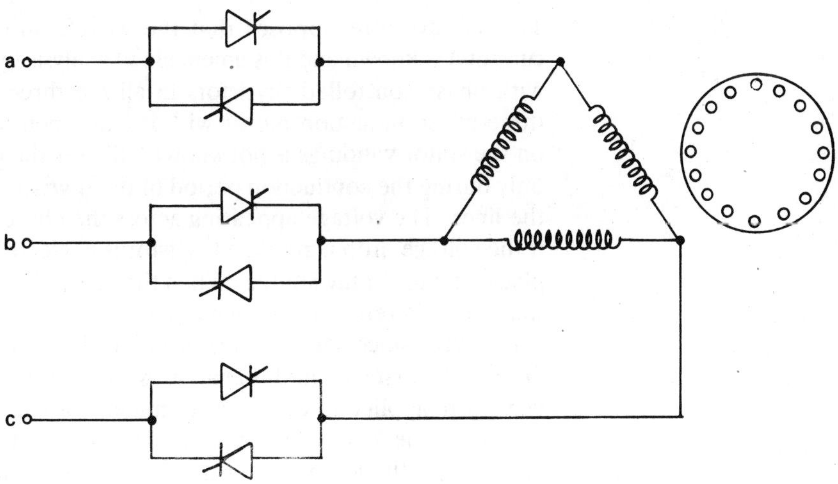

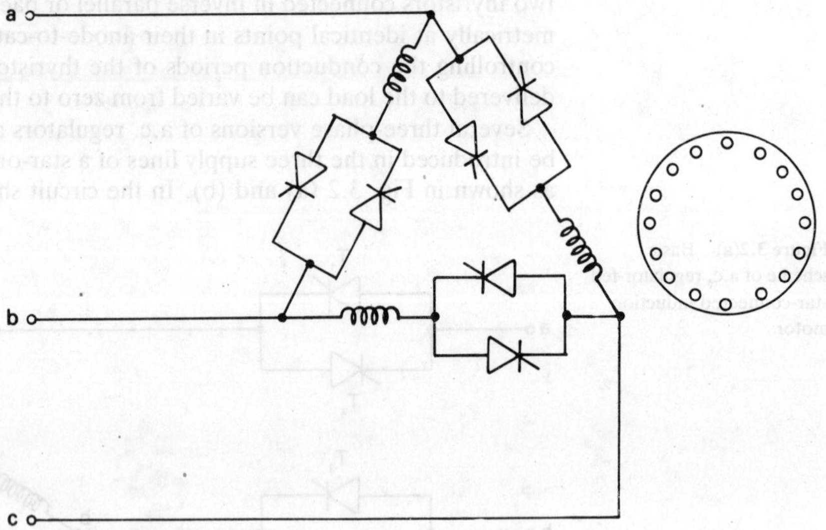

Figure 3.2(c) Another basic scheme of a.c. regulator-fed delta-connected motor.

back-to-back thyristors controls the voltage delivered to one phase of the stator of the motor. Of these, the six-thyristor power-control circuit in conjunction with a star-connected motor has been found to be the best as regards limiting the input current drawn by the motor. Hence, while analyzing the performance of the stator voltage-controlled induction-motor drive in the next section, such a power controller is assumed.

3.2 Steady-State Analysis

This method presupposes that the waveform of the input voltages (or currents) is known and it is amenable to analysis by Fourier series. However, with phase-controlled thyristors in all the three lines of a star-connected three-phase induction motor with isolated neutral, the voltage impressed on the stator windings is not known fully for the period of a half-cycle, but only during the conduction period of the thyristors connected in series with the lines. The voltage appearing across the phase winding is sinusoidal and if the voltage drop across the thyristor is neglected, it is exactly equal to the phase voltage of the source. When the series thyristor is 'off', the current in that phase is zero, being open-circuited, and the voltage across that phase is not zero, since some voltage is induced due to currents in other phases. Hence, the first step in this analysis is to determine the nature of the voltage waveform applied to the stator terminals for a half-cycle.[14]

Line-to-line voltages are easily accessible for motors with isolated neutrals and, hence, the waveform of the voltage between any two lines is deduced first.. When SCRs T_1 and T_6 in Fig. 3.2a are 'on', v_{ab}, the stator voltage across a–b, is directly given by the sinusoidal phase voltages v_{as} and v_{bs}

($v_{ab} = v_{as} - v_{bs}$). However, when SCRs T_1 and T_6 are 'off', v_{ab} is dependent on the voltage induced in the open-circuited phase by other currents. It is observed that the induced voltage in phase 'a' is sinusoidal and v_{ab} is in phase with the corresponding source voltage, but of lower amplitude. By symmetry of the waveform, the induced voltage in phase 'b' when SCR T_6 is turned 'off' can be determined from the induced voltage in phase 'a' when SCR T_1 was 'off'. Fixing the induced voltage arbitrarily at the beginning, the half-cycle line-voltage waveform for v_{ab} is obtained as shown in Fig. 3.3. The sequence of conduction in phases 'a' and 'b' indicated in the figure is as follows.

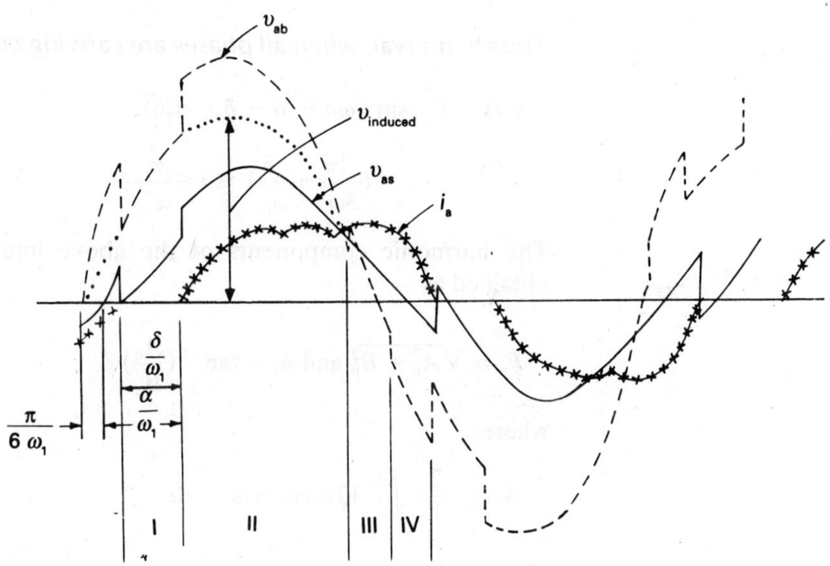

Figure 3.3 Half-cycle line-voltage waveform.

Starting from the instant when phase 'a' is on open-circuit and SCR T_6 conducts, SCRs T_1 and T_6 conduct, SCR T_1 conducts and phase 'b' is on open-circuit, and finally SCRs T_1 and T_4 conduct. The duration of open-circuit is fixed a priori to be the same for both phases.

The line-to-line voltage waveform obtained as explained above can be expressed mathematically as follows.

First interval, when phase 'a' is open-circuited

$$v(t) = V_{ind} \sin\left(\omega_1 t + \alpha - \delta + \frac{\pi}{6}\right); 0 \leq t \leq \frac{\delta}{\omega_1} \quad [3.1]$$

where α and δ denote the firing angle of the SCR and some arbitrary phase angle respectively.

Second interval, when all phases are carrying current

$$v(t) = V_{ab} \sin(\omega_1 t + \alpha - \delta + \frac{\pi}{6}); \frac{\delta}{\omega_1} \leqslant t \leqslant \frac{2\pi}{3\omega_1} \quad [3.2]$$

Third interval, when phase 'b' is open-circuited

$$v(t) = V_{ab} \sin(\omega_1 t + \alpha - \delta + \pi/6)$$

$$-V_{ind} \sin(\omega_1 t + \alpha - \delta - \frac{\pi}{2}); \frac{\omega\pi}{3\omega_1} \leqslant t \leqslant (\frac{2\pi}{3\omega_1} + \frac{\delta}{\omega_1}) \quad [3.3]$$

Fourth interval, when all phases are carrying current

$$v(t) = V_{ab} \sin(\omega_1 t + \alpha - \delta + \pi/6);$$

$$(\frac{2\pi}{3\omega_1} + \frac{\delta}{\omega_1}) \leqslant t \leqslant \frac{\pi}{\omega_1} \quad [3.4]$$

The harmonic components of the above line-to-line voltage can be obtained as

$$F_n = \sqrt{A_n^2 + B_n^2} \text{ and } \delta_n = \tan^{-1}(\frac{A_n}{B_n}) \quad [3.5]$$

where

$$A_n = \frac{2}{T_1} \int_0^{T_1} V(t) \cos n\omega_1 t \cdot dt \quad [3.6]$$

$$B_n = \frac{2}{T_1} \int_0^{T_1} V(t) \sin n\omega_1 t \cdot dt \quad [3.7]$$

F_n and δ_n denote the amplitude and phase angle of the nth harmonic component of the voltage waveform of period T_1. It may be noted that due to X-axis symmetry of the waveform, only odd harmonics will be present and within those, triplen harmonics will be absent since the motor has an isolated neutral.

The harmonic components of the phase voltage are given by

$$F_{n(phase)} = \frac{F_n}{\sqrt{3}} \text{ and } \delta_{n(phase)} = \delta_n \pm \frac{\pi}{6} \quad [3.8]$$

The positive sign is applicable for the order of harmonic 5, 11, 17, ... and the negative sign for 7, 13, 19, ... The next step is to apply these harmonics to corresponding harmonic steady-state equivalent circuits in order to determine the currents and steady torques caused by each one of the harmonic applied voltages and then, to find out the r.m.s. value of the current drawn and the net torque developed by the motor, using the principle of superposition.

Figure 3.4 shows the steady-state equivalent circuit of the motor which can be used for analysis corresponding to the nth order of harmonic excitation.

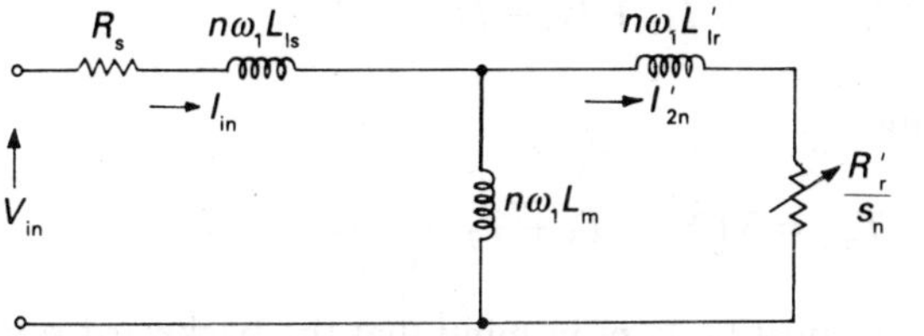

Figure 3.4 Steady-state nth-harmonic equivalent circuit.

R_s = stator resistance per phase (could be corrected for skin effect, if necessary)
L_{ls} = stator leakage reactance per phase and is expressed as
L_{ls} = 1.5 ($L_{ss} - aM$), where L_{ss}, a and M represent the stator self-inductance per phase, stator-to-rotor turns ratio and the maximum value of mutual inductance between the stator and rotor phases respectively.
L_m = magnetizing inductance per phase and is equal to 1.5 $a\,M$.
L'_{lr} = rotor leakage inductance per phase referred to stator and is expressed as
L'_{lr} = 1.5 ($a^2 L_{rr} - a\,M$), where L_{rr} indicates the actual rotor self-inductance per phase.
R'_r = $a^2 R_r$, the rotor resistance per phase referred to stator, where R_r is the actual rotor resistance per phase (must necessarily be corrected for skin effect).

s_n = slip corresponding to the nth harmonic and is equal to $\frac{(n \pm 1) \pm s_1}{n}$,

where s_1 is the fundamental slip and negative sign within brackets is valid for positive-sequence harmonics like 7, 13, 19, etc.

For chosen values of speed of rotation of the motor (fundamental slip) and firing angle α, the currents and torques corresponding to each harmonic can be obtained from the following expressions.

$$I_{1n} = V_{1n}/Z_{1n} \qquad [3.9]$$

where

$$Z_{1n} = R_s + jn\,\omega_1\,L_{1s} + \frac{jn\,\omega_1\,L_m \cdot (\frac{R'_r}{s_n} + jn\,\omega_1\,L'_{1r})}{jn\,\omega_1\,(L_m + L'_{1r}) + \frac{R'_r}{s_n}} \qquad [3.10]$$

$$I'_{2n} = I_{1n} \frac{jn\omega_1 L_m}{\dfrac{R'_r}{s_n} + jn\omega_1 (L_m + L'_{1r})} \quad [3.11]$$

$$T_n = (I'_{2n})^2 \frac{R'_r}{s_n} \quad [3.12]$$

$$I_{r.m.s.} = \sqrt{I_{11}^2 + I_{15}^2 + I_{17}^2 + \ldots} \quad [3.13]$$

and

$$T_{net} = 3\,(T_1 - T_5 + T_7 - \ldots) \quad [3.14]$$

It must be kept in mind that the backward-rotating fields caused by the negative-sequence harmonics would produce steady torques of opposite sign to those caused by the forward fields.

A family of speed/torque curves as shown in Fig. 3.5 can be obtained for various applied voltages, by giving various values of the firing angle α.

Figure 3.5 Speed/torque curves of induction motor for different applied voltages.

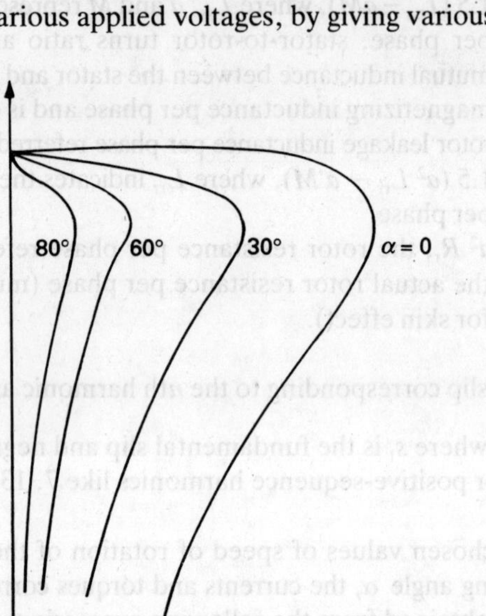

3.3 Transient Analysis

3.3.1 *Assumptions*

The following assumptions are made:

(i) Core losses, m.m.f. space harmonics and magnetic saturation effects are negligible.
(ii) The resistances of both stator and rotor are constants.
(iii) SCRs are ideal switches.

3.3.2 *Modes of Operation*

In three-phase motors controlled by back-to-back line SCRs, both two-phase and three-phase modes of operation can take place cyclically. The former mode of operation occurs when, after a zero-crossing of a phase voltage, the current in that phase remains at zero value until the appropriate complementary SCR starts conduction. However, if the firing angle, measured from the zero-crossing of the corresponding phase voltage, is such that the complementary SCR is turned on before the current has reached zero value, then the current in that line continues to flow uninterrupted and three-phase mode of operation takes place. The extent and duration of these modes depend on the firing angle of the SCRs and also on the circuit parameters.[15]

The two-phase mode of conduction is possible with any two of the three phases, i.e. a−b, b−c or c−a. For purposes of reference, it is desirable to identify by some subscript the various modes of conduction encountered. When all three stator phases conduct, the three-phase mode is designated mode 0. For the two-phase mode, when lines a−b are connected it is referred to as mode 1. Similarly, mode 2 and mode 3 represent b−c and c−a operations respectively.

3.3.3 *Derivation of Equations of Performance*

3.3.3.1 *Mode 0*

A coupled-circuit model of a three-phase induction motor is shown in Fig 3.6. The following voltage equations can be written by adding the voltage around the closed circuit of each of the stator and rotor phases.

$$v_{as} = \frac{d\psi_{mas}}{dt} + \frac{d\psi_{las}}{dt} + R_s\, i_{as} = p\,\psi_{as} + R_s\, i_{as}$$

$$v_{bs} = \frac{d\psi_{mbs}}{dt} + \frac{d\psi_{lbs}}{dt} + R_s\, i_{bs} = p\,\psi_{bs} + R_s\, i_{bs} \qquad [3.15]$$

$$v_{cs} = \frac{d\psi_{mcs}}{dt} + \frac{d\psi_{lcs}}{dt} + R_s\, i_{cs} = p\,\psi_{cs} + R_s\, i_{cs}$$

$$v_{ar} = 0 = \frac{d\psi_{mar}}{dt} + \frac{d\psi_{lar}}{dt} + R_r\, i_{ar} = p\,\psi_{ar} + R_r\, i_{ar}$$

$$v_{br} = 0 = \frac{d\psi_{mbr}}{dt} + \frac{d\psi_{lbr}}{dt} + R_r\, i_{br} = p\,\psi_{br} + R_r\, i_{br} \qquad [3.15]$$

Contd.

$$v_{cr} = 0 = \frac{d\psi_{mcr}}{dt} + \frac{d\psi_{lcr}}{dt} + R_r\, i_{cr} = p\,\psi_{cr} + R_r\, i_{cr}$$

ψ_m and ψ_l denote the flux-linkages due to mutual airgap flux and leakage flux respectively.

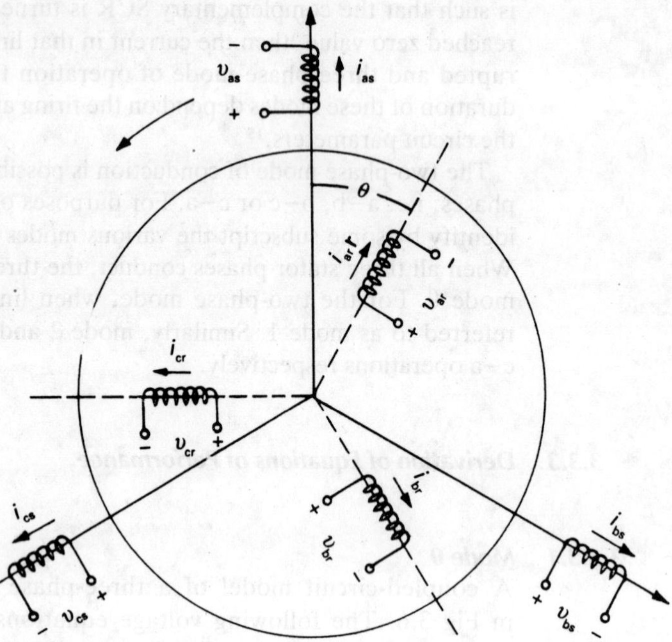

Figure 3.6 Coupled-circuit model of 3-phase induction motor.

$$[\psi] = [L]\,[i] \qquad [3.16]$$

where

$$[\psi] = [\psi_{as}\ \psi_{bs}\ \psi_{cs}\ \psi_{ar}\ \psi_{br}\ \psi_{cr}]^t \qquad [3.17]$$

$$[i] = [i_{as}\ i_{bs}\ i_{cs}\ i_{ar}\ i_{br}\ i_{cr}]^t \qquad [3.18]$$

and

$$[L] = \begin{bmatrix} L_{ss} & L_{sm} & L_{sm} & M\cos\theta & M\cos(\theta+\frac{2\pi}{3}) & M\cos(\theta-\frac{2\pi}{3}) \\ L_{sm} & L_{ss} & L_{sm} & M\cos(\theta-\frac{2\pi}{3}) & M\cos\theta & M\cos(\theta+\frac{2\pi}{3}) \\ L_{sm} & L_{sm} & L_{ss} & M\cos(\theta+\frac{2\pi}{3}) & M\cos(\theta-\frac{2\pi}{3}) & M\cos\theta \\ M\cos(\theta+\frac{2\pi}{3}) & M\cos(\theta-\frac{2\pi}{3}) & M\cos(\theta+\frac{2\pi}{3}) & L_{rr} & L_{rm} & L_{rm} \\ M\cos(\theta+\frac{2\pi}{3}) & M\cos\theta & M\cos(\theta-\frac{2\pi}{3}) & L_{rm} & L_{rr} & L_{rm} \\ M\cos(\theta-\frac{2\pi}{3}) & M\cos(\theta+\frac{2\pi}{3}) & M\cos\theta & L_{rm} & L_{rm} & L_{rr} \end{bmatrix} \quad [3.19]$$

where L_{ss}, L_{sm}, L_{rr} and L_{rm} are self and mutual inductances of phase windings in the stator and rotor respectively,
M is the maximum value of the mutual inductance between a stator phase and a rotor phase, and
θ is the electrical rotor-position angle.

Equation [3.15] can be expressed in the matrix form as

$$[v] = p\,[L]\,[i] + [R]\,[i] \quad [3.20]$$

where

$$[v] = [v_{as}\ v_{bs}\ v_{cs}\ v_{ar}\ v_{br}\ v_{cr}]^t \quad [3.21]$$

and

$$[R] = [R_s\ R_s\ R_s\ R_r\ R_r\ R_r]^t \quad [3.22]$$

Since three-phase, three-wire supply to the motor is assumed, line voltages rather than phase voltages are used in eqns [3.20] and [3.21].

Also

$$i_{cs} = -(i_{as} + i_{bs}) \quad [3.23]$$

Hence, eqns [3.15] to [3.19] can be modified to reduce their order.

$$[L_o]=\begin{bmatrix} (L_{ss}-L_{sm}) & (L_{sm}-L_{ss}) & M[\cos\theta - \cos(\theta-\frac{2\pi}{3})] & M[\cos(\theta+\frac{2\pi}{3}) - \cos\theta] & M[\cos(\theta-\frac{2\pi}{3}) - \cos(\theta+\frac{2\pi}{3})] \\ 2(L_{ss}-L_{sm}) & -(L_{sm}-L_{ss}) & M[\cos\theta - \cos(\theta+\frac{2\pi}{3})] & M[\cos(\theta+\frac{2\pi}{3}) - \cos(\theta-\frac{2\pi}{3})] & M[\cos(\theta-\frac{2\pi}{3}) - \cos\theta] \\ M[\cos\theta - \cos(\theta+\frac{2\pi}{3})] & M[\cos(\theta-\frac{2\pi}{3}) - \cos(\theta+\frac{2\pi}{3})] & L_{rr} & L_{rm} & L_{rm} \\ M[\cos(\theta+\frac{2\pi}{3}) - \cos(\theta-\frac{2\pi}{3})] & M[\cos\theta - \cos(\theta-\frac{2\pi}{3})] & L_{rm} & L_{rr} & L_{rm} \\ M[\cos(\theta-\frac{2\pi}{3}) - \cos\theta] & M[\cos(\theta+\frac{2\pi}{3}) - \cos\theta] & L_{rm} & L_{rm} & L_{rr} \end{bmatrix} \quad [3.24]$$

$$[R_0] = \begin{bmatrix} R_s & R_s & 0 & 0 & 0 \\ 2R_s & R_s & 0 & 0 & 0 \\ 0 & 0 & R_r & 0 & 0 \\ 0 & 0 & 0 & R_r & 0 \\ 0 & 0 & 0 & 0 & R_r \end{bmatrix} \quad [3.25]$$

$$[v_0] = [(v_{as} - v_{bs})\ (v_{as} - v_{cs})\ v_{ar}\ v_{br}\ v_{cr}]^t \quad [3.26]$$

$$[i_0] = [i_{as}\ i_{bs}\ i_{ar}\ i_{br}\ i_{cr}]^t \quad [3.27]$$

The new voltage equation becomes

$$[v_0] = p\,[L_0]\,[i_0] + [R_0]\,[i_0] \quad [3.28]$$

$$= [L_0]\,p\,[i_0] + [G_0]\,[i_0]\,p\,\theta + [R_0]\,[i_0] \quad [3.29]$$

where

$$
[G_o] = \begin{bmatrix}
0 & 0 & -M[\sin\theta - \sin(\theta-\frac{2\pi}{3})] & -M[\sin(\theta+\frac{2\pi}{3}) - \sin\theta] & -M[\sin(\theta-\frac{2\pi}{3}) - \sin(\theta+\frac{2\pi}{3})] \\
0 & 0 & -M[\sin\theta - \sin(\theta+\frac{2\pi}{3})] & -M[\sin(\theta+\frac{2\pi}{3}) - \sin(\theta-\frac{2\pi}{3})] & -M[\sin(\theta-\frac{2\pi}{3}) - \sin\theta] \\
-M[\sin\theta - \sin(\theta+\frac{2\pi}{3})] & -M[\sin(\theta-\frac{2\pi}{3}) - \sin(\theta+\frac{2\pi}{3})] & 0 & 0 & 0 \\
-M[\sin(\theta+\frac{2\pi}{3}) - \sin(\theta-\frac{2\pi}{3})] & -M[\sin\theta - \sin(\theta-\frac{2\pi}{3})] & 0 & 0 & 0 \\
-M[\sin(\theta-\frac{2\pi}{3}) - \sin\theta] & -M[\sin(\theta+\frac{2\pi}{3}) - \sin\theta] & 0 & 0 & 0
\end{bmatrix} \qquad [3.30]
$$

From eqn [3.29] the current derivative is found as

$$p\,[i_0] = [L_0]^{-1}\,[v_0] - [G_0]\,[i_0]\,p\theta - [R_0]\,[i_0] \qquad [3.31]$$

The instantaneous electromagnetic torque is given as

$$
\begin{aligned}
T_e = -M\,[&(i_{as}\,i_{ar} + i_{bs}\,i_{br} + i_{cs}\,i_{cr})\sin\theta \\
&+(i_{as}\,i_{br} + i_{bs}\,i_{cr} + i_{cs}\,i_{ar})\sin(\theta + \frac{2\pi}{3}) \\
&+(i_{as}\,i_{cr} + i_{bs}\,i_{ar} + i_{cs}\,i_{br})\sin(\theta - \frac{2\pi}{3})]
\end{aligned} \qquad [3.32]
$$

The equation of motion is expressed as

$$J \frac{d^2\theta_m}{dt^2} + B \frac{d\theta_m}{dt} + T_L = T_e \quad [3.33]$$

where

$$\theta_m = \frac{2}{P} \theta \quad [3.34]$$

and

$$\Omega = p\,\theta_m \quad [3.35]$$

3.3.3.2 *Mode 1*

In this mode of operation, phases 'a' and 'b' are connected to the supply and phase 'c' is open due to the blocking action of the SCRs in that phase. The third row and the third column in the inductance matrix $[L]$ in eqn [3.19] are omitted.

The voltage equation can be modified and expressed as

$$[v_1] = [(v_{as} - v_{bs})\,(v_{ar} - v_{br})\,(v_{cr} - v_{ar})]^t \quad [3.36]$$

and the corresponding current vector is

$$[i_1] = [i_{as}\, i_{ar}\, i_{br}]^t \quad [3.37]$$

During this mode

$$i_{bs} = -i_{as}$$

and

$$i_{cr} = -(i_{ar} + i_{br})$$

Omitting the third row and third column in the inductance matrix $[L]$ and using eqns [3.36] and [3.37], a 3×3 inductance matrix $[L_1]$ is obtained as

$$[L_1] = \begin{bmatrix} 2(L_{ss} - L_{sm}) & -3M\cos(\theta - \frac{2\pi}{3}) & 3M\cos(\theta + \frac{2\pi}{3}) \\ 3M\cos\theta & (L_{rr} - L_{rm}) & -(L_{rr} - L_{rm}) \\ -3M\cos(\theta - \frac{2\pi}{3}) & -2(L_{rr} - L_{rm}) & -(L_{rr} - L_{rm}) \end{bmatrix} \quad [3.38]$$

The corresponding resistance matrix $[R_1]$ is given as

$$[R_1] = \begin{bmatrix} 2R_s & 0 & 0 \\ 0 & R_r & -R_r \\ 0 & -2R_r & -R_r \end{bmatrix} \qquad [3.39]$$

The corresponding voltage equation is expressed as

$$[v_1] = p\,[L_1]\,[i_1] + [R_1]\,[i_1] \qquad [3.40]$$

$$= [L_1]\,p\,[i_1] + [G_1]\,[i_1]\,p\,\theta + [R_1]\,[i_1] \qquad [3.41]$$

where

$$[G_1] = \begin{bmatrix} 0 & 3M\sin(\theta - \frac{2\pi}{3}) & -3M\sin(\theta + \frac{2\pi}{3}) \\ -3M\sin\theta & 0 & 0 \\ -3M\sin(\theta - \frac{2\pi}{3}) & 0 & 0 \end{bmatrix} \qquad [3.42]$$

From eqn [3.41] the current vector of derivatives is found as

$$p\,[i_1] = [L_1]^{-1}\{[v_1] - [G_1]\,[i_1]\,p\theta - [R_1]\,[i_1]\} \qquad [3.43]$$

After substituting the modified values of currents in this mode, namely $i_{as} = 0$ and $i_{bs} = -i_{as}$, we get the expression for electromagnetic torque as

$$T_{e_1} = -M\,[(i_{as}\,i_{ar} - i_{as}\,i_{br})\sin\theta$$

$$+ (i_{as}\,i_{br} - i_{as}\,i_{cr})\sin(\theta + \frac{2\pi}{3})$$

$$+ (i_{as}\,i_{cr} - i_{as}\,i_{ar})\sin(\theta - \frac{2\pi}{3})] \qquad [3.44]$$

3.3.3.3 *Mode 2*

In this mode of operation, phases 'b' and 'c' are conducting and phase 'a' is open-circuited. Hence, the first row and first column are redundant. Therefore, the new voltage and current vectors are expressed as

$$[v_2] = [(v_{bs} - v_{cs})\,(v_{ar} - v_{br})\,(v_{cr} - v_{ar})]^t \qquad [3.45]$$

$$[i_2] = [i_{bs}\,i_{ar}\,i_{br}]^t \qquad [3.46]$$

The stator current constraints are

$$i_{as} = 0, i_{bs} = -i_{cs}$$

and the rotor current must fulfill the usual condition

$$i_{cr} = -(i_{ar} + i_{br})$$

Using eqns [3.45] and [3.46] and matrix reduction, we get the following new 3 × 3 inductance matrix $[L_2]$ as

$$[L_2] = \begin{bmatrix} 2(L_{ss} - L_{sm}) & -3M\cos(\theta + \frac{2\pi}{3}) & 3M\cos\theta \\ 3M\cos(\theta - \frac{2\pi}{3}) & (L_{rr} - L_{rm}) & (L_{rm} - L_{rr}) \\ 3M\cos(\theta + \frac{2\pi}{3}) & 2(L_{rm} - L_{rr}) & (L_{rm} - L_{rr}) \end{bmatrix} \quad [3.47]$$

The corresponding resistance matrix $[R_2]$ is given as

$$[R_2] = \begin{bmatrix} R_s & 0 & 0 \\ 0 & R_r & -R_r \\ 0 & -2R_r & R_r \end{bmatrix} \quad [3.48]$$

The voltage equation becomes

$$[v_2] = p[L_2][i_2] + [R_2][i_2] \quad [3.49]$$

$$= [L_2]p[i_2] + [G_2][i_2]p\theta + [R_2][i_2] \quad [3.50]$$

where

$$[G_2] = \begin{bmatrix} 0 & 3M\sin(\theta - \frac{2\pi}{3}) & -3M\sin\theta \\ -3M\sin(\theta - \frac{2\pi}{3}) & 0 & 0 \\ -3M\sin(\theta + \frac{2\pi}{3}) & 0 & 0 \end{bmatrix} \quad [3.51]$$

The current-derivative vector can be found from

$$p[i_2] = [L_2]^{-1}\{[v_2] - [G_2][i_2]p\theta - [R_2][i_2]\} \quad [3.52]$$

The electromagnetic torque developed during this mode is given by

$$T_{e_2} = -M\,[(i_{bs}\,i_{br} - i_{bs}\,i_{cr})\sin\theta + (i_{bs}\,i_{cr} - i_{bs}\,i_{ar})\sin(\theta + \frac{2\pi}{3}) + (i_{bs}\,i_{ar} - i_{bs}\,i_{br})\sin(\theta - \frac{2\pi}{3})] \quad [3.53]$$

3.3.3.4 *Mode 3*

During this mode, phase 'b' is open-circuited and phases 'c' and 'a' are conducting. Following the procedure adopted for modes 1 and 2, we have

$$p[i_3] = [L_3]^{-1}\{[v_3] - [G_3][i_b]\,p\theta - [R_3][i_3]\} \quad [3.54]$$

$$[v_3] = [(v_{cs} - v_{as})\ (v_{ar} - v_{br})\ (v_{cr} - v_{ar})]^t \quad [3.55]$$

$$[i_3] = [i_{cs}\ i_{ar}\ i_{br}]^t \quad [3.56]$$

$$[L_3] = \begin{bmatrix} 2(L_{sm} - L_{ss}) & -M\cos\theta & 3M\cos(\theta - \frac{2\pi}{3}) \\ -3M\cos(\theta + \frac{2\pi}{3}) & (L_{rr} - L_{rm}) & (L_{rm} - L_{rr}) \\ -3M\cos\theta & 2(L_{rm} - L_{rr}) & (L_{rm} - L_{rr}) \end{bmatrix} \quad [3.57]$$

$$[R_3] = \begin{bmatrix} -2R_s & 0 & 0 \\ 0 & R_r & -R_r \\ 0 & -2R_r & -R_r \end{bmatrix} \quad [3.58]$$

$$[G_3] = \begin{bmatrix} 0 & 3M\sin\theta & -3M\sin(\theta - \frac{2\pi}{3}) \\ 3M\sin(\theta + \frac{2\pi}{3}) & 0 & 0 \\ 3M\sin\theta & 0 & 0 \end{bmatrix} \quad [3.59]$$

and

$$T_{e_3} = -M\,[(i_{as}\,i_{ar} - i_{as}\,i_{cr})\sin\theta + (i_{as}i_{br} - i_{as}i_{ar})\sin(\theta + \frac{2\pi}{3}) + (i_{as}i_{cr} - i_{as}i_{br})\sin(\theta - \frac{2\pi}{3}) \quad [3.60]$$

3.3.4 *Digital Solution of Performance Equations*

The basic differential equations governing the performance of the motor

for both three and two-phase modes of operation involve products of currents as well as speed and current. Consequently, the equations become non-linear whenever the speed is varying. Numerical solution only can be attempted to determine the current, speed and torque for sudden changes in load torque or firing angle of the thyristor.
The general form of the current-derivative vector is written as

$$p[i] = [L]^{-1}[V] \qquad [3.61]$$

where

$$[V] = [v]-[G][i]p\theta - [R][i] \qquad [3.62]$$

For any mode of operation, the first step of the solution involves the evaluation of vector $[V]$. Once $[V]$ is reduced to a column vector, matrix $[L]$ is inverted with the help of a suitable sub-routine. Then $[L]^{-1}$ is pre-multiplied with $[V]$. The result is again a column matrix. Hence, eqn [3.61] is reduced to a set of differential equations ready for digital solution.

For example, $[V_1]$ during mode 1 is given by

$$[V_1] = \begin{bmatrix} (v_{as}-v_{bs}) - 3p\theta\, M \sin(\theta - \frac{2\pi}{3})\, i_{ar} + 3p\theta\, M \sin(\theta + \frac{2\pi}{3})\, i_{br} - 2R_s i_{as} \\ (v_{ar}-v_{br}) + 3p\theta\, M \sin\theta\, i_{as} - R_r i_{ar} + R_r i_{br} \\ (v_{ar}-v_{cr}) + 3p\theta\, M \sin(\theta - \frac{2\pi}{3})\, i_{as} + 2R_r i_{ar} + R_r i_{br} \end{bmatrix} \qquad [3.63]$$

Although the differential equations are now in a form suitable for digital-computer solution, solving is still difficult because the motor is supplied from a solid-state voltage regulator and at every instant the actual operating mode must be determined and taken into account for deciding which set of differential equations are to be solved.

The SCR switching constraints can be obtained by referring to Fig. 3.3. It may be noted that the six SCRs are triggered in a sequential manner with T_1 in phase 'a' as the datum. For a specified firing angle α, the switching instants for all six SCRs are calculated and included with the computer input data. For example, the switching points SWT_1 of thyristor T_1 are

$$SWT_1 = \alpha + 6 \cdot \frac{\pi}{3} + 6 \cdot \frac{\pi}{3}(K-1) \qquad [3.64]$$

where

$$K = 1,2,3,\ldots$$

$$\left.\begin{aligned}
SWT_2 &= \alpha + \frac{\pi}{3} + 6 \cdot \frac{\pi}{3}(K-1) \\
SWT_3 &= \alpha + 2 \cdot \frac{\pi}{3} + 6 \cdot \frac{\pi}{3}(K-1) \\
SWT_4 &= \alpha + 3 \cdot \frac{\pi}{3} + 6 \cdot \frac{\pi}{3}(K-1) \\
SWT_5 &= \alpha + 4 \cdot \frac{\pi}{3} + 6 \cdot \frac{\pi}{3}(K-1) \\
SWT_6 &= \alpha + 5 \cdot \frac{\pi}{3} + 6 \cdot \frac{\pi}{3}(K-1)
\end{aligned}\right\} \quad [3.65]$$

According to this sequence T_1 is turned on at α..($\pi/3$) radians later, T_2 is triggered. Conduction begins at ($\alpha + \pi/3$), When SCRs T_1 and T_2 are both turned on.

At the beginning of each step of numerical integration, a check is made to determine whether the present solution-point coincides with the instant at which the triggering of the next SCR in sequence is to occur. If it does, transfer to a new mode may take place, depending on the present mode and the position of the SCR just triggered.

Let us assume that we are presently operating in mode 1 and the time for SCR T_5 to be triggered is approaching. Transition to mode 0 will then be necessary. The programme sets this new mode and continues with computations. However, if the step-size is such that the instant ωt to which calculations refer does not coincides with the triggering instant of T_5 and the next integration point bypasses it, the programme adjusts the step-size so that it precisely coincides with the firing instant of the incoming SCR T_5. This check must be carried out at the start of every integration step.

While operating in three-phase mode, it may happen that the current in a particular phase becomes zero. Hence, the SCR that has been conducting that current will effectively be turned off, as it cannot conduct current in the reverse direction. But, depending on the firing angle and the machine parameters, the complementary SCR in the same line may be the one that has been triggered most recently. In that case, the current will continue to flow uninterrupted. The current in the reverse direction would flow through the complementary SCR. In case the complementary SCR is not the one that has been triggered most recently and the current in the other SCR of the same phase is approaching zero, the programme must resort to iteration to reach current zero as nearly as possible.

4 Stator frequency-controlled induction motors

It is well known that the speed of an induction motor can be varied easily by changing its supply frequency, since this changes its synchronous speed. However, simply varying the stator frequency, keeping the applied voltage constant does not provide an efficient drive system.

Induction motors, for that matter any a.c. excited device, normally operate near saturation in order to give maximum utilization of the magnetic core. When the stator frequency is decreased from its rated value, the flux density increases ($\Phi_{max} \propto E/f$, i.e. $\approx \propto V/f$), creating excessive iron losses and demanding more magnetizing current. When the supply frequency is increased, keeping the applied voltage at its rated value, the flux reduces and the magnetic core remains underutilized. Hence, in order to operate the induction motor efficiently and economically at various frequencies, the flux established in the airgap must be maintained constant, that is, the ratio E/f should remain unchanged. As it is difficult to set the induced e.m.f. E directly, it is convenient to adjust the stator voltage V, which differs from E only by the stator leakage impedance drop, to maintain approximately constant flux, by keeping V/f constant. However, when the stator supply frequency is low, this is not valid since the stator leakage reactance drop reduces with frequency, becoming comparable to the stator resistance drop, which does not change with frequency. This necessitates a boosting of the stator applied voltage V from the fixed V/f ratio value to maintain constant flux. Further, with a change in motor load, the stator leakage impedance drop varies and thus calls for a change in the set V/f ratio. However, maintaining the flux constant at its rated value in order to obtain high torque is possible only at speeds below the rated one. For operating the motor at speeds above the rated value, the applied voltage has to be greater than the rated voltage of the motor, if the flux is to be kept constant. The motor may not be able to withstand these higher voltages; hence during such high-speed operations, the applied voltage is kept fixed at the rated value and the frequency alone is varied. Obviously, this causes reduced flux and, hence, torque, but an approximately constant-power operation of the motor takes place.

4.1 Steady-State Analysis of Induction Motor Under Different Operating Constraints

The performance of the polyphase induction motor operated from a voltage source or current source of variable magnitude and frequency under constant airgap flux or constant slip frequency condition can be easily determined from a clear understanding of the basic operation of the motor and its steady-state equivalent circuit.

4.1.1 *Speed/Torque Characteristics Under Constant-Flux Conditions*

The torque developed by an induction motor depends on the magnitude of the airgap flux and the relative speed of the rotor with respect to the speed of the stator magnetic field, i.e., the slip speed. Even when the stator

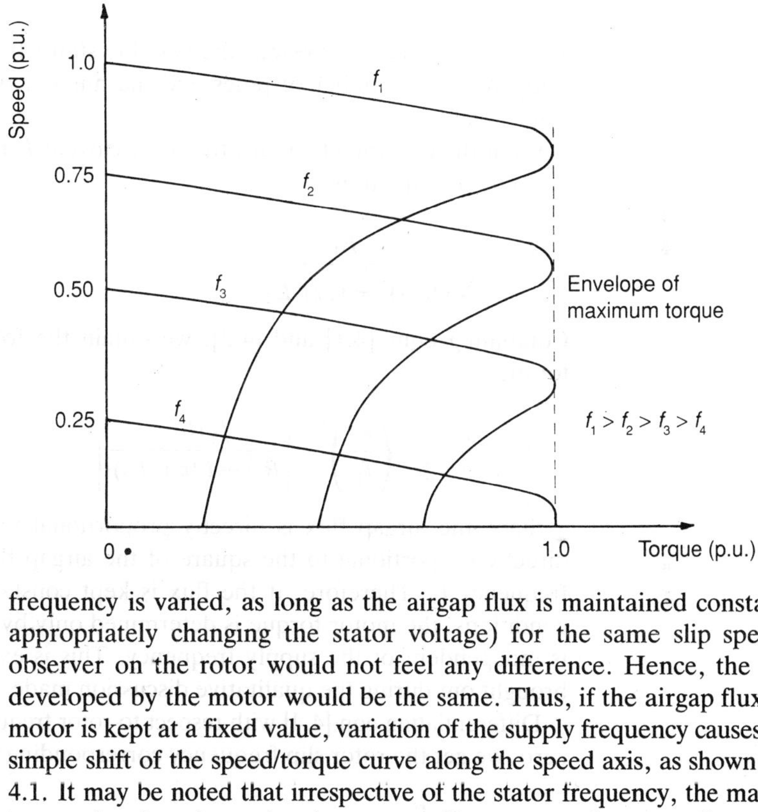

Figure 4.1 Speed/torque curves for variable-frequency operation of induction motor at constant flux.

frequency is varied, as long as the airgap flux is maintained constant (by appropriately changing the stator voltage) for the same slip speed, an observer on the rotor would not feel any difference. Hence, the torque developed by the motor would be the same. Thus, if the airgap flux in the motor is kept at a fixed value, variation of the supply frequency causes only a simple shift of the speed/torque curve along the speed axis, as shown in Fig. 4.1. It may be noted that irrespective of the stator frequency, the maximum torque developed remains the same and it occurs at the same slip speed.

Quantitatively, the torque developed by the motor under constant flux conditions can be derived from the commonly used stator-referred equivalent circuit of the induction motor shown in Fig. 4.2.

In terms of the equivalent circuit parameters, the torque is expressed as

$$T_e = \frac{P}{2}\frac{M}{2\pi f_1}\,(I_2')^2\,\frac{R_2'}{s} \tag{4.1}$$

where

$$s = \frac{f_2}{f_1} \tag{4.2}$$

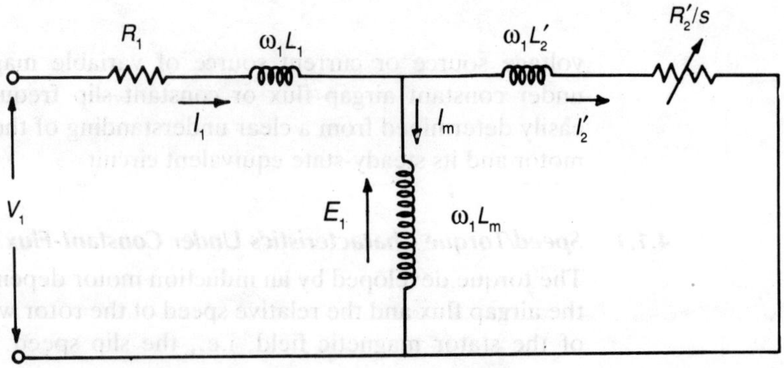

Figure 4.2 Equivalent circuit of the induction motor.

and f_1, f_2, P and m represent the variable stator frequency, the rotor slip frequency, the number of poles and the number of phases of the motor respectively.

From the equivalent circuit, the rotor current I_2' referred to the stator is given by the equation

$$I_2' = \frac{E_1}{\sqrt{(R_2'/s)^2 + (2\pi f_1 L_2')^2}} \tag{4.3}$$

Combining eqns [4.1] and [4.3], we obtain the following expression for torque:

$$T_e = \frac{P}{2} \cdot \frac{m}{2\pi} \left(\frac{E_1}{f_1}\right)^2 \left[\frac{f_2 R_2'}{R_2'^2 + (2\pi f_2 L_2')^2}\right] \tag{4.4}$$

Since the airgap flux is directly proportional to (E_1/f_1), the torque is directly proportional to the square of the airgap flux at a specified rotor frequency f_2. Therefore, if the flux is kept constant under all operating conditions, the motor torque is determined only by the slip frequency and is independent of the supply frequency. This is exactly the fact that was brought out during the qualitative discussion made earlier.

Differentiating eqn [4.4] with respect to rotor frequency f_2 and equating to zero, we get the rotor slip frequency corresponding to maximum torque as

$$f_{2\,max} = \frac{R_2'}{2\pi L_2'} \tag{4.5}$$

On substituting the value of f_{2max} into eqn [4.4], the maximum torque is obtained as

$$T_{e\,max} = \frac{P}{2}\,\frac{m}{2\pi}\left(\frac{E_1}{f_1}\right)^2 \frac{1}{4\pi L_2'} \tag{4.6}$$

Equations [4.5] and [4.6] also show that whatever may be the stator frequency, the maximum torque developed remains the same and it occurs at the same slip frequency. It is also seen that the rotor resistance does not affect the maximum torque, but influences the rotor frequency at which the breakdown occurs, as in the case of a constant-voltage, constant-frequency fed induction motor.

Furthermore, from the equivalent circuit, the stator current I_1 is given by

$$\dot{I}_1 = \dot{I}_m + \dot{I}'_2 \qquad [4.7]$$

$$= \frac{\dot{E}_1}{j\omega_1 L_m} + \frac{E_1}{(R'_2/s) + j\omega_1 L'_2}$$

$$= \left(\frac{\dot{E}_1}{f_1}\right)\left[\frac{1}{j2\pi L_m} + \frac{1}{(R'_2/f_2 + j2\pi L'_2)}\right] \qquad [4.8]$$

Equation [4.8] shows that the stator current $\dot{I}_1$ is also independent of the supply frequency f_1 and is determined solely by the rotor frequency, when the airgap flux is maintained constant.[16]

4.1.2 Speed/Torque Characteristics when Operated from a Current Source

Variable-frequency operation of the motor fed from a constant-current source rather than a voltage source has certain definite advantages. Since the current in the inverter is kept at a fixed value, no transient surges can occur. Also, there is no need for any over-current capacity. This makes it possible to design an economic inverter.

The performance of the motor could, again, be easily determined with the help of the equivalent circuit shown in Fig. 4.2.

From the equivalent circuit, the following phasor equations relating rotor current and stator current can be obtained:

$$j\omega_1 L_m (\dot{I}_1 - \dot{I}'_2) = \left(\frac{R'_2}{s} + j\omega_1 L'_2\right)\dot{I}'_2 \qquad (4.9)$$

Considering the magnitude only, the rotor current I'_2 referred to stator can be found in terms of the stator current I_1 as

$$I'_2 = \frac{\omega_1 L_m I_1}{\sqrt{(R'_2/s)^2 + \omega_1^2 (L'_2 + L_m)^2}} \qquad (4.10)$$

Substituting eqns [4.10] and [4.2] in eqn [4.1], the torque developed can be written as

$$T_e = \frac{P}{2}\frac{m}{2\pi} I_1^2 \left[\frac{f_2 R_2' (2\pi L_m)^2}{R_2'^2 + [2\pi f_2 (L_2' + L_m)]^2} \right] \tag{4.11}$$

It must be noted that the torque developed for specified values of stator current and rotor frequency depends only on the parameters of the motor and is independent of the stator frequency.

For a given stator current, the maximum torque occurs when

$$R_2' = 2\pi f_2 (L_2' + L_m) \tag{4.12}$$

i.e, when

$$f_2 = \frac{R_2'}{[2\pi (L_2' + L_m)]} \tag{4.13}$$

At this frequency of the rotor current, the torque per ampere of the motor has an optimum value. The maximum torque is obtained by substituting eqn [4.12] into eqn [4.11] as

$$T_{e\,max} = \frac{P}{2} \cdot m I_1^2 \frac{L_m^2}{2(L_2' + L_m)} \tag{4.14}$$

The speed/torque curves at various stator currents but at any fixed value of stator frequency, are shown in Fig. 4.3. It may be observed that the starting torque is very low even when the motor is operated at rated current. This would be lower than that developed by the motor operated at rated voltage and rated frequency from a voltage source. This is due to the significant difference in the magnitudes of the flux created during both

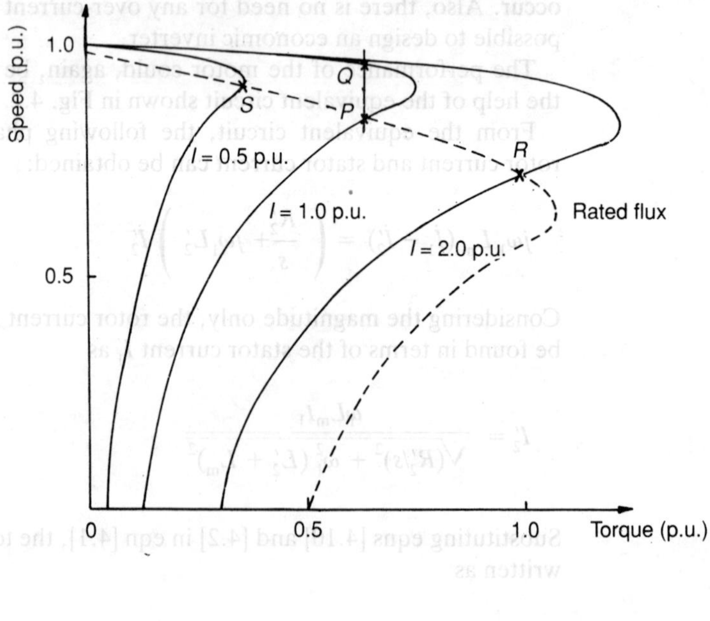

Figure 4.3 Speed/torque curves of current-fed induction motor for different stator currents.

these operations. While rated flux is produced by a voltage-fed machine at rated voltage, only a low value of airgap flux (low magnetizing current since the input current to the motor itself is limited to rated value) would be created by the current-fed machine. As the speed increases, the impedance of the motor increases, causing a rise in the motor applied voltage which, in turn, creates higher airgap flux and larger developed torque. If saturation is neglected, the torque rises to a high value and then falls to zero with a steep slope at synchronous speed. In an actual motor, however, saturation will limit the developed torque as shown by the solid line. A speed/torque curve at rated flux is also shown in Fig. 4.3, where the portion of the curve with negative slope can be considered to have stable operation for a constant torque load. This curve intersects the speed/torque curve at rated current of the current-fed motor at P. The motor can be operated either at P or Q for the same torque demand, when it is drawing rated current from the current source. At point Q, the slip is smaller than that at P and, hence, the rotor circuit impedance is larger. Therefore, for the same input current to the motor, the rotor current is lower at Q. But, the magnetizing current and, hence, the airgap flux is slightly higher resulting in partial saturation of the magnetic circuit and higher iron losses. The stator copper loss is the same at P and Q, but the rotor copper loss is slightly higher at P. Since the point P corresponds to a constant-voltage fed operation with rated current and airgap flux, the operation of the motor at that point is preferred to that at Q. However, point P is in the unstable region of the motor characteristics for a constant load torque and, therefore, closed loop operation of the drive system is a must. The torque at rated flux can be varied by varying both the current and the slip as indicated by the points R and S in Fig. 4.3, so that the operation lies on the negative slope of the speed/torque curve corresponding to rated voltage and flux.[16, 17]

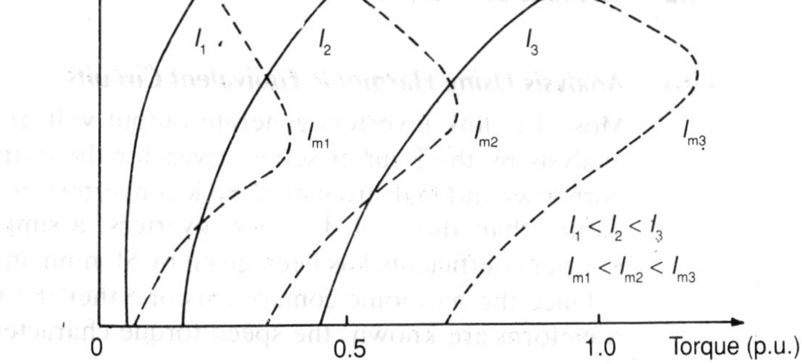

Figure 4.4 Speed/torque curves of induction motor under constant slip frequency for various values of magnetizing currents.

4.1.3 *Speed/Torque Characteristics with Constant Slip Frequency Operation*

If the slip frequency is kept constant at a low value such that the operation of the motor always occurs at a small value of slip, efficiency need not be sacrificed at low speed operation and a speed unaffected by load variation may be obtained.

From eqn [4.11], it is obvious that the motor torque is directly proportional to I_1^2, if the slip frequency is kept constant. This is true for all stator frequencies. The speed/torque characteristics of a motor operating with a constant slip frequency for various values of stator current can be obtained using the same expression and will be as shown in Fig. 4.4.

From the equivalent circuit shown in Fig. 4.2, a relationship between the stator current I_1 and the magnetizing current I_m can be obtained as

$$I_m = I_1 \frac{\sqrt{(R_2'/s)^2 + (2\pi f_1 L_2')^2}}{\sqrt{(R_2'/s)^2 + [2\pi f_1 (L_2' + L_m)]^2}} \qquad [4.15]$$

Substituting f_2/f_1 for s, we get

$$I_m = I_1 \sqrt{\frac{1 + (f_2)^2 (2\pi L_2'/R_2')^2}{1 + (f_2)^2 [2\pi(L_2'/L_m')/R_2']^2}} \qquad [4.16]$$

From eqn [4.16], it is clear that I_m is proportional to I_1 when slip frequency is kept constant.[16] Neglecting the effect of saturation, we observe that the airgap flux is directly proportional to the magnetizing current and hence, to the stator current under constant slip frequency condition. The speed/torque curves corresponding to different values of airgap flux or magnetising current under constant slip frequency can be determined using eqns [4.11] and [4.16]. They are also shown in Fig. 4.4. It is clearly seen that various load torques can be supplied at the same speed. They correspond to different values of stator current or airgap flux.

4.2 Methods of Analysis of Inverter-Fed Induction Motors

4.2.1 *Analysis Using Harmonic Equivalent Circuits*

Most d.c. link inverters generate output voltage waveforms amenable to analysis by the Fourier series. Even for the output voltage waveforms of both low- and high-frequency cycloconverters, which are more complex in nature than those of d.c. link inverters, a simple method to obtain the Fourier coefficients has been given by Sloninn and Biringer.[18]

Once the harmonic components of either the voltage or current output waveform are known, the speed/torque characteristic at a specified stator frequency can be obtained by using the harmonic equivalent circuit and the equations derived in Section 3.2. By choosing different values for stator frequency ω_1, the family of speed/torque curves shown in Fig. 4.5 for constant volts/hertz operation can be determined.

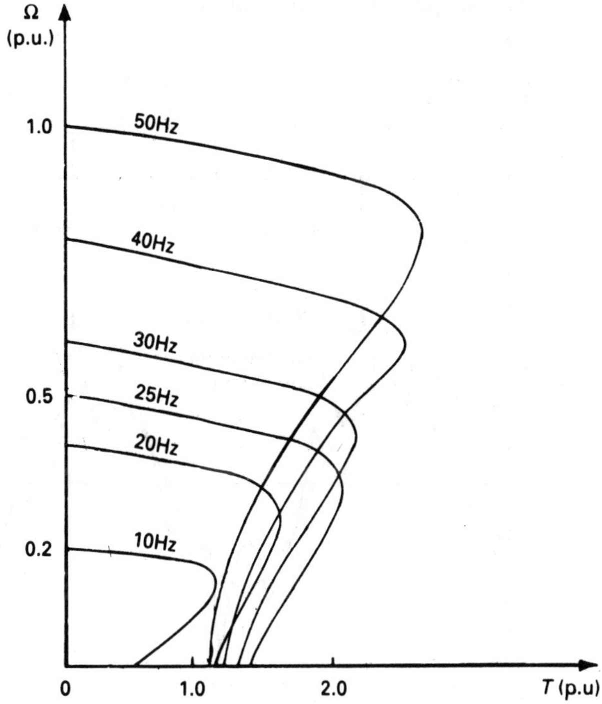

Figure 4.5 Speed/torque curves of motor for constant *V/f* operation

The waveform of the stator phase current can be determined from the expression

$$i_1 = I_{11} \sin(\omega_1 t + \delta_1 - \theta_1) + I_{15} \sin(5\omega_1 t + \delta_5 - \theta_5) + I_{17} \sin(7\omega_1 t + \delta_7 - \theta_7) + \ldots + I_{1k} \sin(k\omega_1 t + \delta_k - \theta_k) + \ldots \quad [4.17]$$

where θ_1, θ_5, etc. denote phase angles corresponding to the power factor of respective harmonic currents. A typical current waveform obtained when an induction motor is fed from an inverter that provides a six-step supply voltage is illustrated in Fig. 4.6. The time harmonics present in the applied voltage not only increase the r.m.s. value of the current drawn by the motor, but also generate large current peaks which impose a more severe commutating duty on the inverter.

4.2.2 *Analysis Using Generalized Machine Theory*

From the unified machine theory, it is well known that a multipolar, polyphase symmetrical machine can be reduced to an equivalent two-phase machine, whose operation can be described by a minimum number of differential equations that can be solved with the help of a digital computer. Of course, the machine is assumed to be ideal, that is the stator as well as the rotor circuit have both magnetic and electrical symmetry, the magnetic circuit remains unsaturated, the core losses are negligible, the m.m.f. and flux density distribution in the airgap is sinusoidal and the machine parameters are constant.

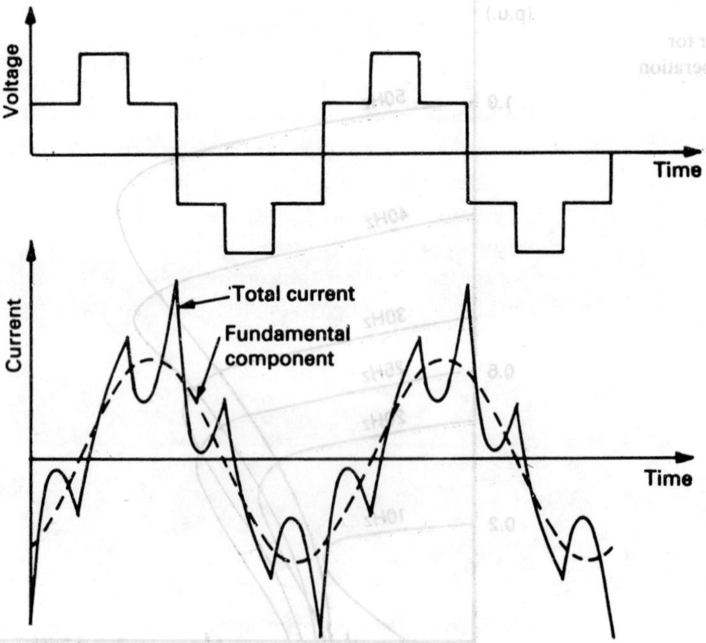

Figure 4.6 Stator current waveform corresponding to 6-step voltage waveform.

For steady-state and transient analysis of induction motors fed from static power converters, it is advantageous to write the machine equations in a system of orthogonal axes α and β stationary in space. With such a choice of stator-fixed axes, the frequency of the stator voltages remains the same as that of the supply and the expressions for stator voltages do contain fewer terms compared to those of the original machine.[19,20]

The voltage/current relations in terms of the $\alpha - \beta$ axes for a two-pole, two-phase induction machine having a stator-to-rotor turns ratio of unity are given by

$$\bar{v} = [R]\, i + p\,[L]\, \bar{i} \qquad [4.18]$$

where

$$\bar{v} = [v_{\alpha s} \mid v_{\beta s} \mid v_{\alpha r} \mid v_{\beta r}]^t \qquad [4.19]$$

$$\bar{i} = [i_{\alpha s} \mid i_{\beta s} \mid i_{\alpha r} \mid i_{\beta r}]^t \qquad [4.20]$$

$$[R] = \text{diag.}\ [R_s, R_s, R_r, R_r] \qquad [4.21]$$

$$[L] = \begin{bmatrix} L_{ss} & & M & \\ & L_{ss} & & M \\ M & \omega_r M & L_{rr} & \omega_r L_{rr} \\ -\omega_r M & M & -\omega_r L_{rr} & L_{rr} \end{bmatrix} \quad [4.22]$$

$v_{\alpha s}$, $v_{\beta s}$, $v_{\alpha r}$, $v_{\beta r}$ and $i_{\alpha s}$, $i_{\beta s}$, $i_{\alpha r}$, $i_{\beta r}$ denote the voltages and currents in the stator and rotor windings along the α and β axes respectively; R_s and R_r indicate the stator and rotor resistance per phase respectively; M represents the mutual inductance between stator and rotor phases; L_{ss} and L_{rr} denote the self inductance per phase of stator and rotor winding respectively; and ω_r indicates the speed of rotation of the rotor in *electrical* radians/second.

In case the actual rotor winding has a different number of turns from that of the stator, it is necessary to replace R_r, M, L_{rr}, $v_{\beta r}$, $v_{\alpha r}$, $i_{\alpha r}$ and $i_{\beta r}$ by their referred quantities depending on the ratio of stator turns per phase/rotor turns per phase. For a rotio a, the referred quantities would be given by

$$R'_r = a^2 R_r,\ M' = aM,\ L'_{rr} = a^2 L_{rr},$$

$$v'_{\alpha r} = a v_{\alpha r},\ v'_{\beta r} = a v_{\beta r},\ i'_{\alpha r} = i_{\alpha r/a} \text{ and}$$

$$i'_{\beta r} = i_{\beta r/a}$$

The relations between the applied stator phase voltages and their values referred to the α and β axes, for a balanced three-phase system, are

$$\begin{bmatrix} v_\alpha \\ \\ v_\beta \end{bmatrix} = \frac{2}{3} \begin{bmatrix} 0 & -\dfrac{\sqrt{3}}{2} & \dfrac{\sqrt{3}}{2} \\ & & \\ 1 & -\dfrac{1}{2} & -\dfrac{1}{2} \end{bmatrix} \begin{bmatrix} v_A \\ v_B \\ v_C \end{bmatrix} \quad [4.23]$$

and the inverse relationship is given by

$$\begin{bmatrix} v_A \\ v_B \\ v_C \end{bmatrix} = \begin{bmatrix} 0 & 1 \\ -\dfrac{\sqrt{3}}{2} & -\dfrac{1}{2} \\ \dfrac{\sqrt{3}}{2} & -\dfrac{1}{2} \end{bmatrix} \begin{bmatrix} v_\alpha \\ v_\beta \end{bmatrix} \quad [4.24]$$

The constant 2/3 has been chosen so that the power developed by the actual three-phase machine and the equivalent two-phase machine will be the same on a per-phase basis.

The torque developed by the equivalent two-pole, two-phase machine is given as

$$T_e = M' \,(i_{\beta s}\, i'_{\alpha r} - i_{\alpha s}\, i'_{\beta r}) \tag{4.25}$$

Hence, the electromagnetic torque developed by a *m*-phase balanced machine wound for *P*-poles is given by

$$T_e = \frac{P}{2}\,\frac{m}{2}\,M' \,(i_{\beta s}\, i'_{\alpha r} - i_{\alpha s}\, i'_{\beta r}) \tag{4.26}$$

The equation of motion is expressed as

$$J\frac{d\Omega}{dt} + B\Omega\, T_L = T_e \tag{4.27}$$

For digital computation, it is convenient to rearrange eqn [4.18].

$$p\bar{i} = [L]^{-1}\,[\bar{v} - [R]\,\bar{i}\,] \tag{4.28}$$

$$p\Omega = \frac{1}{J}\,(T_e - T_L - B\Omega\,) \tag{4.29}$$

Also, it is preferable to express both the electrical and mechanical quantities in eqns [4.28] and [4.29] in per-unit values by using the following base values:

Base power	— Rated apparent power, W
Base voltage	— Peak value of rated phase voltage, V
Base current	— Peak value of rated phase current, A
Base impedance	— Base voltage/Base current, Ω
Base speed	— Synchronous speed, mechanical radians/second
Base torque	— Base power/Base speed, Nm
Base angular frequency	— Rated angular frequency, electrical radians/second
Inertia constant	— $\dfrac{\text{Moment of inertia}}{\text{Base power}}$ (Base speed)^2, seconds

Under steady-state conditions, the acceleration of the rotor $\dfrac{d\Omega}{dt} = 0$ and hence

$$T_e = T_L + B\Omega \tag{4.30}$$

Before proceeding to solve eqns [4.28] and [4.29] to determine the transient performance, care must be taken to see whether correct values of L_{ss}, M' and L'_{rr} have been substituted. Very often, these parameters are deduced from the per-phase equivalent circuit of the actual m-phase machine, which gives the values of stator leakage inductance per phase (L_1), rotor leakage inductance per phase referred to stator (L'_2) and the magnetizing inductance (L_m). From these values, the magnitudes of the desired quantities can be obtained from the following expressions:

$$\left.\begin{aligned} L_1 &= L_{ss} - \frac{m}{2}M' \\ L'_2 &= L'_{rr} - \frac{m}{2}M' \end{aligned}\right\} \qquad [4.31]$$

and

$$L_m = \frac{m}{2} M' \qquad [4.32]$$

While solving eqns [4.28] and [4.29], the solutions are advanced in a step-by-step fashion, assuming that no significant change of variables has occurred during a particular step and hence the step-length for the solution must be carefully chosen to give as accurate results as possible.

4.2.3 *Space Vector Method of Analysis*

The commonly used steady-state equivalent circuit model and the matrix equations, which represent the induction motor and enable us to determine the transient performance are, however, not adequate for understanding the design and operation of controlled induction motor drives capable of as high a dynamic performance as that of the separately-excited, voltage-controlled d.c. motor drives. Using the space vector theory proposed by Kovacs and Racz,[21, 22] it is possible to construct such a model, valid for any instantaneous variation of voltage and current generated by the inverter supplying the motor. It also adequately describes both the steady-state and transient operation of the machine. The space vector theory is very much related to the two-axis theory of electrical machines enunciated by Park. Hence space vectors (phasors) are also known as Park vectors. The method of analysis using space vectors is simple and enables us to appreciate the physical nature of the various phenomena involved.

4.2.3.1 *Space vector of stator mmfs, currents, flux-linkages and voltages*

Figure. 4.7 shows the cross-sectional view of a smooth airgap machine with balanced two-pole, three-phase windings. It is assumed that the permeability of the iron used is infinity and the flux density is radial in the airgap. The effects of slotting, iron losses and the end effects are neglected. Although the stator and rotor windings are shown as single, full-pitched coils located on two sides of the airgap, they actually represent distributed windings which, at every instant, produce sinusoidal m.m.f. waves centered on the magnetic axes of the respective phases.

Figure 4.7 Cross-section of a basic balanced three-phase machine.

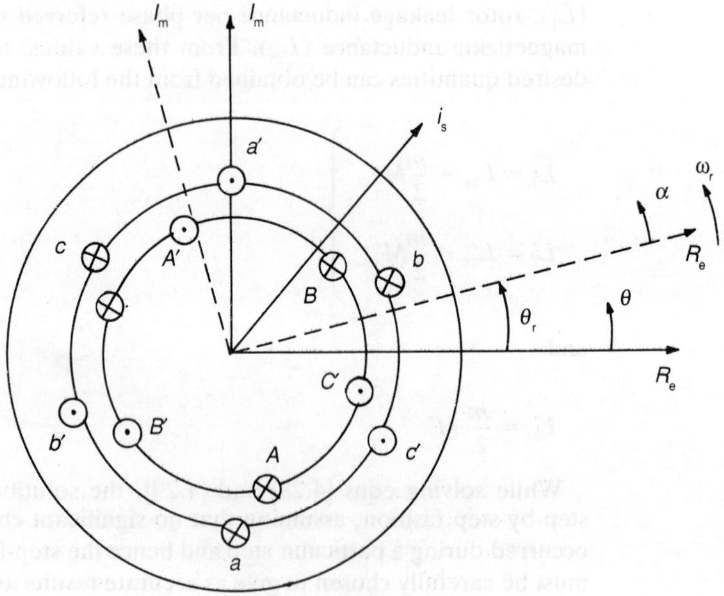

Let us assume that the stator windings are supplied by a system of three-phase currents $i_{sa}(t)$, $i_{sb}(t)$ and $i_{sc}(t)$, which vary arbitrarily with time. Then, with the neutral point isolated, there will not be any zero-sequence stator currents.

The distribution of the resultant m.m.f. produced by the stator currents is given by

$$f_s(\theta, t) = N_s\,[i_{sa}(t)\cos\theta + i_{sb}(t)\cos(\theta - 2\pi/3) + i_{sc}(t)\cos(\theta - 4\pi/3)] \quad (4.33)$$

where N_s represents the effective turns per phase of the stator and θ is the angle measured around the periphery with respect to the magnetic axis of phase a, which coincides with the real axis of the stator reference frame.

Equation [4.33] can also be written as

$$f_s(\theta, t) = \frac{3}{2} N_s \operatorname{Re}\left\{ \frac{2}{3}\left[i_{sa}(t) + a\, i_{sb}(t) + a^2\, i_{sc}(t) \right] e^{-j\theta} \right\} \quad [4.34]$$

where a and a^2 are space operators equal to $e^{j2\pi/3}$ and $e^{j4\pi/3}$ respectively. It must be noted that the symbols a and a^2 used in the theory of symmetrical components have a different meaning. They refer to phase differences in time and are used to indicate the vectors of the three-phase balanced voltage or current systems.

Now, let us denote

$$\frac{2}{3}\left[i_{sa}(t)+a\, i_{sb}(t)+a^2 i_{sc}(t) \right] = \bar{i}_s(t) = |\, i_{sa}\,|\, e^{j\theta_s} \quad [4.35]$$

$\bar{i}_s(t)$ is the complex space vector of the three-phase currents in the complex plane with respect to the stationary reference frame fixed to the stator. $|\,\bar{i}_s\,|$ is the modulus of the stator current space vector and θ_s its phase angle with respect to the real axis. Since, in general, currents vary with time, the modulus and the phase angle also vary with time. Physically, the space vector of the stator currents determines the instantaneous magnitude and space displacement of the peak of the stator mmf produced by the three-phase stator windings.[23]

The space vector of the stator mmfs is defined as

$$\bar{f}_s(t) = N_s \bar{i}_s(t) = \bar{f}_{sa}(t) + \bar{f}_{sb}(t) + \bar{f}_{sc}(t) \quad [4.36]$$

where $f_{sa}(t)$, $f_{sb}(t)$ and $f_{sc}(t)$ are the space vectors of the individual phase mmfs.

From eqn [4.35], it follows that the space vector of the three-phase stator currents can be obtained by adding the space vectors corresponding to each phase current, namely,

$$\bar{i}_{sa} = i_{sa}(t),$$

$$\bar{i}_{sb} = a\, i_{sb}(t),$$

$$\bar{i}_{sc} = a^2 i_{sc}(t).$$

If the three-phase currents belong to a balanced system and are sinusoidal in nature as given by

$$i_{sa} = I_s\cos(\omega_s t - \varphi),$$

$$i_{sb} = I_s\cos(\omega_s t - \varphi - 2\pi/3),$$

$$i_{sc} = I_s\cos(\omega_s t - \varphi - 4\pi/3),$$

the space vector of these stator currents will be given by

$$i_s = \frac{2}{3}[i_{sa}(t) + a\, i_{sb}(t) + a^2 i_{sc}(t)]$$
$$= I_s e^{j(\omega_s t - \varphi)} \quad [4.37]$$

As I_s is of fixed magnitude and independent of time, the locus of the stator current vector is a circle along which the tip of this space vector moves in the anticlockwise direction in space. The angular velocity of this space vector is constant and equal to the synchronous speed ω_s. In this particular case of three-phase sinusoidal balanced currents, the space vector of the stator currents is identical to the positive-sequence complex vector of the three-phase currents. Therefore, the time vector diagrams are identical to the space vector diagrams.

But, in other cases the space vectors and complex phasors are not identical.

In the same manner as it was done with the stator current space vector, it is possible to define flux linkage and voltage space vectors.

The space vector for stator flux linkage is given as

$$\bar{\psi}_s = \frac{2}{3}(\psi_{sa} + a\psi_{sb} + a^2\psi_{sc}) \qquad [4.38]$$

where ψ_{sa}, ψ_{sb} and ψ_{sc} represent the total flux linking with the stator phases, a, b and c respectively.

Secondly, the space vector for stator voltage is expressed as

$$\bar{v}_s = \frac{2}{3}(v_{sa} + a\,v_{sb} + a^2 v_{sc}) \qquad [4.39]$$

where v_{sa}, v_{sb} and v_{sc} denote the instantaneous values of the phase voltages of the stator.

Using space vectors, it is possible to write the stator voltage equations of a three-phase machine into a single space vector equation. The voltage equations of the individual stator phase are known to be

$$v_{sa} = i_{sa} R_s + \frac{d\,\psi_{sa}}{dt} \qquad [4.40]$$

$$v_{sb} = i_{sb} R_s + \frac{d\,\psi_{sb}}{dt} \qquad [4.41]$$

$$v_{sc} = i_{sc} R_s + \frac{d\,\psi_{sc}}{dt} \qquad [4.42]$$

Multiplying eqn [4.40] by 2/3, eqn [4.41] by 2/3 a and eqn [4.42] by 2/3 a^2 and adding the left and right hand sides of the expressions obtained, we get

$$\frac{2}{3}(v_{sa} + av_{sb} + a^2v_{sc}) = \frac{2}{3}(i_{sa} + ai_{sb} + a^2i_{sc})R_s$$

$$+ \frac{2}{3}\frac{d}{dt}(\psi_{sa} + a\psi_{sb} + a^2\psi_{sc}) \qquad [4.43]$$

Using the definition of space vectors, eqn [4.44] can be expressed as

$$\bar{v}_s = \bar{i}_s R_s + \frac{d}{dt} \bar{\psi}_s \qquad [4.44]$$

4.2.3.2 *Determination of instantaneous values of space vector quantities*

If the space vectors for stator current ($\bar{i}_s$), flux-linkage ($\bar{\psi}_s$) and voltage ($\bar{v}_s$) were known, that is, if we know the modulus and space phase angle of these quantities, the projections of any one of these space vectors on to the magnetic axes of stator phases a, b and c would give the instantaneous phase values of the said electrical or magnetic quantity. For example, v_{sc}, instantaneous value of the voltage across phase c is the magnitude of the projection of $\bar{v}_s$ on to the axis of c.

In order to determine the projection of $\bar{v}_s$ on to the axis of c, let us rotate the space vector $\bar{v}_s$ by an angle of $2\pi/3$ radians in the anticlockwise direction, as the rotation of the axis of c by $2\pi/3$ radians in the anticlockwise direction makes it coincide with the real axis of the complex plane. It must be noted that the relative positions of the space vector and the axis of c have not changed. Therefore, the magnitude of the projection of $\bar{v}_s$ on to the axis of c is equal to the projection on to the real axis of the rotated space vector, namely $a\,\bar{v}_s$. Let us find its value using eqn [4.39].

$$\text{Re}(a\bar{v}_s = \text{Re}\left[\frac{2}{3}(a\,v_{sa} + a^2 v_{sb} + a^3 v_{sc})\right] \qquad [4.45]$$

Since

$$a = -\frac{1}{2} + j\frac{\sqrt{3}}{2},\; a^2 = \frac{1}{2} - j\frac{\sqrt{3}}{2} \text{ and } a^3 = 1,$$

$$\text{Re}\,(a\,\bar{v}_s = \frac{2}{3}\left(-\frac{v_{sa}}{2} - \frac{v_{sb}}{2} + v_{sc}\right)$$

$$= \frac{2}{3}\left(-\frac{v_{sc}}{2} + v_{sc}\right) \text{ since } v_{sa} + v_{sb} + v_{sc} = 0$$

$$= v_{sc} \qquad [4.46]$$

v_{sc} is nothing but the instantaneous value of the voltage across phase c.

Thus, we can conclude that the projections of the space vector of an electrical or magnetic quantity on to the axes of the phase windings always give the instantaneous values of that quantity provided no zero-sequence term of that quantity exists. In other words, there exists a direct correspondence between the space vectors and the instantaneous values of the phase quantities in three-phase machines [22].

4.2.3.3 Space vector of rotor quantities

The resultant mmf produced by the balanced three-phase distributed rotor windings A, B and C having N_r effective turns per phase and carrying time-varying currents i_{rA}, i_{rB} and i_{rC}, respectively, can be expressed as

$$f_r(\theta, t) = N_r[i_{rA}(t)\cos\alpha + i_{rB}(t)\cos(\alpha - 2\pi/3) + i_{rC}(t)\cos(\alpha - 4\pi/3)] \qquad [4.47]$$

where α is the angle measured around the periphery with respect to the magnetic axis of the rotor phase A.

Equation [4.46] can be written in complex form as

$$f_r(\theta, t) = \frac{3}{2} N_r \,\mathrm{Re}\left\{ \frac{2}{3}\,[i_{rA}(t) + a\, i_{rB}(t) + a^2\, i_{rC}(t)]\, e^{-j\alpha} \right\} \qquad [4.48]$$

Now, the expression

$\frac{2}{3}[i_{rA}(t) + a\, i_{rB}(t) + a^2\, i_{rC}(t)]$ can be defined as being equal to

$$\bar{i}_r = |\bar{i}_r|\, e^{j\alpha_r} \qquad [4.49]$$

expressed in the reference frame fixed to the rotor. $|\bar{i}_r|$ is the modulus of the rotor current space vector and α_r is its phase angle measured from the real axis of the reference frame fixed to the rotor. The speed of this reference frame is given by

$$\omega_r = \frac{d\theta_r}{dt} \qquad [4.50]$$

where θ_r is the angle between the real axes of reference frames fixed to the stator and rotor and measured from the former. The rotor current space vector determines the instantaneous magnitude and angular displacement of the peak of the sinusoidally distributed rotor mmf.

Thus, it can be generalized that the definitions of the space vector quantities in their own reference frames are similar. Hence, the space vector expressions for rotor flux-linkages and voltages are

$$\bar{\psi}_r = \frac{2}{3}[\psi_{rA}(t) + a\psi_{rB}(t) + a^2\psi_{rC}(t)] \qquad [4.51]$$

and

$$\bar{v}_r = \frac{2}{3}[v_{rA}(t) + a v_{rB}(t) + a^2 v_{rC}(t)] \qquad [4.52]$$

As in the case of the stator voltage space vector, the space vector equations for rotor voltage can be written as

$$\bar{v}_r = \bar{i}_r R_r + \frac{d\bar{\psi}_r}{dt} \qquad [4.53]$$

4.2.3.4 *Relationship between quantities expressed in stationary and rotating reference frames*

So far the stator space vector quantities were expressed in a reference frame fixed to the stator and those of the rotor were given in a reference frame fixed to the rotor. Hence, to overcome the difficulties that arise while determining the effect of the interaction between stator and rotor quantities, it is necessary to refer these quantities to a common reference frame.

Figure 4.8 shows three reference frames—one stationary in space, another fixed to the rotor and hence moving with an angular velocity ω_r in the anticlockwise direction, and the third rotating with an arbitrary angular velocity ω_k in the anticlockwise direction. The real axis of the rotor reference frame is displaced from the real axis of the stationary reference frame by an angle θ_r, while that of the general rotating frame is displaced from the real axis of the stationary frame by an angle θ_k.

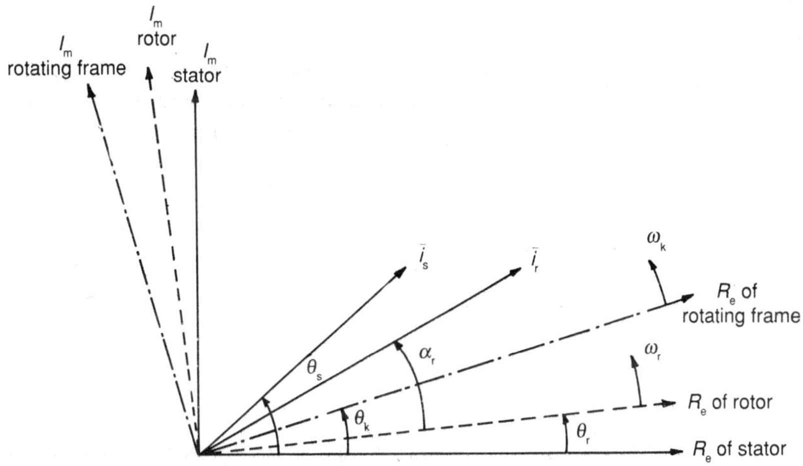

Figure 4.8 Co-ordinate transformation between stationary and rotating reference frames.

The stator current space vector $\bar{i}_s$ is defined by its modulus $|\bar{i}_s|$ and the phase angle θ_s. Therefore, in the stator reference frame, the current space vector is

$$\bar{i}_s = |\bar{i}_s| e^{j\theta_s} \qquad [4.54]$$

Equation [4.54] is the same as eqn [4.35].

Using Fig.4.8, the same space vector expressed in a reference frame rotating with an angular velocity ω_k can be written as

$$\bar{i}_s^k = |\bar{i}_s| e^{j(\theta_s - \theta_k)} = \bar{i}_s e^{-j\theta_k} \qquad [4.55]$$

where θ_k is determined from the expression

$$\frac{d\theta_k}{dt} = \omega_k \qquad [4.56]$$

If the general rotating reference frame were the same as that for the rotor, which moves with an angular velocity ω_r, the stator current space vector expressed in the rotor reference frame is given by

$$\bar{i}_s^{\,r} = |\bar{i}_s| \, e^{j(\theta_s - \theta_r)} = \bar{i}_s e^{-j\theta_r} \qquad [4.57]$$

where

$$\frac{d\theta_r}{dt} = \omega_r \qquad [4.58]$$

Similarly, the rotor current space vector in the rotor reference frame is

$$\bar{i}_r = |\,\bar{i}_r\,| \, e^{j\alpha_r} \qquad [4.59]$$

Equation [4.59] is the same as eqn [4.49].
In the general reference frame rotating with an angular velocity ω_k, the rotor current space vector becomes

$$\bar{i}_r^{\,k} = |\,\bar{i}_r\,| \, e^{j(\alpha_r - \overline{\theta_k - \theta_r})}$$

$$= |\,\bar{i}_r\,| \, e^{j\alpha_r} e^{-j(\theta_k - \theta_r)}$$

$$= \bar{i}_r \, e^{-j(\theta_k - \theta_r)} \qquad [4.60]$$

The rotor current space vector expressed in the stationary reference frame is given by

$$\bar{i}_r^{\,s} = \bar{i}_r \, e^{j\theta_r} \qquad [4.61]$$

4.2.3.5 *Transformation of voltage equations from one frame to another*

Let us transform the stator space vector voltage equation from the stationary reference frame to a general reference frame moving with an angular velocity ω_k.

According to eqn [4.44],

$$\bar{v}_s = \bar{i}_s R_s + \frac{d\bar{\psi}_s}{dt} \quad \text{in the stator frame.}$$

Substituting $\bar{i}_s = \bar{i}_s^k e^{j\theta_k}$ (obtained from eqn [4.55]), $\bar{\psi}_s = \bar{\psi}_s^k e^{j\theta_k}$ and

$\bar{v}_s = \bar{v}_s^k e^{j\theta_k}$ (by similarity), we have

$$\bar{v}_s^k e^{j\theta_k} = \bar{i}_s^k e^{j\theta_k} R_s + \frac{d}{dt}(\bar{\psi}_s^k e^{j\theta_k})$$

$$= \bar{i}_s^k e^{j\theta_k} R_s + e^{j\theta_k} \frac{d\bar{\psi}_s^k}{dt} + \bar{\psi}_s^k e^{j\theta_k} j \frac{d\theta_k}{dt} \qquad [4.62]$$

Hence

$$\bar{v}_s^k = \bar{i}_s^k R_s + \frac{d\bar{\psi}_s^k}{dt} + j\omega_k \bar{\psi}_s^k \qquad [4.63]$$

The first, second and third terms in the right-hand side of eqn [4.63] denote the voltage drop due to resistance, the transformer voltage and the speed voltage respectively. It follows from eqn [4.63] that the transformation of the stator voltage space vector equation from the stator to the rotor reference frame can be expressed as

$$\bar{v}_s^r = \bar{i}_s^r R_s + \frac{d\bar{\psi}_s^r}{dt} + j\omega_r \bar{\psi}_s^r \qquad [4.64]$$

In eqns [4.63] and [4.64], it is unnecessary to use the superscripts *k* or *r* due to the presence of the speed voltage terms.

Now, let us deal with the transformation of the rotor space vector voltage equation expressed in its own reference frame to the general reference frame rotating with an angular velocity ω_k.

As per eqn [4.53],

$$\bar{v}_r = \bar{i}_r R_r + \frac{d\bar{\psi}_r}{dt} \quad \text{in the rotor reference frame.}$$

Substituting $\bar{i}_r = \bar{i}_r^k . e^{j(\theta_k - \theta_r)}$ (from eqn [4.60]) and $\bar{\psi}_r = \bar{\psi}_r^k . e^{j(\theta_k - \theta_r)}$

and $\bar{v}_r = \bar{v}_r^k . e^{j(\theta_k - \theta_r)}$ into the above equation and simplifying, we get

$$\bar{v}_r^k = \bar{i}_r^k R_r + \frac{d\bar{\psi}_r^k}{dt} + j(\omega_k - \omega_r)\bar{\psi}_r^k \qquad [4.65]$$

Now, the rotor voltage equation in the rotor reference frame can be transformed to the stator reference frame as

$$\text{(from eqn [4.61])},\ \bar{i}_r = \bar{i}_r^{\,s}\ e^{-j\theta_r} \qquad [4.66]$$

By similarity,

$$\bar{\psi}_r = \bar{\psi}_r^{\,s}\ e^{-j\theta_r}$$

and

$$\bar{v}_r = \bar{v}_r^{\,s}\ e^{-j\theta_r}$$

Substituting eqn [4.66] in eqn [4.53] and simplifying, we obtain

$$\bar{v}_r^{\,s} = \bar{i}_r^{\,s} R_r + \frac{d\,\bar{\psi}_r^{\,s}}{dt} - j\omega_r\,\bar{\psi}_r^{\,s} \qquad [4.67]$$

In eqns [4.65] and [4.67] also, the superscripts *k* or *s* can be omitted due to the existence of the speed voltage terms.

4.2.3.6 *Space vectors and two-axis theory*

It is also possible to express space vectors by means of the two-axis theory as was originally done by Park.

The space vector of the stator currents can be defined as a vector whose real part is the instantaneous value of the direct-axis stator current component $i_{s\alpha}(t)$, and whose imaginary part is equal to the quadrature-axis stator current component $i_{s\beta}(t)$. Thus, the stator current space vector in the stationary reference frame can be expressed as

$$i_{s\alpha}(t) + j i_{s\beta}(t) \qquad [4.68]$$

In balanced three-phase machines, the direct and quadrature-axis stator current components $i_{s\alpha}$ and $i_{s\beta}$ are fictitious two-phase current-components, which are related to the actual three-phase stator currents as

$$i_{s\alpha} = \frac{2}{3}\left(i_{sa} - \frac{1}{2} i_{sb} - \frac{1}{2} i_{sc}\right) \qquad [4.69]$$

$$i_{s\beta} = \frac{1}{\sqrt{3}}\left(i_{sb} - i_{sc}\right) \qquad [4.70]$$

It follows from the definition of the space vector of stator currents that its real-axis component gives

$$\mathrm{Re}(\bar{i}_s) = \mathrm{Re}\left[\frac{2}{3}(i_{sa} + a\, i_{sb} + a^2 i_{sc})\right]$$

$$= \frac{2}{3}\left[i_{sa} - \frac{1}{2} i_{sb} - \frac{1}{2} i_{sc}\right] \qquad [4.71]$$

It may be noted that eqn [4.71] is the same as eqn [4.69].
The imaginary-axis component of the stator current space vector is given by

$$\mathrm{Im}(\bar{i}_s) = \mathrm{Im}\left[\frac{2}{3}(i_{sa} + a\, i_{sb} + a^2 i_{sc})\right]$$

$$= \frac{2}{3}\left[\frac{\sqrt{3}}{2} i_{sb} - \frac{\sqrt{3}}{2} i_{sc}\right] = \frac{1}{\sqrt{3}}(i_{sb} - i_{sc}) \qquad [4.72]$$

Equation [4.72] agrees with eqn [4.70].

In a two-phase machine, $i_{s\alpha}$ and $i_{s\beta}$ are the actual currents that flow in the two stator windings α and β, which are in space quadrature. Similarly, if i_{rd} and i_{rq} are the instantaneous values of the direct and quadrature-axis rotor current components of the three-phase rotor currents, i_{rA}, i_{rB} and i_{rC} are related to them by the expression

$$i_{rd} = \frac{2}{3}\left(i_{rA} - \frac{1}{2} i_{rB} - i_{rC}\right) \qquad [4.73]$$

and

$$i_{rq} = \frac{1}{\sqrt{3}}(i_{rB} - i_{rC}) \qquad [4.74]$$

The space vector of the rotor currents in a reference frame fixed to the rotor can be expressed as

$$\bar{i}_r = \bar{i}_{rd} + j\, i_{rq} \qquad [4.75]$$

Similarly, the two-axis representation of flux-linkages and voltages is as follows:

$$\bar{\psi}_s = \psi_{s\alpha} + j\psi_{s\beta} \qquad [4.76]$$

$$v_s = v_{s\alpha} + jv_{s\beta} \qquad [4.77]$$

$$\bar{\psi}_r = \psi_{rd} + j\psi_{rq} \qquad [4.78]$$

$$\bar{v}_r = v_{rd} + jv_{rq} \qquad [4.79]$$

It must be remembered that while $\bar{\psi}_s$ and $\bar{v}_s$ are associated with the stationary reference frame, $\bar{\psi}_r$ and $\bar{v}_r$ are expressed in terms of the rotor reference frame.

4.2.3.7 *Park transformation*

Park transformation deals with the derivation of stator voltages in terms of the direct (d) and quadrature (q) axes of the rotor, that is, in the real and imaginary axes of a reference frame fixed on the rotor.

The space vector stator voltage equation referred to the rotor reference frame as given by eqn [4.64] is

$$\bar{v}_s = \bar{i}_s R_s + \frac{d\,\bar{\psi}_s}{dt} + j\omega_r \bar{\psi}_s$$

Substituting

$$\bar{v}_s = v_{sd} + jv_{sq} \tag{4.80}$$

$$\bar{i}_s = i_{sd} + ji_{sq} \tag{4.81}$$

$$\bar{\psi}_s = \psi_{sd} + j\psi_{sq} \tag{4.82}$$

into eqn [4.64], and equating the real and imaginary terms on either side of that equation, we obtain

$$v_{sd} = i_{sd} R_s + \frac{d\,\psi_{sd}}{dt} - \omega_r \psi_{sq} \tag{4.83}$$

$$v_{sq} = i_{sq} R_s + \frac{d\,\psi_{sq}}{dt} + \omega_r \psi_{sd} \tag{4.84}$$

These are the well-known Park equations expressing the stator voltages of the a.c. machine in the rotor reference frame.

The rotor voltage components are given by

$$v_{rd} = i_{rd} R_r + \frac{d\,\psi_{rd}}{dt} \tag{4.85}$$

$$v_{rq} = i_{rq} R_r + \frac{d\,\psi_{rq}}{dt} \tag{4.86}$$

The voltage equations derived so far contain the term or terms involving the magnetic quantity, flux-linkage, either in space vector form or its two-axis components. However, for the purpose of analysis of electrical machines, it is convenient to express the flux-linkage in terms of currents and inductances.

4.2.3.8 *Stator flux-linkage space vector*

Similar to the stator current space vector, the stator flux-linkage space vector in the stator reference frame can be expressed in terms of the instantaneous values of the flux- linkages of the three stator phases as given in eqn [4.38], i.e.

$$\bar{\psi}_s = \frac{2}{3}(\psi_{sa} + a\psi_{sb} + a^2\psi_{sc})$$

where the instantaneous values of the flux-linkages associated with the phases a, b and c are given by

$$\psi_{sa} = L_s i_{sa} + M_s i_{sb} + M_s i_{sc} + M_{sr}\cos\theta_r i_{rA}$$

$$+ M_{sr}\cos(\theta_r + 2\pi/3) i_{rB} + M_{sr}\cos(\theta_r + 4\pi/3) i_{rC} \quad [4.87]$$

$$\psi_{sb} = M_s i_{sa} + L_s i_{sb} + M_s i_{sc} + M_{sr}\cos(\theta_r + 4\pi/3)\, i_{rA}$$

$$+ M_{sr}\cos\theta_r i_{rB} + M_{sr}\cos(\theta_r + 2\pi/3) i_{rC} \quad [4.88]$$

and

$$\psi_{sc} = M_s i_{sa} + M_s i_{sb} + L_s i_{sc} + M_{sr}\cos(\theta_r + 2\pi/3)\, i_{rA}$$

$$+ M_{sr}\cos(\theta_r + 4\pi/3) i_{rB} + M_{sr}\cos\theta_r i_{rC} \quad [4.89]$$

where L_s denotes the self-inductance of a stator phase winding, M_s denotes the mutual inductance between two stator phases, and M_{sr} denotes the maximum value of the mutual inductance, which varies sinusoidally with respect to rotor angular position, between a stator phase and a rotor phase respectively. Substitution of eqns [4.87]–[4.89] into eqn [4.38] and use of eqns [4.35], [4.49] and [4.61] gives the space vector equation for the stator flux- linkages in the stationary reference frame as

$$\bar{\psi}_s = L_{ss}\bar{i}_s + L_m \bar{i}_r e^{j\theta_r}$$

$$= L_{ss}\bar{i}_s + L_m \bar{i}_r^{\,s} \quad [4.90]$$

where $L_{ss} = L_s - M_s$ is the total three-phase stator inductance and L_m is the three-phase magnetizing inductance equal to 3/2 M_{sr}.

The space vector of the stator flux-linkages can be expressed in terms of the two axes α and β fixed on the stator as

$$\psi_s = \psi_{s\alpha} + j\psi_{s\beta} \tag{4.91}$$

where

$$\psi_{s\alpha} = L_{ss} i_{s\alpha} + L_m i_{r\alpha} \tag{4.92}$$

and

$$\psi_{s\beta} = L_{ss} i_{s\beta} + L_m i_{r\beta} \tag{4.93}$$

$i_{s\alpha}$, $i_{s\beta}$ and $i_{r\alpha}$, $i_{r\beta}$ are the instantaneous values of the α and β - axis stator current components and rotor current components respectively, and all the four currents are related to the stator reference frame.
It must be noted that

$$i_{r\alpha} + j\, i_{r\beta} = \bar{i}_r^{\,s} = \bar{i}_r e^{j\theta_r} \tag{4.94}$$

The two-axis components of the rotor current space vector in the reference frame fixed to the rotor are given by

$$\bar{i}_r = i_{rd} + j i_{rq} \tag{4.95}$$

Therefore, the relationship between the α, β and d, q components of the rotor current space vector is given by [23]

$$\begin{vmatrix} i_{r\alpha} \\ i_{r\beta} \end{vmatrix} = \begin{vmatrix} \cos\theta_r & -\sin\theta_r \\ \sin\theta_r & \cos\theta_r \end{vmatrix} \begin{vmatrix} i_{rd} \\ i_{rq} \end{vmatrix} \tag{4.96}$$

4.2.3.9 *Rotor flux-linkage space vector*

The space vector of the rotor flux-linkages expressed in the rotor reference frame rotating with an angular velocity ω_r is

$$\bar{\psi}_r = \frac{2}{3}\left[\ \psi_{rA}(t) + a\psi_{rB}(t) + a^2\psi_{rC}(t)\ \right] \tag{4.97}$$

where

$$\psi_{rA} = L_r i_{rA} + M_r i_{rB} + M_r i_{rC} + M_{sr}\cos\theta_r i_{sa}$$

$$+ M_{sr}\cos(\theta_r + 4\pi/3) i_{sb} + M_{sr}\cos(\theta_r + 2\pi/3) i_{sc} \quad [4.98]$$

$$\psi_{rB} = M_r i_{rA} + L_r i_{rB} + M_r i_{rC} + M_{sr}\cos(\theta_r + 2\pi/3) i_{sa}$$

$$+ M_{sr}\cos\theta_r i_{sb} + M_{sr}\cos(\theta_r + 4\pi/3) i_{sc} \quad [4.99]$$

and

$$\psi_{rC} = M_r i_{rA} + M_r i_{rB} + L_r i_{rC} + M_{sr}\cos(\theta_r + 2\pi/3) i_{sa}$$

$$+ M_{sr}\cos(\theta_r + 4\pi/3) i_{sb} + M_{sr}\cos\theta_r i_{sc} \quad [4.100]$$

where L_r and M_r denote the self-inductance of the rotor phase and the mutual inductance between two rotor phases, respectively.

Substituting eqns [4.98] to [4.100] into eqn [4.97] and using eqns [4.35], [4.49] and [4.57], we get the space vector equation for the rotor flux-linkages in the rotor reference frame as

$$\bar{\psi}_r = L_{rr}\bar{i}_r + L_m\bar{i}_s^{\,r} \quad [4.101]$$

where L_{rr} is the total three-phase rotor inductance and is given by $L_{rr} = L_r - M_r$

In terms of its two-axis components

$$\bar{\psi}_r = \psi_{rd} + j\psi_{rq} \quad [4.102]$$

where

$$\psi_{rd} = L_{rr}\, i_{rd} + L_m i_{sd} \quad [4.103]$$

and

$$\psi_{rq} = L_{rr}\, i_{rq} + L_m i_{sq} \quad [4.104]$$

In the above equations, i_{rd}, i_{rq}, i_{sd} and i_{sq} are the direct and quadrature components of the rotor and stator currents respectively, and all of them are expressed in the reference frame fixed to the rotor.

It must be noted that

$$i_{sd} + j\, i_{sq} = \bar{i}_s^{\,r} = \bar{i}_s e^{-j\theta_r} \qquad [4.105]$$

Also, $\bar{i}s = i_{s\alpha} + j\ i_{s\beta}$ in the stationary reference frame. Therefore,

$$\begin{vmatrix} i_{sd} \\ i_{sq} \end{vmatrix} = \begin{vmatrix} \cos\theta_r & \sin\theta_r \\ -\sin\theta_r & \cos\theta_r \end{vmatrix} \begin{vmatrix} i_{s\alpha} \\ i_{s\beta} \end{vmatrix} \qquad [4.106]$$

gives the relationship between the α, β and d, q components of the stator currents.[23]

4.2.3.10 Space vector voltage equations in the stationary reference frame

The stator and rotor voltage equations expressed in space vectors referred to the stator frame as given by eqns [4.44] and [4.67] are

$$\bar{v}_s = R_s\, \bar{i}_s + \frac{d\,\bar{\psi}_s}{dt}$$

and

$$\bar{v}_r^{\,s} = R_r\, \bar{i}_r^{\,s} + \frac{d\,\bar{\psi}_r^{\,s}}{dt} - j\omega_r \bar{\psi}_r^{\,s}$$

Expressing the flux-linkage space vectors in terms of inductances and currents, we get

$$\bar{v}_s = R_s \bar{i}_s + \frac{d}{dt}(L_{ss}\bar{i}_s) + \frac{d}{dt}(L_m \bar{i}_r^{\,s}) \qquad [4.107]$$

$$\bar{v}_r^{\,s} = R_r \bar{i}_r^{\,s} + \frac{d}{dt}(L_{rr}\bar{i}_r^{\,s}) + \frac{d}{dt}(L_m \bar{i}_s) - j\omega_r (L_{rr}\bar{i}_r^{\,s} + L_m\, \bar{i}_s) \qquad [4.108]$$

4.2.3.11 Space vector voltage equations in a general rotating reference frame

The stator and rotor voltage equations in space vectors with respect to a reference frame rotating at an angular velocity ω_k, as given by eqns [4.63] and [4.65], are

$$\bar{v}_s^{\,k} = R_s\, \bar{i}_s^{\,k} + \frac{d\bar{\psi}_s^{\,k}}{dt}\ j\omega_k\, \bar{\psi}_s^{\,k}$$

and

$$\bar{v}_r^{\,k} = R_r\, \bar{i}_r^{\,k} + \frac{d\bar{\psi}_r^{\,k}}{dt} + j\,(\omega_k - \omega_r)\ \bar{\psi}_r^{\,k}$$

Expressing the flux-linkage space vectors in terms of inductances and currents, we obtain

$$\bar{v}_s^{\,k} = R_s\,\bar{i}_s^{\,k} + \frac{d}{dt}\,(L_{ss}\,\bar{i}_s^{\,k}) + \frac{d}{dt}(L_m\,\bar{i}_r^{\,k})$$

$$+ j\omega_k\,(L_{ss}\,\bar{i}_s^{\,k} + L_m\,\bar{i}_r^{\,k}) \qquad [4.109]$$

and

$$\bar{v}_r^{\,k} = R_r\,\bar{i}_r^{\,k} + \frac{d}{dt}\,(L_{rr}\,\bar{i}_r^{\,k}) + \frac{d}{dt}(L_m\,\bar{i}_s^{\,k})$$

$$+ j(\omega_k - \omega_r)\,(L_{rr}\bar{i}_r^{\,k} + L_m\,\bar{i}_s^{\,k}) \qquad [4.110]$$

4.2.3.12 *Instantaneous power and torque expressions*

The instantaneous power in a three-phase system is given by

$$p = v_{sa}\,i_a + v_{sb}i_b + v_{sc}\,i_c \qquad [4.111]$$

where v_{sa}, v_{sb} and v_{sc} are the instantaneous values of the input voltages and i_a, i_b and i_c are the input currents to the phases *a, b* and *c* respectively.

In terms of space vector quantities, instantaneous power is given by

$$p = \frac{3}{2}\text{Re}\,(\bar{v}_s^{\,*}\,\bar{i}_s) \text{ or } = \frac{3}{2}\text{Re}\,(\bar{v}_s\,\bar{i}_s^{\,*}) \qquad [4.112]$$

In order to obtain an expression for the instantaneous torque in terms of space vector quantities, the basic energy-balance equation of an electromechanical system is used. In differential form, the equation is written as

$$dW_{elec} = dW_{loss} + dW_{field} + dW_{mech} \qquad [4.113]$$

In general, for a doubly-fed, three-phase machine, the differential electrical energy input can be expressed, using eqn [4.112], as

$$dW_{elec} = p.dt = \frac{3}{2}\,\text{Re}\,(\,\bar{v}_s\,\bar{i}_s^{\,*} + \bar{v}_r^{\,s}\,\bar{i}_r^{\,s*})\,dt \qquad [4.114]$$

where the stator voltage and current vectors as well as the rotor voltage and current vectors are referred to the stator reference frame.
Substituting eqns [4.44] and [4.67] in eqn [4.114], we get

$$dW_{\text{elec}} = \frac{3}{2}\text{Re}\left[\left(\bar{i}_s R_s + \frac{d\bar{\psi}_s}{dt}\right)\bar{i}_s^* + \left(\bar{i}_r^s R_r + \frac{d\bar{\psi}_r^s}{dt} - j\omega_r \bar{\psi}_r^s\right)\bar{i}_r^{s*}\right] dt$$

$$= \frac{3}{2}\left(|\bar{i}_s|^2 R_s + |\bar{i}_r^s|^2 R_r\right) dt$$

$$+ \frac{3}{2}\text{Re}\left[\frac{d\bar{\psi}_s}{dt}\bar{i}_s^* + \left(\frac{d\bar{\psi}_r^s}{dt} - j\omega_r \bar{\psi}_r^s\right)\bar{i}_r^{s*}\right] dt \quad [4.115]$$

Neglecting magnetic and mechanical losses, dW_{loss} is only due to the stator and rotor winding copper losses and, therefore,

$$dW_{\text{loss}} = \frac{3}{2}\left(|\bar{i}|^2 R_s + |\bar{i}_r^s|^2 R_r\right) dt \quad [4.116]$$

If mechanical motion were to be absent, the stored energy in the magnetic field is nothing but electrical energy input minus the losses that take place. Hence, dW_{field} can be found using eqn [4.115] and substituting $\omega_r = 0$. Thus,

$$dW_{\text{field}} = \frac{3}{2}\text{Re}\left[\frac{d\bar{\psi}_s}{dt}\bar{i}_s^* + \frac{d\bar{\psi}_{rs}}{dt}\bar{i}_r^{s*}\right] dt \quad [4.117]$$

If T is the torque developed and $d\theta$ the virtual angular rotation, the dW_{mech} can be expressed as

$$dW_{\text{mech}} = T.\,d\theta = T.\,\omega_r.\,dt \quad [4.118]$$

Substituting eqns [4.115]–[4.118] in eqn [4.113], we get

$$T = \frac{3}{2}\text{Re}\,(-j\bar{\psi}_r^s\,\bar{i}_r^{s*})$$

$$= -\frac{3}{2}(\bar{\psi}_r^s \times \bar{i}_r^{s*}) \text{ (vector product)} \quad [4.119]$$

For a pole machine, eqn [4.119] must be multiplied by $P/2$; hence its instantaneous electromagnetic torque is given by

$$T = -\frac{3}{2}\frac{P}{2}(\bar{\psi}_r^s \times \bar{i}_r^{s*}) \quad [4.120]$$

Since the torque does not vary with change of reference frame, it can be expressed as

$$T = -\frac{3}{2}\frac{P}{2}(\bar{\psi}_r \times \bar{i}_r) \quad [4.121]$$

where $\bar{\psi}_r$ and $\bar{i}_r$ are the space vectors of the rotor flux-linkages and currents referred to the actual rotor frame, or

$$T = -\frac{3}{2}\frac{P}{2}(\bar{\psi}_r^{\,k} \times \bar{i}_r^{\,k}) \quad [4.122]$$

where $\bar{\psi}_r^{\,k}$ and $\bar{i}_r^{\,k}$ are the space vectors of the rotor flux-linkages and currents in a general frame 'k' rotating with a uniform angular velocity ω_k, and whose real and imaginary axes are denoted by x and y .

By the action-reaction principle, eqn [4.122] can be written as

$$T = \frac{3}{2}\frac{P}{2}(\bar{\psi}_s^{\,k} \times \bar{i}_s^{\,k}) \quad [4.123]$$

By splitting the total stator flux-linkage into the sum of a leakage flux-linkage $\bar{\psi}_{sl}^{\,k}$ and magnetizing flux-linkage $\bar{\psi}_m^{\,k}$, we get

$$\bar{\psi}_s^{\,k} = \bar{\psi}_{sl}^{\,k} + \bar{\psi}_m^{\,k} \quad [4.124]$$

where

$$\bar{\psi}_{sl}^{\,k} = L_{sl}\,\bar{i}_s^{\,k} \quad [4.125]$$

where L_{sl} is the leakage inductance of a stator winding.

If the stator and rotor windings have equal number of effective turns, the space vector of the magnetizing flux-linkages in the general reference frame is given by

$$\bar{\psi}_m^{\,k} = L_m\,\bar{i}_m^{\,k} \quad [4.126]$$

where L_m is the magnetizing inductance and $\bar{i}_m^{\,k}$ is the space vector of the magnetizing current in the general reference frame itself. It is expressed as

$$\bar{i}_m^{\,k} = \bar{i}_s^{\,k} + \bar{i}_r^{\,k} \quad [4.127]$$

where $\bar{i}_s^{\,k}$ and $\bar{i}_r^{\,k}$ are the space vectors of the stator and rotor currents in the general reference frame.

Substituting eqns [4.124]–[4.127] in eqn [4.123], we get

$$T = \frac{3}{2}\,\frac{P}{2}\left(\left[\, L_{\rm sl}\,\bar{i}_{\rm s}^{\,k} + L_{\rm m}\,\bar{i}_{\rm m}^{\,k}\,\right] \times \bar{i}_{\rm s}^{\,k}\right)$$

$$= \frac{3}{2}\,\frac{P}{2}\left(L_{\rm m}\bar{i}_{\rm m}^{\,k} \times \bar{i}_{\rm s}^{\,k}\right)$$

$$= \frac{3}{2}\,\frac{P}{2}\left(\bar{\psi}_{\rm m}^{\,k} \times \bar{i}_{\rm s}^{\,k}\right) \qquad [4.128]$$

From eqn [4.128] it is seen that the torque is expressed as the vector product of the magnetizing current and stator current space vectors. Also, as may be expected, the stator leakage fluxes do not contribute to the development of torque.[23]

Alternatively, the torque can be expressed in terms of the two-axis components of the general reference frame by resolving all the space vectors into their real and imaginary axis components.

Substituting $\bar{\psi}_{\rm m}^{\,k} = \bar{\psi}_{\rm mx} + j\psi_{my}$ and $\bar{i}_{\rm s}^{\,k} = i_{\rm sx} + ji_{\rm sy}$

in eqn [4.128], we get

$$T = \frac{3}{2}\,\frac{P}{2}\left(\psi_{\rm mx}\, i_{\rm sy} - \psi_{\rm my}\, i_{\rm sx}\right) \qquad [4.129]$$

The instantaneous torque can be expressed in terms of the two-axis components of rotor flux-linkage and stator current as explained below.

The rotor flux-linkage space vector in the general reference frame is given by

$$\bar{\psi}_{\rm r}^{\,k} = \left(L_{\rm rr}\,\bar{i}_{\rm r}^{\,k} + L_{\rm m}\,\bar{i}_{\rm s}^{\,k}\right) \qquad [4.130]$$

Substituting eqn [4.130] in eqn [4.122], we get

$$T = \frac{3}{2}\,\frac{P}{2}\left(L_{\rm m}\bar{i}_{\rm s}^{\,k} \times \bar{i}_{\rm r}^{\,k}\right) \qquad [4.131]$$

From eqn [4.131], we have

$$T = \frac{3}{2}\,\frac{P}{2}\left(L_m \bar{i}_r^{\,k} \times \bar{i}_s^{\,k}\right)$$

$$= \frac{3}{2}\,\frac{P}{2}\,\frac{L_m}{L_{rr}}\left(L_{rr}\bar{i}_r^{\,k} + L_m \bar{i}_s^{\,k}\right) \times \bar{i}_s^{\,k}$$

$$= \frac{3}{2}\,\frac{P}{2}\,\frac{L_m}{L_{rr}}\left(\bar{\psi}_r^{\,k} \times \bar{i}_s^{\,k}\right) \qquad [4.132]$$

Substituting $\bar{\psi}_r^{\,k} = \psi_{rx} + j\psi_{ry}$ and

$\bar{i}_s^{\,k} = i_{sx} + j\,i_{sy}$ in eqn [4.132]

we get

$$T = \frac{3}{2}\,\frac{P}{2}\,\frac{L_m}{L_{rr}}\left(\psi_{rx}\,i_{sy} - \psi_{ry}\,i_{sx}\right) \qquad [4.133]$$

It may be noted that

$$\psi_{rx} = L_{rr}\,i_{rx} + L_m\,i_{sx} \qquad [4.134]$$

and

$$\psi_{ry} = L_{rr}\,i_{ry} + L_m\,i_{sy} \qquad [4.135]$$

By using special reference frames fixed to the stator flux-linkage space vector, rotor flux-linkage space vector or the magnetizing flux-linkage space vector, it is possible to obtain expressions for the instantaneous torque developed in a form which enables independent control of the torque and flux-producing current components as in the case of a separately-excited d.c. motor. This actually constitutes the basis for vector control[24] of a.c. motors.

4.2.3.13 *Use of a reference frame fixed to the stator flux-linkage space vector*

As can be seen from eqn [4.123], the instantaneous torque can be expressed in terms of the vector product of the stator flux-linkage and current space vectors in any general reference frame. Suppose we choose a special reference frame (with real and imaginary axes x and y) which rotates at the speed of the stator flux-linkage space vector and has its real axis coaxial with the stator flux-linkage space vector, i.e., the imaginary axis component of the stator flux-linkage is zero, as shown in Fig.4.9. Then, both in the steady-state and transient conditions, the torque of a P-pole machine is given by

$$T = \frac{3}{2}\frac{\mathrm{P}}{2}\,\psi_{sx}\,i_{sy} \tag{4.136}$$

where ψ_{sx} is the real axis component of the stator flux-linkage space vector in the specially chosen reference frame, and i_{sy} is the imaginary axis component of the stator current space vector in the same reference frame.

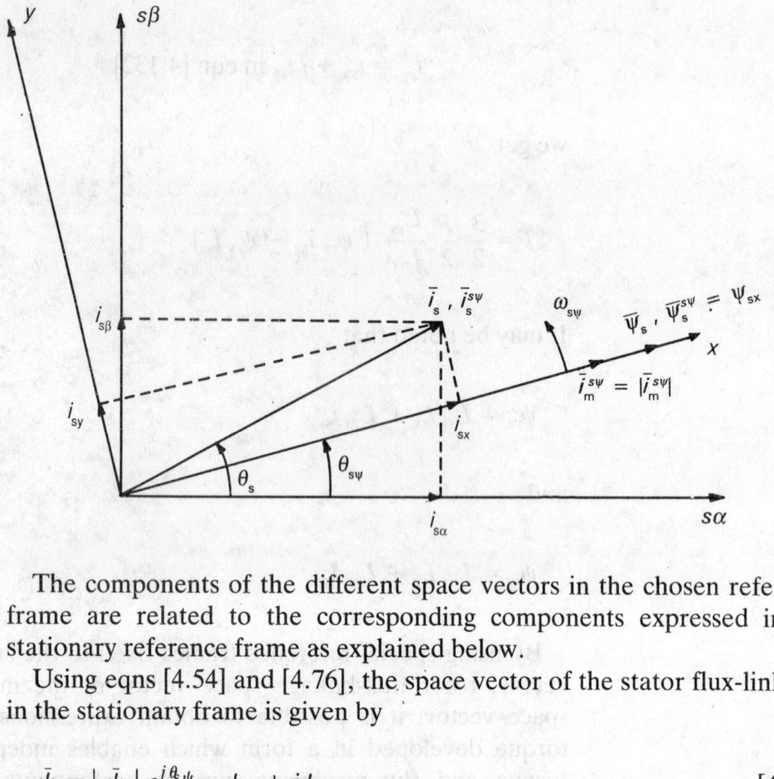

Figure 4.9 Relation between the stator reference frame and a reference frame fixed to the stator flux-linkage space vector.

The components of the different space vectors in the chosen reference frame are related to the corresponding components expressed in the stationary reference frame as explained below.

Using eqns [4.54] and [4.76], the space vector of the stator flux-linkages in the stationary frame is given by

$$\bar{\psi}_s = |\,\bar{\psi}_s\,|\,e^{j\theta_{s\psi}} = \psi_{s\alpha} + j\psi_{s\beta} \tag{4.137}$$

where $\psi_{s\alpha}$ and $\psi_{s\beta}$ are the real and imaginary axis components in the stator reference frame of the stator flux-linkage space vector, $|\,\bar{\psi}_s\,|$ is its modulus and $\theta_{s\psi}$ its space phase angle with respect to the real axis of the stator reference frame α. The speed of the chosen reference frame is expressed as

$$\omega_{s\psi} = \frac{d\,\theta_{s\psi}}{dt} \tag{4.138}$$

Figure 4.9 shows the relationship between the chosen and stationary reference frames. Using this figure, we can write the space vectors of the stator current and stator flux-linkages in the chosen reference frame as

$$\bar{i}_s^{s\psi} = \bar{i}_s e^{-j\theta_{s\psi}} = (i_{s\alpha} + j\, i_{s\beta})\, e^{-j\theta_{s\psi}}$$

$$= i_{sx} + j i_{sy} \qquad [4.139]$$

and

$$\bar{\psi}_s^{s\psi} = \bar{\psi}_s e^{-j\theta_{s\psi}} = (\psi_{s\alpha} + j\psi_{s\beta})\, e^{-j\theta_{s\psi}}$$

$$= \psi_{sx} + j\, \psi_{sy} \qquad [4.140]$$

where the two-axis stator current and stator flux-linkage components in the specially chosen frame are i_{sx}, i_{sy} and ψ_{sx}, ψ_{sy} respectively; in the stationary reference frame they are $i_{s\alpha}$, $i_{s\beta}$ and $\psi_{s\alpha}$, $\psi_{s\beta}$ respectively.

But substitution of eqn [4.137] into eqn [4.140] gives

$$\bar{\psi}_s^{s\psi} = |\, \bar{\psi}_s \,|\, e^{j\theta_{s\psi}}\, e^{-j\theta_{s\psi}} = |\, \bar{\psi}_s \,|$$

$$= \psi_{sx} + j\,0 = \psi_{sx} \qquad [4.141]$$

This proves mathematically that in the chosen reference frame, the space vector of the stator flux-linkages consists only of a real axis component which is equal to the modulus of the stator-flux linkage space vector.

The relationship between $i_{s\alpha}$, $i_{s\beta}$ and the referred currents i_{sx}, i_{sy}, given by eqn [4.139] can be expressed in matrix form as

$$\begin{vmatrix} i_{sx} \\ i_{sy} \end{vmatrix} = \begin{vmatrix} \cos\theta_{s\psi} & \sin\theta_{s\psi} \\ -\sin\theta_{s\psi} & \cos\theta_{s\psi} \end{vmatrix} \begin{vmatrix} i_{s\alpha} \\ i_{s\beta} \end{vmatrix} \qquad [4.142]$$

Now, the stator flux-linkage ψ_{sx} appearing in eqn [4.136] can be expressed in terms of current and inductance as

$$\text{(from eqn [4.141])}\ \psi_{sx} = \bar{\psi}_s^{s\psi} \qquad [4.143]$$

Let us define a space vector representing the stator magnetizing current in the chosen reference frame as

$$\bar{i}_{m}^{\,s\psi} = \frac{\bar{\psi}_{s}^{\,s\psi}}{L_{m}} \quad [4.144]$$

From eqn [4.144] it is obvious that the stator magnetizing current space vector is coaxial with $\bar{\psi}_{s}^{\,s\psi}$ and hence has only one component along the real axis.

$$\bar{i}_{m}^{\,s\psi} = i_{msx} + j\,i_{msy} = i_{msx} + j0$$

$$= |\,\bar{i}_{m}^{\,s\psi}| = \frac{|\,\bar{\psi}_{s}^{\,s\psi}|}{L_{m}} = \frac{\psi_{sx}}{L_{m}} \quad [4.145]$$

Substituting eqn [4.145] into eqn [4.136] we get

$$T = \frac{3}{2}\,\frac{P}{2}\,L_{m}\,|\,\bar{i}_{m}^{\,s\psi}\,|\,i_{sy} \quad [4.146]$$

$|\,\bar{i}_{m}^{\,s\psi}\,|$ and i_{sy} are the flux-producing and torque-producing components respectively of the stator current. Equation [4.146] is similar to the expression for electromagnetic torque developed by the separately-excited compensated d.c. machine. The torque can, thus, be controlled independently by controlling these two currents.[23]

4.2.3.14 Use of a reference frame fixed to the rotor flux-linkage space vector

From eqn [4.132] written in the general reference frame, it is clear that the torque is proportional to the vector product of the rotor flux-linkage and the stator current space vectors expressed in the general reference frame. Now, if such a rotating reference frame that nullifies the imaginary axis component of the rotor flux-linkage space vector is chosen, the torque will be proportional to the real axis component of the rotor flux-linkage space vector in the specially chosen frame and the imaginary axis component of the stator current space vector expressed in the same reference frame.

The space vector of the rotor flux-linkage in the stationary reference frame is given by

$$\bar{\psi}_{r}^{\,s} = \bar{\psi}_{r}\,e^{j\theta_{r}} = \psi_{r\alpha} + j\psi_{r\beta}$$

$$= |\,\bar{\psi}_{r}\,|\,e^{j\theta_{r\psi}} \quad [4.147]$$

where $\psi_{r\alpha}$ and $\psi_{r\beta}$ are the stationary reference frame components of the rotor flux-linkage space vector, $|\bar{\psi}_r|$ is its modulus and $\theta_{r\psi}$ is its spatial angle with respect to the real axis of the stationary reference frame. They are illustrated in Fig.4.10 which gives the relationship between stator current components in the stationary reference frame and those in the specially chosen reference frame fixed to the rotor flux-linkage space vector.

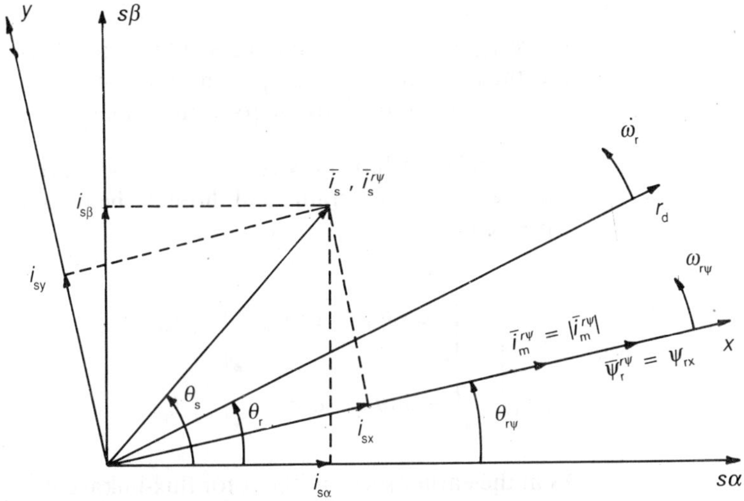

Figure 4.10 Relation between the stationary reference frame and a reference frame fixed to the rotor flux-linkage space vector.

The real and imaginary axes x and y of the chosen reference frame shown in Fig.4.10 rotate at the speed of the rotor flux-linkage space vector given by

$$\omega_{r\psi} = \frac{d\,\theta_{r\psi}}{dt} \qquad [4.148]$$

The stator current space vector in the chosen reference frame can be expressed as

$$\bar{i}_s^{r\psi} = \bar{i}_s e^{-j\theta_{r\psi}} = \bar{i}_{sx} + j\,i_{sy} \qquad [4.149]$$

Also,

$$\bar{\psi}_r^{r\psi} = \bar{\psi}_r e^{-j(\theta_{r\psi} - \theta_r)} = \psi_r e^{j\theta_r} e^{-j\theta_{r\psi}}$$

$$= \bar{\psi}_r^s e^{-j\theta_{r\psi}} = |\bar{\psi}_r| e^{j\theta_{r\psi}} e^{-j\theta_{r\psi}}$$

$$= |\bar{\psi}_r| = \psi_{rx} \qquad [4.150]$$

This proves that in the chosen reference frame, the rotor flux-linkage space vector has only a real axis component.

Substitution of eqn [4.150] into eqn [4.133] gives the torque expression as

$$T = \frac{3}{2}\frac{P}{2}\frac{L_m}{L_{rr}}\psi_{rx}\, i_{sy} \qquad [4.151]$$

where ψ_{rx} (= | ψ_r | is the modulus of the rotor flux-linkage space vector and i_{sy} is the imaginary axis component of the stator current space vector in the reference frame fixed to the rotor flux-linkage space vector.

The relationship between the stator current components in the stationary reference frame and those in the chosen reference frame can be expressed as

$$\begin{vmatrix} i_{sx} \\ i_{sy} \end{vmatrix} = \begin{vmatrix} \cos\theta_{r\psi} & \sin\theta_{r\psi} \\ -\sin\theta_{r\psi} & \cos\theta_{r\psi} \end{vmatrix} \begin{vmatrix} i_{s\alpha} \\ i_{s\beta} \end{vmatrix} \qquad [4.152]$$

As in the earlier section, the rotor flux-linkage ψ_{rx} appearing in eqn [4.151] can be expressed in terms of current and inductance as

$$\text{(from eqn [4.150])}\ \psi_{rx} = \psi_r^{\,r\psi} \qquad [4.153]$$

Now, let us define a space vector for the rotor magnetizing current in the specially chosen reference frame as

$$\bar{i}_m^{\,r\psi} = \frac{\bar{\psi}_r^{\,r\psi}}{L_m} \qquad [4.154]$$

It is apparent from the above equation that the rotor magnetizing current space vector is coaxial with the rotor flux-linkage space vector in the chosen reference frame and has only one component in the real axis.

Hence,

$$\bar{i}_m^{\,r\psi} = i_{mrx} = |\,\bar{i}_m^{\,r\psi}| = \frac{|\,\bar{\psi}_r^{\,r\psi}|}{L_m}$$

$$= \frac{\psi_{rx}}{L_m} \qquad [4.155]$$

Substituting eqn [4.155] into eqn [4.151] we get

$$T = \frac{3}{2}\frac{P}{2}\frac{L_m^2}{L_{rr}}|\bar{i}_m^{r\psi}|i_{sy} \qquad [4.156]$$

Equation [4.156] shows that the electromagnetic torque can be controlled by independently controlling the flux-producing component $|\bar{i}_m^{r\psi}|$ and the torque-producing stator current component i_{sy}. It must be noted that both of them are in space quadrature. On the assumption of linear magnetic circuit, L_m and L_{rr} are constants and, hence, the expression for torque is similar to that of the separately-excited d.c. machine having compensating windings.[23,25]

4.2.3.15 Use of a reference frame fixed to the magnetizing flux-linkage space vector

In this case, the torque expression will be derived in terms of the modulus of the magnetizing flux-linkage space vector and the quadrature axis stator current component referred to a rotating frame fixed to the magnetizing flux-linkage space vector.

A special reference frame with the real and imaginary axes x and y rotating at the speed of the magnetizing flux-linkage space vector has its real axis coaxial with the magnetizing flux-linkage space vector as shown in Fig. 4.11. It is clear from the figure that if, in the stationary reference frame, the magnetizing flux-linkage space vector is defined as

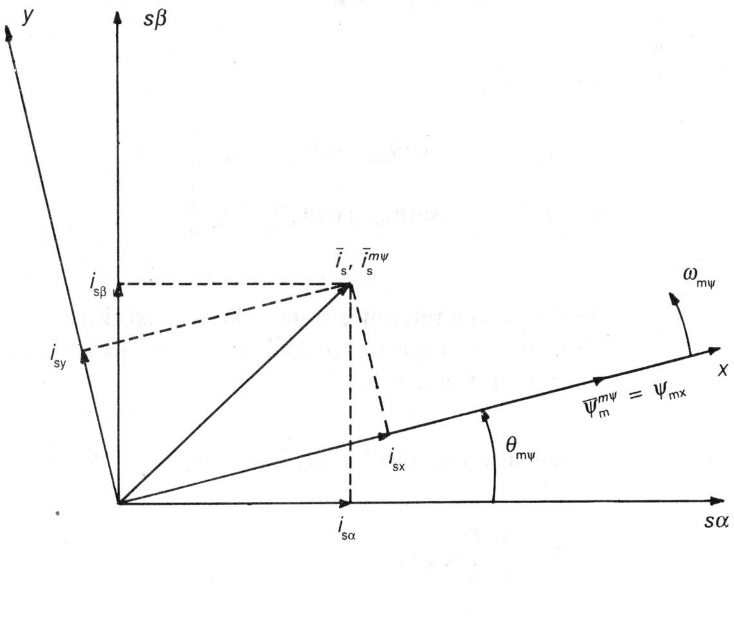

Figure 4.11 Relation between the stationary reference frame and the reference frame fixed to the magnetizing flux-linkage space vector.

$$\bar{\psi}_m{}^s = |\bar{\psi}_m| e^{j\theta_{m\psi}} = \psi_{m\alpha} + j\,\psi_{m\beta} \qquad [4.157]$$

where $|\bar{\psi}_m|$ and $\theta_{m\psi}$ are the modulus and space phase angle respectively of the magnetizing flux-linkage space vector, and $\psi_{m\alpha}$ and $\psi_{m\beta}$ are the stationary axis components of the magnetizing flux-linkage, space vector, the space vector of the stator currents in the specially chosen reference frame rotating at a speed

$$\omega_{m\psi} = \frac{d\,\theta_{m\psi}}{dt} \qquad [4.158]$$

is

$$\bar{i}_s{}^{m\psi} = \bar{i}_s\, e^{-j\theta_{m\psi}} = i_{sx} + j\, i_{sy} \qquad [4.159]$$

where $\bar{i}_s$ is the space vector of the stator currents in the stator reference frame.

The relationship between the stator current-components in the stationary reference frame and those in the chosen reference frame can be obtained using the expression

$$\bar{i}_s{}^{m\psi} = i_{sx} + j\, i_{sy} = (i_{s\alpha} + j i_{s\beta})\, e^{-j\theta_{m\psi}} \qquad [4.160]$$

as

$$\begin{vmatrix} i_{sx} \\ i_{sy} \end{vmatrix} = \begin{vmatrix} \cos\theta_{m\psi} & \sin\theta_{m\psi} \\ -\sin\theta_{m\psi} & \cos\theta_{m\psi} \end{vmatrix} \begin{vmatrix} i_{s\alpha} \\ i_{s\beta} \end{vmatrix} \qquad [4.161]$$

In the special reference frame, the real axis is coaxial with the magnetizing flux-linkage space vector and, therefore, its imaginary axis component is zero, that is, $\psi_{my} = 0$.

Substituting zero for ψ_{my} into eqn [4.129], we get

$$T = \frac{3}{2}\,\frac{P}{2}\,\psi_{mx}\, i_{sy} \qquad [4.162]$$

As in the previous section, the magnetizing flux-linkage ψ_{mx} appearing in eqn [4.162] can be expressed in terms of current and inductance.

It is known that

$$\psi_{mx} = \bar{\psi}_m^{\;m\psi} \qquad [4.163]$$

Defining a space vector for the magnetizing current in the chosen reference frame as

$$\bar{i}_m^{\;m\psi} = \frac{\bar{\psi}_m^{\;m\psi}}{L_m} \qquad [4.164]$$

we get

$$\bar{i}_m^{\;m\psi} = i_{mx} = |\;\bar{i}_m^{\;m\psi}| = \frac{|\bar{\psi}_m^{\;m\psi}|}{L} = \frac{\psi_{mx}}{L_m} \qquad [4.165]$$

Substituting eqn [4.165] into eqn [4.162], the torque is obtained as

$$T = \frac{3}{2}\,\frac{P}{2} L_m\, i_{mx}\, i_{sy} \qquad [4.166]$$

where i_{mx} is the main flux-producing current component and i_{sy} is the torque-producing component of the stator current in quadrature to i_{mx}.[23]

4.3 Effect of Non-Sinusoidal Supply Voltages on the Performance of Induction Motors

The presence of time harmonics in the supply voltage waveform causes harmonic currents, which in turn produce additional harmonic torques and losses, thereby affecting the efficiency and smooth running of the motor. Attention is focussed, in the following sections, on each one of the above factors.

4.3.1 *Harmonic Currents*

It may be noted that the slip corresponding to the nth harmonic

$$s_n = \left[\frac{(n \pm 1) \pm s_1}{n}\right]$$

is close to unity at all motor speeds from standstill to synchronism. Hence, the equivalent circuit for harmonic excitations is almost independent of motor speed and, therefore, the harmonic currents practically remain constant during no-load to full-load operation of the motor. Neglecting the circuit resistance in comparison with the reactance at the harmonic frequencies and omitting the shunt-magnetizing reactance which is much larger than the leakage reactance, the harmonic current can be deduced to be inversely proportional to the sum of the leakage reactance of the motor and to the square of the order of the harmonic. As the order of the harmonic increases, the magnitude of the harmonic current decreases and the total r.m.s. harmonic current given by

$$I_{\text{har}} = \sqrt{[(I_{15})^2 + (I_{17})^2 + \ldots + (I_{1n})^2 + \ldots]} \qquad [4.167]$$

would be more or less dependent on the first few terms in the right-hand side of eqn [4.167]. The normal three-phase induction motor has a percentage leakage reactance in the range of 10 to 20 and the total r.m.s. current at full-load on a usual six-step voltage supply is from 2 percent to 10 percent greater than the fundamental current.

The presence of harmonic currents and the leakage fluxes associated with them increase saturation of iron present in the leakage flux paths and, hence, reduce the value of the magnetizing inductance. This results in an increased magnetizing current and, therefore, slightly larger fundamental current itself.

4.3.2 Harmonic Torques

The additional harmonic currents produce both steady and pulsating harmonic torques.

Steady harmonic torques are developed by interaction of harmonic airgap fluxes and harmonic rotor currents of the same order. However, these constitute a very small fraction compared to the torque due to the fundamental. This follows from the ratio of the *n*th harmonic torque to that due to the fundamental which is given by

$$\frac{T_n}{T_1} = \frac{1}{n} \cdot \frac{s_1}{s_n} \left(\frac{I_{2n}}{I_{21}}\right)^2 \cdot \left(\frac{R_{2n}}{R_{21}}\right) \qquad [4.168]$$

It may be noted that although R_{2n} is slightly greater than R_{21}, $n > 1$, $(s_1 / s_n) < 1$ and $(I_{2n} / I_{21}) < 1$ and hence (T_n / T_1) will always be < 1 and will be decreasing rapidly as n increases.

Also, the harmonic torques are alternately negative and positive for the harmonics listed in the ascending order. Therefore the resultant torque developed, which is the algebraic sum of that due to the fundamental and harmonics of the applied voltage, will be slightly less than that due to the fundamental alone.

Pulsating torques with an average value of zero are created by the reaction of harmonic rotating fluxes with harmonic rotor currents of a different order. The dominant pulsating torques arise from the interaction between the fundamental rotating field and the harmonic rotor currents. The most dominant amongst them is the one that pulsates at six times the fundamental frequency produced by the reaction of the fundamental rotating flux with both the fifth and the seventh harmonic rotor currents. Actually, torques that pulsate at integral multiples of six times the supply frequency are developed, but the sixth harmonic torque has the largest amplitude in the case of six-step voltage supply to the motor. If a pulse-width modulated inverter with a low switching frequency is used, violent torque pulsations can occur at the switching frequency.

Pulsating torques cause oscillations in rotor speed. At very low speeds of operation, rotation occurs with a series of jerks. Therefore, the pulsating torques may fix the lower limit of speed range of the motor, depending on the inertia of the rotating parts of the drive system. These torques can be reduced by reducing the harmonic contents, especially of the lower order in the supply voltage waveform, with the help of twelve-step inverters or pulse-width modulated inverters with a high switching frequency. Introduction of appropriate series inductors in the stator phases will reduce the magnitude of harmonic currents and thereby create fewer torque pulsations. However, this will cause a slight reduction in the fundamental steady torque also. Increasing the number of phases, especially the use of a six-phase induction motor with an unbalanced stator winding, also reduces the amplitude of pulsating torques.

4.3.3 Harmonic Losses

The additional losses which are present in the induction motor due to the harmonics in the supply voltage waveform are termed harmonic losses.

The stator copper loss increases not only due to the existence of harmonic currents but also due to the increase in the fundamental current itself, as explained earlier. The resistance of the stator winding also increases due to skin effect, especially for higher-order harmonic currents flowing in stator windings of medium- and large-power motors.

The additional rotor copper loss is primarily due to the significant increase in the rotor resistance due to skin effect, particularly in the case of deep-bar rotors. With a constant-torque load, a very small increase in the fundamental rotor current may occur in order to overcome the small net negative torque produced by the harmonic currents.

The core loss in the motor also increases slightly due to the higher peak value of the flux density wave caused by non-sinusoidal excitation. The end-leakage and skew-leakage fluxes, which normally contribute to the so-called stray load loss, may produce an appreciable core ioss at harmonic frequencies.

The friction and windage loss remains the same, since it depends only on the speed of rotation and not on the voltage waveform.

4.3.4 Efficiency of the Motor

For a given load torque to be operated at a desired speed, the efficiency of the motor depends only on the total losses in the motor. The magnitude of the additional losses created by the harmonics depends essentially on the nature of the applied voltage waveform. Most static inverters do not generate harmonics of lower order than the fifth and the higher-order ones have small amplitudes. For motors fed from such inverters, only a slight reduction in efficiency occurs.[16] Even if there occurs an overall increase of 25 percent in motor losses, a motor having an efficiency of 88 percent on a 50 Hz sinusoidal supply will have its losses increased from 12 percent to 15 percent, thereby having only a 3 percent reduction in its efficiency.

5 Slip power-controlled induction motor

An examination of the division of power in the rotor circuit of an induction motor indicates that of the total power delivered to the rotor, the fraction $(1-s)$ is transformed to mechanical power and the rest, namely the fraction s of the input power to the rotor is transferred by electromagnetic induction to the rotor circuit. The latter, known as slip power, is dissipated as rotor copper loss if the rotor circuit is short-circuited. This is what happens while controlling the speed of a slip-ring induction motor by the introduction of external rotor resistance. At 10 percent of the synchronous speed, the power input to the rotor is divided between mechanical power developed and rotor copper losses in the ratio of 1:9, giving an overall efficiency of less than 10 percent. However, it is not mandatory that the slip power be dissipated as heat in the rotor circuit, since it can be removed from the rotor ciruit of a slip-ring induction motor and used externally, thereby improving the overall efficiency of the drive system. In fact, the slip power is either returned to the supply network as in the Scherbius scheme or used to drive an auxiliary motor which is mechanically coupled to the induction motor shaft, as in the Kramer scheme. Thus, in general, slip power control of the induction motor involves either a wastage (as in rotor resistance control) or recovery of slip-frequency electric power in appropriate form (as in slip-power recovery schemes).

Let us first investigate the relatively simple and less expensive scheme of static control of rotor resistance, which offers the advantages of controlled starting torque and current and high power factor.

5.1 Static Control of Rotor Resistance Using Chopper

Rotor-resistance control is widely used in applications like cranes, hoists and excavators, which do not require sustained low-speed operation. A high-frequency thyristor chopper circuit which enables the external rotor resistance to be varied smoothly without any mechanical means is often employed, especially when a constant-torque operation is demanded.

The basic circuit for varying the effective resistance of the rotor circuit of a slip-ring induction motor electronically is shown in Fig.5.1. The slip power available at the slip rings is rectified by a full three-phase diode bridge and fed through a filter inductance to a resistance R_{ex}. A thyristor chopper connected across the resistor is switched on and off at a frequency of the order of 300–600 Hz. The effective value of the resistance across the

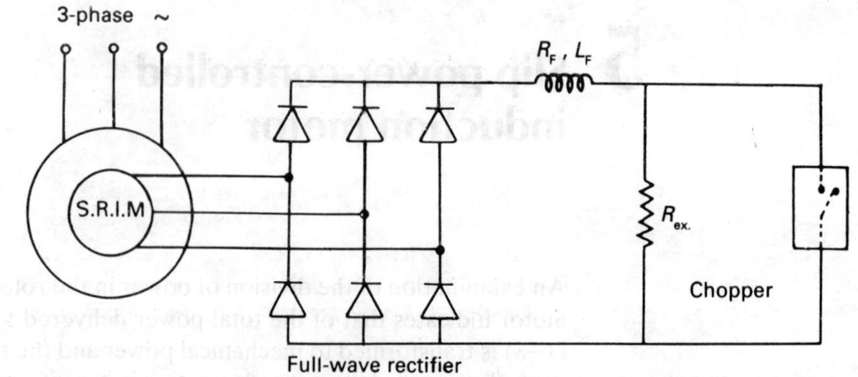

Figure 5.1 Basic scheme for static variation of rotor resistance of induction motor.

rectifier terminals is varied from zero to R_{ex} by controlling the duty cycle δ of the chopper from unity to zero. Figure 5.2 shows the available control range on the speed/torque plane.

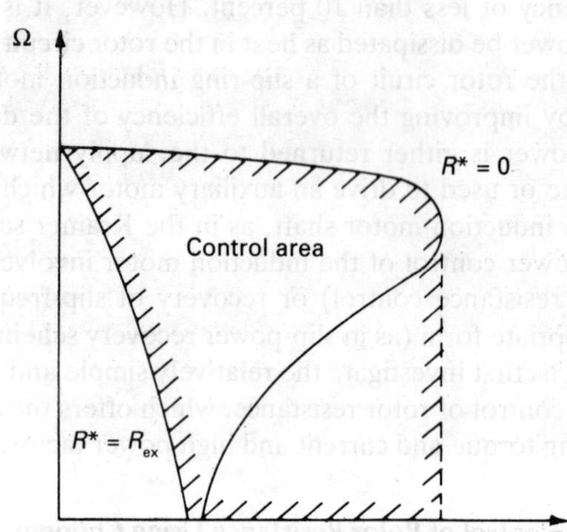

Figure 5.2 Maximum control range.

5.1.1 *Steady-State Analysis Using a d.c. Equivalent Circuit*

A d.c. equivalent circuit[26] that represents the three-phase slip-ring induction motor whose speed is regulated by using a rotor chopper-controlled external resistor is deduced as described below.

Figure 5.3a shows the per-phase equivalent circuit of the induction motor with the stator parameters referred to the rotor side and the rectifier-chopper combination indicated as a single block. Due to both rectification and chopping processes, the rotor current is no longer sinusoidal. The rectified current will be almost a d.c. if the chopping frequency is high and the smoothing filter inductance is large. Thus, the rotor current approximately

Figure 5.3(a) A.C. equivalent circuit of induction motor referred to rotor with rectifier-chopper external resistance block.

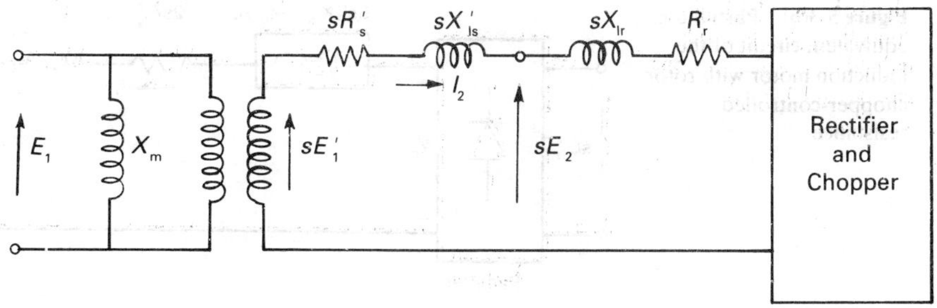

(a)

consists of alternating square pulses of $2\pi/3$ radians duration. The average rectified current I_d is related to rotor r.m.s. per-phase current I_2 as

$$I_2^2 \simeq \frac{2}{3} I_d^2 \quad [5.1]$$

The rectified voltage, neglecting the diode drops, is given as

$$V_d = \frac{3\sqrt{6}}{\pi} s E_1' \quad [5.2]$$

In order to deduce a d.c. equivalent circuit of the actual three-phase system, it is necessary to find equivalent resistances that should be inserted on the d.c. side of the rectifier bridge, representing the stator and rotor copper losses of the motor and the voltage drop due to commutation overlap caused by the stator and rotor leakage reactances.

The total copper loss in the motor for all the three phases is $3I_2^2(sR_s' + R_r)$, which in terms of I_d becomes $2I_d^2(sR_s' + R_r)$. Hence, equivalent resistance representing this power loss is given as $2(sR_s' + R_r)$.

The voltage reduction caused by the leakage reactances is given by

$$V_l = \frac{3s}{\pi} (X_{ls}' + X_{lr}) I_d$$

Thus, the equivalent resistance due to this becomes

$$\frac{3s}{\pi} (X_{ls}' + X_{lr})$$

Hence, the system can be represented by the d.c. equivalent circuit shown in Fig. 5.3b.

Now, the chopper-controlled external resistance R_{ex} can be shown as equivalent to a resistance $R^* = R_{ex}(1 - \delta)$, where δ is the duty cycle of the chopper given by t_{on}/T, in which t_{on} and T denote the on-period and the period of the chopper respectively. By controlling the duty cycle δ in the

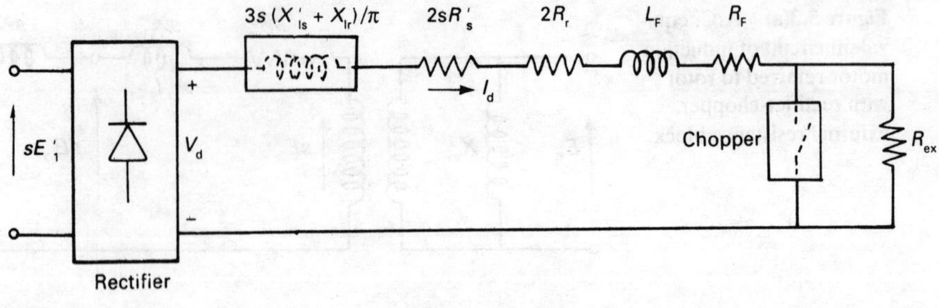

(b)

Figure 5.3(b) Partial d.c. equivalent circuit of the induction motor with rotor chopper-controlled resistance.

range $0 \leqslant \delta \leqslant 1$, R^* will vary within the range $0 \leqslant R^* \leqslant R_{ex}$. Replacing the chopper-controlled external resistor by R^*, we get the equivalent circuit shown in Fig.5.3c.

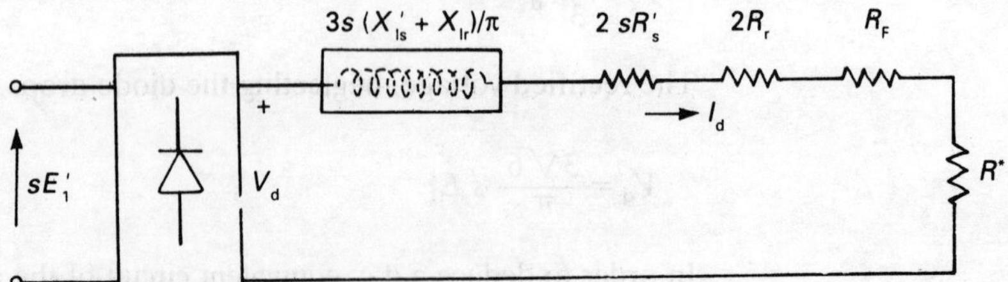

(c)

Figure 5.3(c) Complete d.c. equivalent circuit of the induction motor with rotor chopper-controlled resistance.

Therefore

$$I_d = \frac{V_d}{R_m(s) + R_F + R_{ex}(1 - \delta)} \tag{5.3}$$

where

$$R_m(s) = s\,[2R_s' + \frac{3}{\pi}(X_{ls}' + X_{lr})] + 2R_r$$

Now, the torque developed by the motor at a slip is given by

$$T_e = \frac{P_{cu}}{s}$$

where P_{cu} represents the rotor copper loss. It must be kept in mind that we are dealing with an equivalent circuit of the motor referred to the rotor side. Thus,

$$T_e = \frac{1}{s}\{[V_d - \frac{3s}{\pi}(X'_{ls} + X_{lr})\,I_d]\,I_d - 2sR'_s I_d^2\} \qquad [5.4]$$

For various values of δ and a given external resistance R_{ex}, the speed/torque curves can be determined as shown in Fig. 5.4 using eqns [5.3] and [5.4].

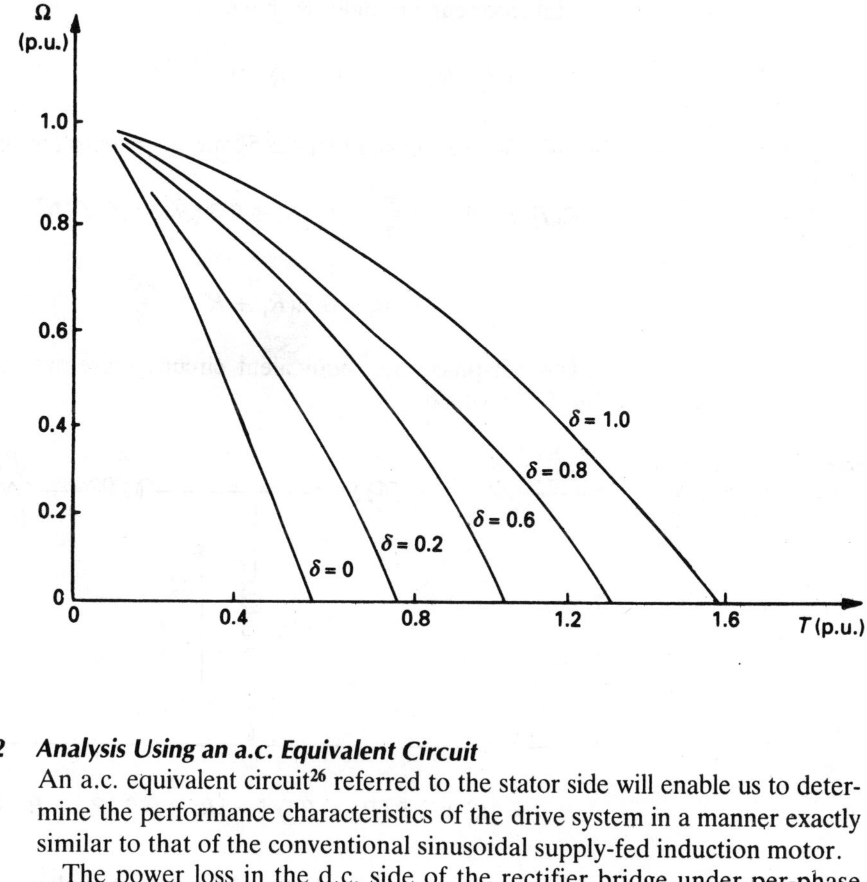

Figure 5.4 Speed/torque curves for various values of effective resistance of rotor.

5.1.2 *Analysis Using an a.c. Equivalent Circuit*

An a.c. equivalent circuit[26] referred to the stator side will enable us to determine the performance characteristics of the drive system in a manner exactly similar to that of the conventional sinusoidal supply-fed induction motor.

The power loss in the d.c. side of the rectifier bridge under per-phase consideration is given by $Id^2/3\ (R^* + R_F)$. This is equivalent to the power dissipation caused by the flow of I_2 in a resistance of magnitude $0.5\ (R_F + R^*)$ in each rotor phase.

The power balance in each rotor phase can be written as

$$E'_2 I'_{21} \cos\theta_2 \; = R'_r I_2'^2 + 0.5\,(R_F + R^*)'\; I_2'^2 + P_{mech} \qquad [5.5]$$

where E'_2 is the induced voltage in the rotor at standstill conditions, referred to the stator;

I'_{21}, is the fundamental of the rotor current referred to the stator;

θ_2 is the phase angle between E'_2 and I'_{21};

R'_r is the rotor resistance referred to the stator;
I_2 is the rotor current in r.m.s. referred to the stator; and
$0.5\ (R_F + R^*)$ is the fictitious resistance $0.5\ (R_F + R^*)$ referred to the stator.

Assuming that the mechanical power developed is caused by the fundamental rotor current only, we have

$$P_{\text{mech}} = I'^2_{21} [R'_r + 0.5\,(R_F + R^*)'] \frac{(1-s)}{s} \qquad [5.6]$$

Substituting eqn [5.6] in eqn [5.5] and $I'_{21} = 3I'_2/\pi$, we get

$$E'_2 I'_{21} \cos\theta_2 = (\frac{\pi^2}{9} - 1)\,[R'_r + 0.5\,(R_F + R^*)']\,I'^2_{21}$$

$$+ [R'_r + 0.5\,(R_F + R^*)']\,\frac{I'^2_{21}}{s} \qquad [5.7]$$

The per-phase a.c. equivalent circuit, therefore, can be as shown in Fig. 5.5 in which

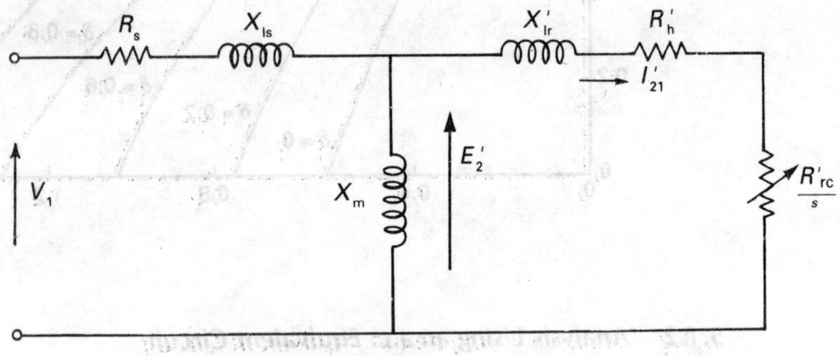

Figure 5.5 A.C. equivalent circuit for rotor chopper-controlled induction motor.

$$R'_{\text{r.c.}} = [R'_r + 0.5\,(R_F + R^*)'] = [R_r + 0.5\,(R_F + R^*)]\,a^2$$

where a = the ratio of stator-to-rotor turns per phase and

$$R'_h = R'_{\text{r.c.}}\,(\frac{\pi^2}{9} - 1)$$

The speed/torque characteristics predicted for various values of δ using the a.c. equivalent circuit are shown in Fig. 5.6.

If the speed/torque curves alone are required, the d.c. equivalent circuit is more convenient to use than the a.c. circuit model. When other performance characteristics such as the input current, power factor and efficiency are also desired, the a.c. equivalent circuit should be employed, since these can be determined simultaneously along with the calculation of torque.

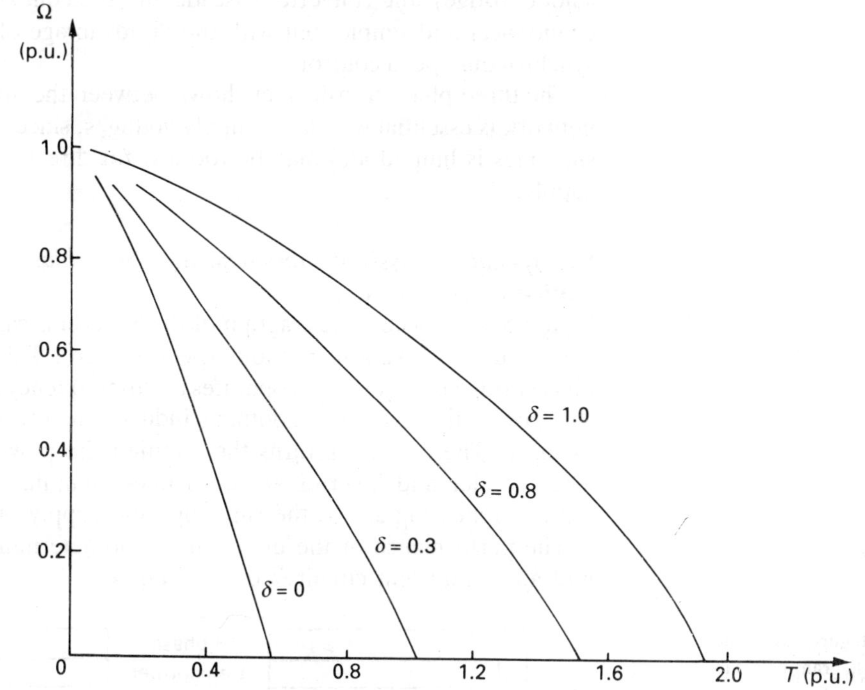

Figure 5.6 Speed/torque curves for various effective resistances of rotor circuit.

5.2 Static Scherbius Scheme

A basic scheme of a Scherbius static-converter cascade that is used for recuperation of slip power in electrical form itself is illustrated in Fig. 5.7. For achieving both subsynchronous and supersynchronous speed control, converters A and B must be fully-controlled thyristor bridges, one functioning at slip frequency as a rectifier or inverter, while the other operates at supply-system frequency as an inverter or rectifier. Not only is the converter cost appreciable, but also a slip-frequency gating circuit is necessary. Moreover, at speeds near synchronous, when the slip-frequency e.m.f.s are inadequate for natural commutation, special connections or forced-commutation methods are essential. If converter A were an uncontrolled one

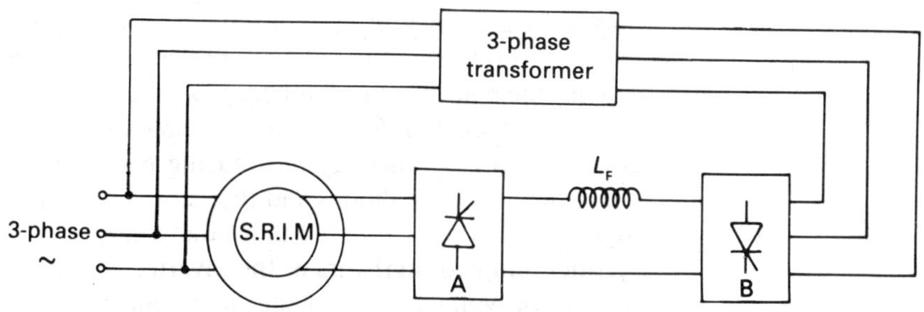

Figure 5.7 Basic scheme for a static Scherbius drive.

(diode bridge), the converter cascade and the control unit would become economical and simple, but with the disadvantage of providing only subsynchronous speed control.

The three-phase transformer shown between the inverter and the supply network is essential with large supply voltages, since the voltage across the slip rings is limited and may be too low for direct inversion into the a.c. supply.

5.2.1 *Steady-State Analysis of Subsynchronous Scherbius Static-Converter Cascade*

Figure 5.8 is a schematic diagram of the Scherbius cascade with static converters used for subsynchronous speed control. This consists of a three-phase bridge rectifier which operates at slip frequency and supplies rectified slip power through the smoothing inductor to the three-phase thyristor inverter. The inverter returns the rectified slip power to the a.c. supply. The rectifier and inverter are both line-commutated by the alternating e.m.f.s appearing across the slip rings and supply busbars respectively.

The performance of the drive can be predetermined by using the d.c. and a.c. equivalent circuits[27] derived below.

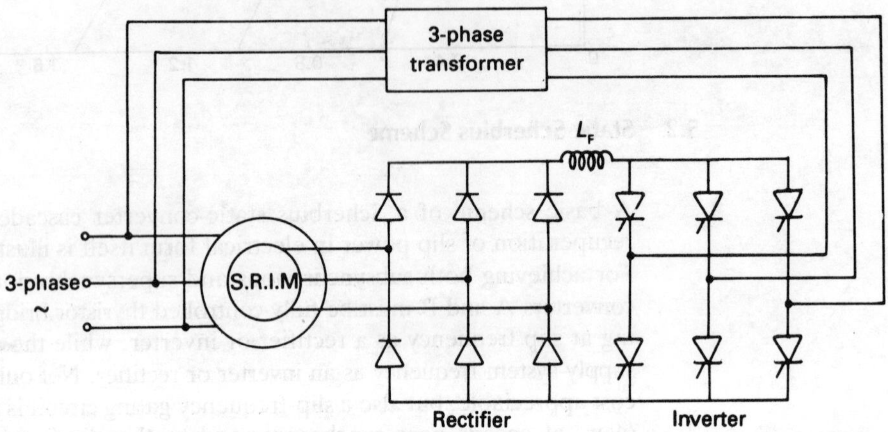

Figure 5.8 Schematic diagram of a subsynchronous static Scherbius drive.

The smoothing inductor L_F is assumed to be infinitely large so as to maintain the rotor rectified current i_d constant over a cycle. Neglecting the magnetizing branch of the normal a.c. equivalent circuit of the induction motor and referring the voltages and currents to the d.c. side of the drive system, the equivalent circuit becomes as shown in Fig. 5.9a. The arguments advanced in Section 5.1.1 while deriving a d.c. circuit model equally hold good in this case also. By introducing two voltage sources of magnitude $2\,\Delta v$ and $2\,\Delta v'$, the diodes and thyristors are replaced by ideal diodes and thyristors. (It may be noted that at any instant of time, two diodes of the rectifier and two thyristors of the inverter will be conducting.) Δv and $\Delta v'$ denote the voltage drop of the diode and thyristor respectively.

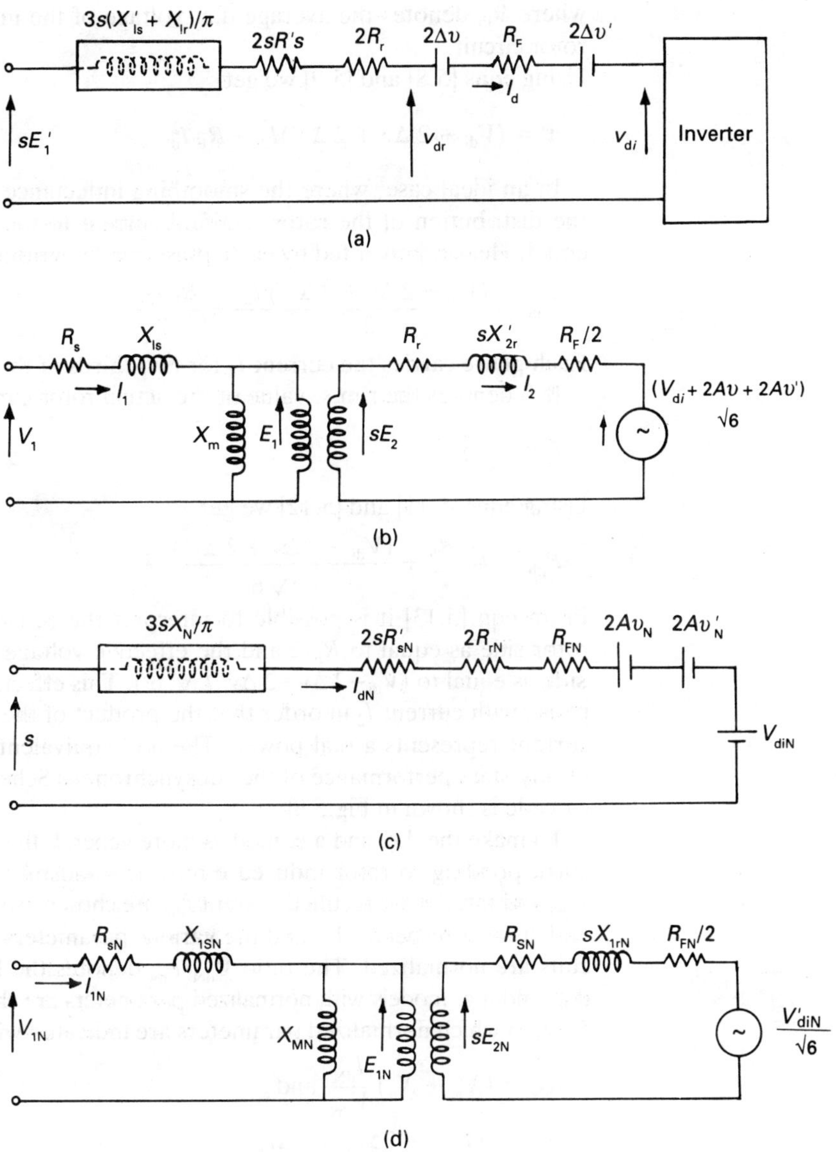

Figure 5.9(a) D.C. equivalent circuit of a subsynchronous static Scherbius drive;

(b) A.C. equivalent circuit of a subsynchronous static Scherbius drive;

(c) D.C. equivalent circuit with normalized parameters;

(d) A.C. equivalent circuit with normalized parameters.

The power fed after rectification is given as

$$P = V_{dr} I_d \quad [5.8]$$

where V_{dr} represents the actual rotor rectified voltage.
But i_d can be written as

$$I_d = \frac{V_{dr} - V_{di} - 2\Delta v - 2\Delta v'}{R_F} \quad [5.9]$$

where V_{di} denotes the average d.c. voltage of the inverter injected to the rotor circuit.
Using eqns [5.8] and [5.9] we get

$$P = (V_{di} + 2\,\Delta v + 2\,\Delta v')I_d + R_F I_d^2 \qquad [5.10]$$

In an ideal case, where the smoothing inductance L_F is infinitely large, the distribution of the rotor rectified current to the three rotor phases is equal. Hence, power fed by each phase can be written as

$$P_{ph.} = \frac{(V_{di} + 2\,\Delta v + 2\,\Delta v')\,I_d}{3} + \frac{R_F I_d^2}{3} \qquad [5.11]$$

Each phase carries the current I_d for two-thirds of the cycle.
If I_2 denotes the r.m.s. value of the actual rotor current, we have

$$I_2^2 = \frac{2}{3} I_d^2 \qquad [5.12]$$

Using eqns [5.11] and [5.12] we get

$$P_{ph.} = I_2^2 \frac{R_F}{2} + \frac{(V_{di} + 2\,\Delta v + 2\,\Delta v')}{\sqrt{6}} I_2 \qquad [5.13]$$

From eqn [5.13] it is possible to interpret the resistance reflected to the rotor side as equal to $R_F/2$ and the effective voltage injected on the rotor side as equal to $(V_{di}+2\,\Delta v+2\,\Delta v' / \sqrt{6})$. This effective voltage must be in phase with current I_2 in order that the product of the effective voltage and current represents a real power. The a.c. equivalent circuit depicting the steady-state performance of the subsynchronous Scherbius static-converter cascade is shown in Fig.5.9b.

To make the d.c. and a.c. models more general, the rotor rectified voltage corresponding to rotor induced e.m.f. at standstill condition of the rotor V_{dN} and rated rotor rectified current I_{dN} are chosen as base values for voltage and current respectively, and the various parameters of the equivalent circuits are normalized. The ratio V_{dN}/I_{dN} denotes the base impedance. The d.c. and a.c. models with normalized parameters are shown in Figs. 5.9c and 5.9d, in which normalized parameters are indicated with an added suffix N.

$$X_N = (X'_{ls} + X_{lr}) \frac{I_{dN}}{V_{dN}} \text{ and}$$

$$V'_{diN} = (V_{diN} + 2\Delta v_N + 2\Delta v'_N).$$

The developed torque T_e is given as

$$T_e = \frac{\text{Rotor power after rectification}}{\Omega_s s}$$

$$= \frac{[sV_1 - (3/\pi)\,s\,(X'_{ls} + X_{lr})I_d - 2R'_s sI_d]\,I_d}{s\Omega_s} \qquad [5.14]$$

where Ω_s is the synchronous speed in mechanical radians/second.

The normalized torque T_N is expressed as

$$T_N = \frac{\Omega_s T_e}{V_{dN} I_{dN}} = I_{dN}\left(1 - \frac{3}{\pi} X_N I_{dN} - 2R'_{sN} I_{dN}\right) \qquad [5.15]$$

and

$$I_{dN} = \frac{s - V_{diN} - 2\Delta v_N - 2\Delta' v_N}{\frac{3}{\pi} X_N s + 2sR'_{sN} + 2R_{rN} + R_{FN}} \qquad [5.16]$$

using the d.c. model of the drive system. Equation [5.15] shows that at constant value of i_{dN}, the torque is constant. It also indicates that there are two values of I_{dN} corresponding to a specified torque.

From eqns [5.15] and [5.16] it follows that for a fixed value of T_N, there exist two values of slip. Thus with V'_{diN} ($= V_{diN} - 2\Delta v_N - 2\Delta v'_N$) as a variable parameter, the speed/torque characteristics of the drive are similar to those of the motor.

Differentiating eqn [5.15] and equating it to zero for for maximum, we find that T_{max} occurs at

$$I_{dN}\big|_{maxT} = \frac{1}{2\left(\frac{3}{\pi} X_N + 2R'_{sN}\right)} \qquad [5.17]$$

Maximum torque is given by

$$T_{max} = \frac{1}{4\left(\frac{3}{\pi} X_N + 2R'_{sN}\right)} \qquad [5.18]$$

Equation [5.18] shows that T_{max} is independent of R_r, R_F and V'_{di} ($= V_{di} - 2\Delta v - 2\Delta v'$). From eqns [5.17] and [5.16], the slip at maximum torque is given by

$$s_{maxT} = 2V'_{diN} + \frac{2R_{rN} + R_{FN}}{\frac{3}{\pi} X_N + 2R'_{sN}} \qquad [5.19]$$

From eqn [5.15], the torque will be zero at $i_d = 0$.
Equation [5.16] shows that the slip at zero torque is given by

$$s_{zeroT} = V'_{diN} \qquad [5.20]$$

The change in slip at zero torque due to change in V'_{diN} is given by

$$\Delta s_{zeroT} = \Delta V'_{diN} \tag{5.21}$$

From eqn [5.19], change in slip at maximum torque due to change in V'_{diN} is given by

$$\Delta s_{maxT} = 2\Delta V'_{diN} \tag{5.22}$$

Hence from eqns [5.21] and [5.22], the nature of the speed/torque characteristics of the drive with slip power recovered electrically can be found as illustrated in Fig. 5.10 for various values of V'_{diN}.

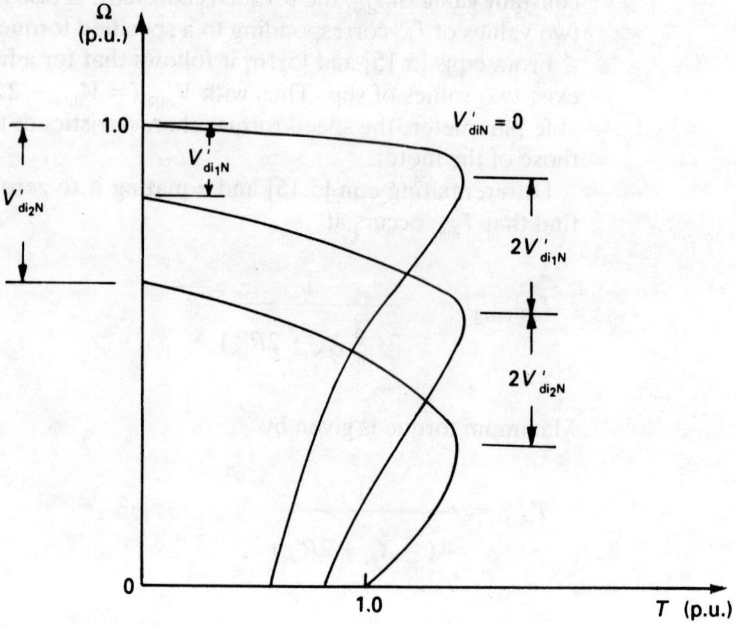

Figure 5.10 Speed/torque characteristics of a static Scherbius drive.

In order to determine the power factor of the input current and efficiency of the drive system, the a.c. equivalent circuit must be used. Neglecting the harmonics in the rotor and stator currents, the performance of the motor can be studied with the help of the phasor diagram shown in Fig. 5.11.

I_{dN} is obtained from eqn [5.16] and I_{2N} is calculated using eqn [5.12]. It must be kept in mind that the current I_{2N} must be in-phase with $V'_{diN}/\sqrt{6}$ and, therefore, the voltage $\frac{I_{2N}}{s}\left(R_{rN} + \frac{R_{FN}}{2}\right)$ is in phase with $\frac{V'_{diN}}{s\sqrt{6}}$. Hence, the phase angle that I_{2N} makes with E_{2N} is known. Once this angle is known, the phase angle of I_{1N} can be found from the phasor diagram (Fig. 5.11).

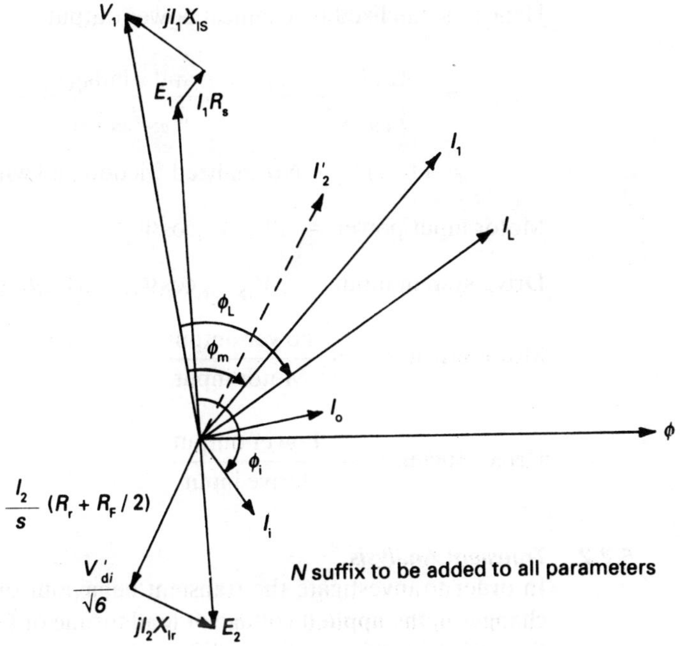

Figure 5.11 Phasor diagram of the induction motor used in static Scherbius drive.

In order to determine the net current drawn from the supply and its power factor, the magnitude and phase angle of the inverter current must be known. The latter is equal to the firing angle α ($\frac{\pi}{2} < \alpha < \pi$). Since power after rectification will be equal to the power fed back to the supply,

$$V_{dr}I_d = 3V_1I_i\cos\Phi_i \qquad [5.23]$$

where V_1 is the phase voltage of the supply network, I_i is the phase current of the inverter and Φ_i is the phase angle of the inverter current.
Hence

$$I_i = \frac{V_{dr}I_d}{3V_1\cos\alpha} \qquad [5.24]$$

Normalizing with respect to the base current, we can get I_{iN}. Having determined I_{iN} and Φ_i ($=\alpha$), it is easy to get the magnitude and phase angle I_{LN} and Φ_{LN} of the phase current drawn from the supply.
Now,

$$\text{mechanical power output} = T\Omega_s(1-s) - \text{Friction and windage losses} \qquad [5.25]$$

Hence, normalized mechanical power output

$$P_{mN} = \frac{T\Omega_s(1-s)}{V_{dN}I_{dN}} - \frac{\text{Friction and windage loss}}{V_{dN}\,I_{dN}}$$

$$= (1-s)T_N - \text{Normalized friction and windage loss}$$

$$\text{Motor input power} = 3V_{1N}\,I_{1N}\cos\Phi_m \qquad [5.26]$$

$$\text{Drive-system input} = 3V_{1N}\,I_{1N}\cos\Phi_m - 3V_{1N}I_{1N}\cos\alpha \qquad [5.27]$$

$$\text{Motor efficiency} = \frac{\text{Power output}}{\text{Motor input}} \qquad [5.28]$$

$$\text{Drive efficiency} = \frac{\text{Power output}}{\text{Drive input}} \qquad [5.29]$$

5.2.2 *Transient Analysis*

In order to investigate the transient behaviour of the drive during sudden changes in the applied voltage or load torque or firing angle of the inverter, the basic two-axis non-linear differential equations of the system describing the performance of the drive are written down in a synchronously rotating reference frame and solved using numerical techniques[28].

Neglecting core losses and saturation and assuming that the mutual inductance between stator and rotor winding varies according to a cosine law, the following equations in per-unit quantities are applicable to a three-phase symmetrical induction motor in the d-q reference frame.

$$\begin{bmatrix} v_{ds} \\ v_{qs} \\ v'_{dr} \\ v'_{qr} \end{bmatrix} = \begin{bmatrix} R_s + X_{ss}\frac{p}{\omega} & -X_{ss} & X_M\frac{p}{\omega} & -X_M \\ X_{ss} & R_s + X_{ss}\frac{p}{\omega} & X_M & X_M\frac{p}{\omega} \\ X_M\frac{p}{\omega} & -s\,X_M & R'_r + X'_{rr}\frac{p}{\omega} & -s\,X'_{rr} \\ s\,X_M & X_M\frac{p}{\omega} & s\,X'_{rr} & R'_r + X'_{rr}\frac{p}{\omega} \end{bmatrix} \begin{bmatrix} i_{ds} \\ i_{qs} \\ i'_{dr} \\ i'_{qr} \end{bmatrix} \qquad [5.30]$$

where $X_M = \omega \cdot aM$.

The electromagnetic torque expressed in per-unit quantities is given by

$$T_e = X_M\,(i_{qs}\,i'_{dr} - i_{ds}\,i'_{qr}) \qquad [5.31]$$

The output voltage of a three-phase uncontrolled bridge rectifier is

$$v_R = \frac{3\sqrt{3}}{\pi}\;E'_{2m} \qquad [5.32]$$

where E'_{2m} denotes the maximum value of the induced e.m.f. in the rotor winding per phase referred to the stator.

If the angular relationship between the q-axis and the magnetic axes of the stator and rotor phases is so chosen that these axes coincide at time zero and the a.c. voltage at the input side of the rectifier is transformed to a synchronously rotating reference frame which corresponds to the frequency of these voltages, then the q-axis voltage is equal to E'_{2m}, while the d-axis voltage is maintained at zero. Thus

$$v'_{dr} = 0 \qquad [5.33]$$

and

$$v'_{qr} = E'_{2m} = \frac{\pi}{3\sqrt{3}} v_R \qquad [5.34]$$

Since v'_{dr} is always zero, the following instantaneous power balance equation for the bridge rectifier is readily established:

$$v_R\, i_R = -\frac{3}{2} v'_{qr}\, i'_{qr} \qquad [5.35]$$

where i'_{qr} is the quadrature component of current fed to the rectifier and the negative sign is because of considering an input power to the rotor. Hence,

$$i_R = -\frac{\pi}{2\sqrt{3}}\, i'_{qr} \qquad [5.36]$$

The voltage equation for the filter circuit is given by

$$v_R = v_I + (R'_F + X'_F \frac{p}{\omega})\, i_R \qquad [5.37]$$

where v_I denotes the input d.c. voltage to the inverter and R'_F and X'_F denote the resistance and reactance of the filter referred to the stator.

Assuming a perfect, smooth d.c. voltage input to the inverter and negligible a.c. source impedance, the counter e.m.f. presented by the inverter can be expressed as

$$v_b = v_I = \frac{3\sqrt{3}}{\pi} V_{Lm} \cos(\pi - \alpha) \qquad [5.38]$$

where V_{Lm} represents the maximum value of a.c. supply voltage and α represents the firing angle of the inverter.

Since at time zero the q-axis of the synchronously rotating reference frame coincides with the magnetic axis of the stator, the quadrature component of the supply voltage v_{qs} is equal to the peak value of line voltage V_{Lm}, and the direct component v_{ds} is equal to zero. Hence, eqn [5.38] can be written as

$$v_I = \frac{3\sqrt{3}}{\pi} v_{qs} \cos(\pi - \alpha) \qquad [5.39]$$

Combining eqns [5.34], [5.36], [5.37] and [5.39] we get

$$v'_{qr} = -v_{qs} \cos\alpha - \frac{\pi^2}{18}\left(R'_F + X'_F \frac{p}{\omega}\right) i'_{qr} \qquad [5.40]$$

Substituting eqn [5.40] and the values of v_{ds} and v'_{dr} in eqn [5.30] we get

$$\begin{bmatrix} 0 \\ v_{qs} \\ 0 \\ v_{qs}\cos\alpha \end{bmatrix} = \begin{bmatrix} R_s + X_{ss}\frac{p}{\omega} & -X_{ss} & X_M\frac{p}{\omega} & -X_M \\ X_{ss} & R_s + X_{ss}\frac{p}{\omega} & X_M & X_M\frac{p}{\omega} \\ X_M\frac{p}{\omega} & -s X_M & R'_r + X'_{rr}\frac{p}{\omega} & -s X'_{rr} \\ s X_M & X_M\frac{p}{\omega} & s X'_{rr} & Z' \end{bmatrix} \times \begin{bmatrix} i_{ds} \\ i_{qs} \\ i'_{dr} \\ i'_{qr} \end{bmatrix} \qquad [5.41]$$

where

$$Z' = \left(R'_r + \frac{\pi^2}{18} R'_F\right) + \left(X'_{rr} + \frac{\pi^2}{18} X'_F\right) \frac{p}{\omega}$$

For digital computation, it is convenient to rearrange the system of equations given by eqn (5.41) in the general form

$$[pi] = [L]^{-1}[v] - [L]^{-1}[R][i]$$

where $[L]^{-1}$ represents the inverse of the inductance matrix given by

$$\begin{bmatrix} X_{ss} & 0 & X_M & 0 \\ 0 & X_{ss} & 0 & X_M \\ X_M & 0 & X'_{rr} & 0 \\ 0 & X_M & 0 & \left(X'_{rr} + \frac{\pi^2}{18} X'_F\right) \end{bmatrix}^{-1} \qquad [5.42]$$

The equation of motion in per-unit quantities is given by

$$2H\frac{d\omega_r}{dt} = T_e - T_L \qquad [5.43]$$

This again can be rewritten as

$$p\omega_r = \frac{1}{2H}[X_M(i_{qs}\,i'_{dr} - i_{ds}\,i'_{qr}) - T_L] \qquad [5.44]$$

The set of five simultaneous first-order differential equations for $p\ i_{ds}$, $p\ i_{qs}$, $p\ i'_{dr}$, $p\ i'_{qr}$ and $p\omega_r$ can be solved for various types of transients using a digital computer.

5.3 Static Kramer Scheme

The static Kramer variable-speed drive system illustrated in Fig. 5.12 consists essentially of a wound-rotor induction motor and a rectifier-fed d.c. motor, the two machines being connected electrically in cascade. The slip-power recovery takes place through the media of the rectifier and the auxiliary d.c. motor, and the recovered power is used directly to contribute to the total developed torque. The speed of the set is controlled by varying the field-current of the d.c. motor.

Since a static Kramer system has no line-commutated inverter, it causes less reactive power and smaller harmonic contents of currents than a static Scherbius system. But it has maintenance problems caused by the brushes and commutator of an auxiliary d.c. motor and the disadvantage of a large moment of inertia.

Figure 5.12 Schematic diagram of a static Kramer drive.

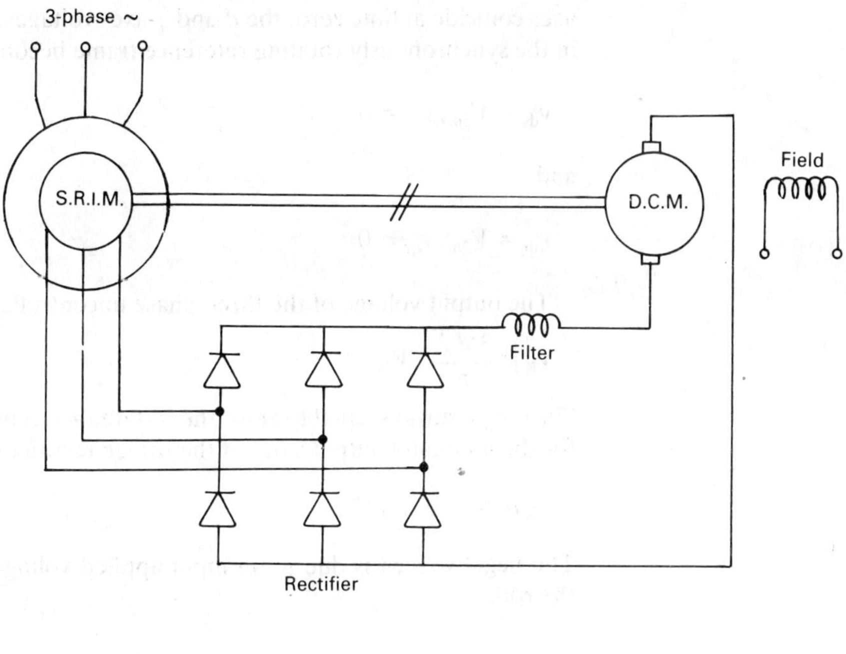

5.3.1 Method of Analysis

With the same assumptions made as in Section 5.2.2, the voltage-current relations of a three-phase symmetrical induction motor in a synchronously rotating frame are given as

$$\begin{bmatrix} v_{ds} \\ v_{qs} \\ v_{dr} \\ v_{qr} \end{bmatrix} = \begin{bmatrix} R_s + X_{ss}\frac{p}{\omega} & -X_{ss} & X_M\frac{p}{\omega} & -X_M \\ X_{ss} & R_s + X_{ss}\frac{p}{\omega} & X_M & X_M\frac{p}{\omega} \\ X_M\frac{p}{\omega} & -s\,X_M & R_r + X_{rr}\frac{p}{\omega} & -s\,X_{rr} \\ s\,X_M & X_M\frac{p}{\omega} & s\,X_{rr} & R_r + X_{rr}\frac{p}{\omega} \end{bmatrix} \begin{bmatrix} i_{ds} \\ i_{qs} \\ i_{dr} \\ i_{qr} \end{bmatrix} \quad [5.45]$$

This differs from eqn [5.30] only with respect to the quantities expressed in the bottom two rows. They are actual rotor quantities and not referred to the stator.

The per-unit electromagnetic torque is given by

$$T_e = X_M\,(i_{qs}\,i_{dr} - i_{ds}\,i_{qr}) \quad [5.46]$$

Let V_{1m} and V_{2m} represent the per-unit peak phase voltages applied to the stator and rotor respectively.

Choosing the angular relationship between the d-axes of the reference frame and the magnetic axes of the stator and rotor phases such that these axes coincide at time zero, the d-and q-axes voltages of the applied voltages in the synchronously rotating reference frame become

$$v_{ds} = V_{1m},\; v_{qs} = 0 \quad [5.47]$$

and

$$v_{dr} = V_{2m},\; v_{qr} = 0 \quad [5.48]$$

The output voltage of the three-phase uncontrolled rectifier is given by

$$v_R = \frac{3\sqrt{3}}{\pi}\,V_{2m} \quad [5.49]$$

Since v_{qr} is always equal to zero, the instantaneous power balance equation for the input and output sides of the bridge rectifier is expressed as

$$v_R\,i_R = -\frac{3}{2}\,v_{dr}\,i_{dr} \quad [5.50]$$

The negative sign is due to an input applied voltage being considered for the rotor.

The voltage equation for the d.c. motor armature is given by

$$v_R = (R_a + X_a \frac{p}{\omega})\, i_R + K_f I_f \omega_r \qquad [5.51]$$

where

$$\omega_r = \omega\,(1-s)$$

The electromagnetic torque developed by the d.c. motor is given by

$$T_e = K_f I_f i_R \qquad [5.52]$$

As $v_{ds} = V_{1m}$ and $v_{qs} = 0$, the stator voltage equations contained in eqn [5.30] or [5.45] are

$$V_{1m} = (R_s + X_{ss}\frac{p}{\omega})\, i_{ds} + X_{ss}\, i_{qs} + X_M \frac{p}{\omega} i_{dr} + X_M\, i_{qr} \qquad [5.53]$$

and

$$0 = X_{ss}\, i_{ds} + (R_s + X_{ss}\frac{p}{\omega})\, i_{qs} + X_M i_{dr} + X_M \frac{p}{\omega} i_{qr} \qquad [5.54]$$

Since the rotor is connected to the armature of the d.c. motor through a rectifier, using eqns (5.45), (5.48), (5.49), (5.50) and (5.51), the *d*-axis rotor equation is obtained as

$$\begin{aligned} \frac{K_f I_f (1-s)\, \omega\, \pi}{3\sqrt{3}} &= X_M \frac{p}{\omega} i_{ds} - s\, X_M\, i_{qs} \\ &\quad + (R_r + \frac{R_a \pi^2}{18})\, i_{dr} + (X_{rr} + \frac{X_a \pi^2}{18})\, \frac{p}{\omega} i_{dr} \\ &\quad - s\, X_{rr}\, i_{qr} \end{aligned} \qquad [5.55]$$

Substituting $v_{qr} = 0$ in the fourth equation of eqn [5.45], the *q*-axis rotor circuit equation becomes

$$0 = s\, X_M\, i_{ds} + X_M \frac{p}{\omega} i_{qs} + s\, X_{rr}\, i_{dr} + (R_r + X_{rr}\frac{p}{\omega})\, i_{qr} \qquad [5.56]$$

Using eqns [5.46], [5.48], [5.49], [5.50] and [5.52], the net electromagnetic torque acting on the shaft of the drive system is given as

$$X_M\,(i_{qs}\, i_{dr} - i_{ds}\, i_{qr}) - K_f\, I_f \frac{\pi\sqrt{3}}{6}\, i_{dr} \qquad [5.57]$$

Hence, the equation of motion of the drive can be written as

$$2H \frac{d\omega_r}{dt} = X_M\,(i_{qs}\, i_{ds} - i_{ds}\, i_{qr}) - K_f I_f \frac{\pi\sqrt{3}}{6} i_{dr} - T_L \qquad [5.58]$$

Equations [5.53] to [5.56] and eqn [5.58] constitute the dynamic equations of the Kramer system[29].

5.3.1.1 *Steady-state analysis*

Ideal no-load speed can be determined corresponding to the condition of zero-current in the rotor circuit. Under ideal no-load conditions, the rectified rotor induced voltage should be equal to the induced voltage in the armature of the d.c. motor. Hence

$$s_0 \frac{3\sqrt{3}}{\pi} \frac{V_{1m}}{a} = K_f I_f \omega (1-s_0) \quad [5.59]$$

where s_0 is the ideal no-load slip.
From eqn [5.59], we get

$$s_0 = \frac{K_f \omega I_f}{K_f \omega I_f + \dfrac{3\sqrt{3}}{\pi} \dfrac{V_{1m}}{a}} \quad [5.60]$$

Obviously, for different values of field current, we get different values of ideal no-load slip for the induction motor.

The steady-state performance of the drive system can be found for any specified slip of the induction motor and field current of the d.c. motor by determining first the steady-state d-and q-axes stator and rotor currents by substituting $p = 0$ in eqns [5.53] to [5.56].
The voltage-current relations under steady state become

$$\begin{bmatrix} V_{1m} \\ 0 \\ \dfrac{K_f I_f (1-s) \omega\pi}{3\sqrt{3}} \\ 0 \end{bmatrix} = \begin{bmatrix} R_s & -X_{ss} & 0 & -X_M \\ X_{ss} & R_s & X_M & 0 \\ 0 & -sX_M & (R_r + R_a \cdot \dfrac{\pi^2}{18}) & -sX_{rr} \\ sX_M & 0 & sX_{rr} & R_r \end{bmatrix} \times \begin{bmatrix} i_{ds} \\ i_{qs} \\ i_{dr} \\ i_{qr} \end{bmatrix} \quad [5.61]$$

The net steady torque developed by the system can be found from eqn [5.57].

The input current drawn by the motor and its power factor are given by

$$I_1 = \sqrt{i_{ds}^2 + i_{qs}^2} \quad [5.62]$$

and

$$\cos\phi_1 = i_{ds} / \sqrt{i_{ds}^2 + i_{qs}^2} \quad [5.63]$$

The variation of total torque developed by the system with slip for different values of field current has been illustrated in Fig. 5.13.

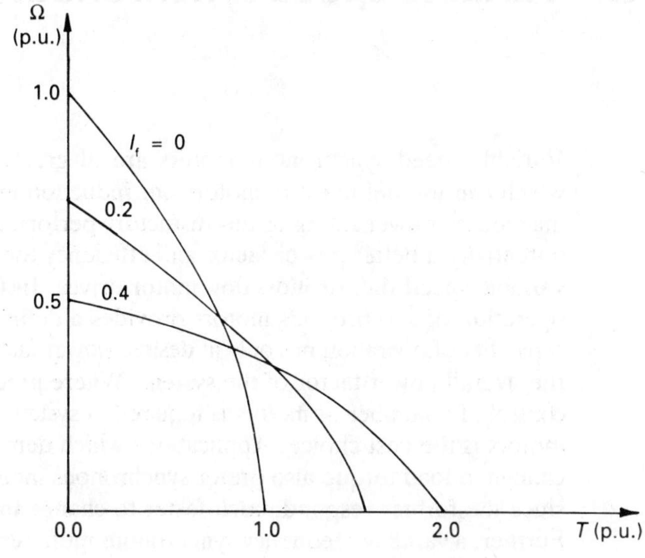

Figure 5.13 Speed/torque curves of the static Kramer drive.

The transient performance can be obtained by solving the dynamic eqns [5.53] to [5.56] and [5.58] by means of a digital computer after rewriting in the form of five simultaneous first-order differential equations for $p\ i_{ds}$, $p\ i_{qs}$, $p\ i_{dr}$, $p\ i_{qr}$ and $p\ \omega_r$.

5.4 Effect of Rectification of Slip Power on the Performance of the Induction Motor

The presence of a rectifier bridge in the rotor circuit causes harmonic currents in the rotor (even when the commutation or overlap angles of the diodes are ignored), which in turn induce associated harmonic currents in the stator winding. These harmonic currents produce harmonic copper losses, which increase the temperature of the induction motor and reduce its rating. Asynchronous harmonic torques are also created (although of small magnitude) by the interaction of a time-harmonic rotor flux and the corresponding induced stator current. This further reduces slightly the rating of the motor.

The commutating reactive power drawn through the induction motor from the stator by the three-phase bridge rectifier also reduces the useful power rating of the motor. Consequently, the induction motor is normally derated by about 10 percent when it is used for slip power control.

The smoothing inductor in the d.c. link is necessary for satisfactory operation of both the chopper and inverter. A large value of inductance is required to limit the magnitude of harmonic currents in the rotor winding.

6 Variable-speed synchronous motors

Variable-speed synchronous motors are of great interest in applications which can use neither d.c. motors nor induction motors either because of inadequate power rating or unsatisfactory performance indices. They have potentially a better power factor and efficiency for a given frame size than variable-speed d.c. or induction motor drives. In fact, variable-frequency operation of synchronous motors provides a definite-speed drive with the capability of operation not only at desired power factor but also of improving the overall power factor of the system. Where precise simultaneous speed control of a number of motors is required, a system comprising synchronous motors is the best choice. Applications which demand a quick response to change in load torque also prefer synchronous motors to induction motors since the former respond much faster to change in torque than the latter. Further, a variable-frequency synchronous motor drive offers the possibility of simple, precise position control.

6.1 Voltage-Source Inverter (VSI)-Fed Synchronous Motor

As in the case of variable-speed induction motor drives, a VSI is employed to give variable-voltage, variable-frequency supply to the synchronous motor. Different speeds are obtained by varying the supply frequency. In order to maintain the flux constant so as to cater to constant torque loads, not only V/f but also the field current is to be kept constant. The latter can conveniently be chosen as that value of field current which enables the motor to operate at or near unity power factor.

The speed/torque curves of the motor with variable-torque, variable-frequency power supply[30] are shown in Fig. 6.1. For a fixed supply voltage and frequency, the developed torque increases in a horizontal line until pull-out torque is reached at point P. At a specified speed, changes in load torque are accommodated by changes in torque angle, which may be oscillatory for sudden changes in load. Different horizontal lines are described corresponding to different voltage and frequency combinations. Beyond the base speed the motor enters into the constant-power region as the maximum torque decreases since the V/f ratio decreases (V cannot exceed the rated voltage and, hence, has to be kept fixed at that value). The field current also goes on decreasing. At any operating condition, the field current can be adjusted independently to maintain the desired power factor at the machine terminal.

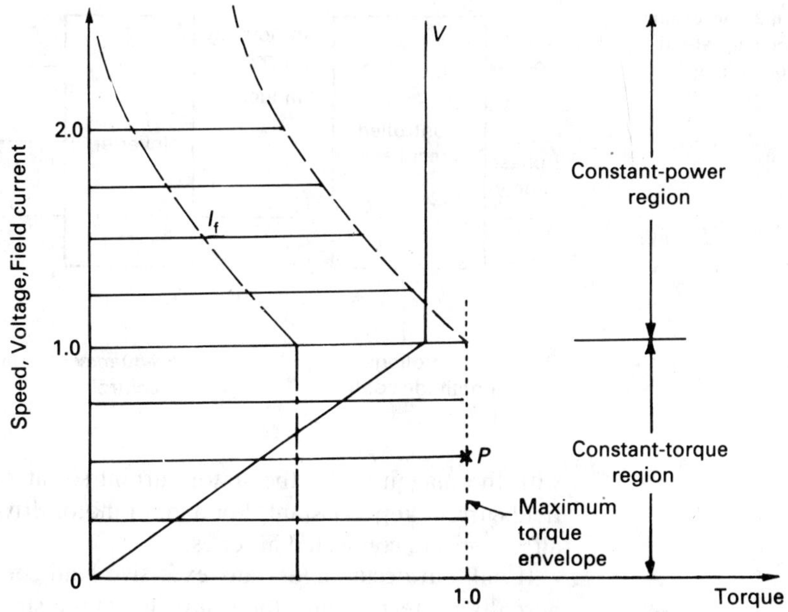

Figure 6.1 Variation of speed, voltage and field current with torque of a frequency-controlled synchronous motor.

The main limitations of synchronous motor systems, which are operated on open-loop, are:

(i) synchronism may be lost with a shock load; and
(ii) starting or resynchronizing requires heavy damper windings.

However, operating open-loop with a current-source instead of a voltage-source inverter, the drive system is free of the spontaneous oscillations which characterize voltage-fed synchronous motors at low voltage and frequency. This is shown to be true even if the motor is of the salient-pole type.

6.2 Current-Source Inverter (CSI)-Fed Synchronous Motor

Figure 6.2 shows the drive configuration for open-loop current-fed synchronous motor control[31]. A six-pulse phase-controlled rectifier operating from a three-phase supply is controlled in such a way as to produce a unidirectional current of controllable magnitude in a smoothing inductor. This current is then switched in a thyristor inverter to give variable-frequency three-phase current to a normal synchronous motor.

Precise speed control can be achieved through control of the inverter frequency. Reversal of rotation is achieved by reversal of the phase sequence of thyristor switching as the frequency goes through zero value. Reversal of power flow is achieved by reversing the polarity of the voltage in the d.c. link between the rectifier and the inverter. Thus, full four-quadrant operation of the drive is provided. In its simplest form, the drive can be operated

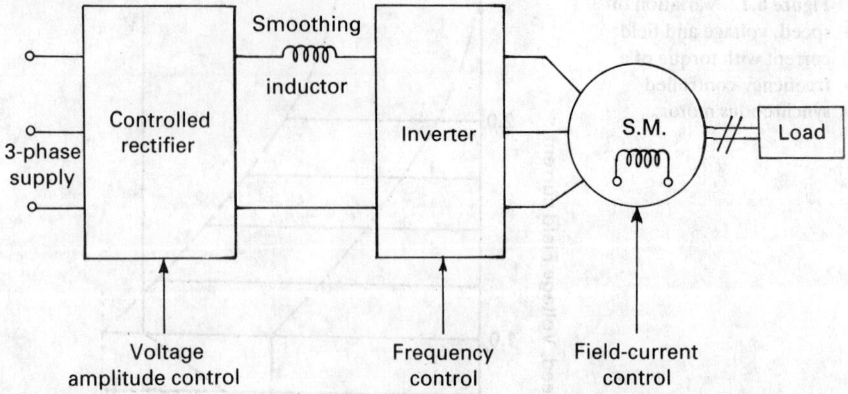

Figure 6.2 Schematic diagram of a CSI-fed synchronous motor.

with the magnitude of the stator current set at rated value and with the field current kept constant. For a multi-motor drive, the stator windings of all motors are connected in series.

If pull-out occurs under any excessive load condition, the system is inherently protected since the source limits the stator current. In that case, however, it is necessary to provide means of adjusting the inverter frequency to restore synchronism.

6.3 Steady-State Analysis of VSI-Fed Synchronous Motor

The analysis uses the Fourier series of the inverter's phase voltage and the d-q equivalent circuit for the synchronous machine[32]. For the sake of generality, a synchronous motor with damper windings has been considered.

The following simplifying assumptions are made.

(i) The inverter is fed by a d.c. voltage free from ripple.
(ii) The inverter has ideal semiconductor devices.
(iii) The output voltage of the inverter is balanced, three-phase in nature.
(iv) Saturation, eddy currents and hysteresis effects in the machine are neglected.
(v) The machine is star-connected with the neutral point electrically isolated.
(vi) The parameters of the machine are constant.
(vii) The rotor speed at any steady-state operating point is constant.

6.3.1 Equivalent Circuit of Synchronous Machine

The synchronous machine with damper bars can be represented in the two-axis theory by three circuits in the d-axis and two circuits in the q-axis.

The synchronous-machine equations transformed to the rotor reference frame, in matrix form, are given as

$$\begin{bmatrix} v_{qs} \\ v_{ds} \\ v_{qr} \\ v_{dr} \\ v_{fr} \end{bmatrix} = \begin{bmatrix} R_s+pL_q & \omega_r L_d & pL_{mq} & \omega_r L_{md} & \omega_r L_{md} \\ -\omega_r L_q & R_s+pL_d & -\omega_r L_{mq} & pL_{md} & pL_{md} \\ pL_{mq} & 0 & R_{qr}+pL_{qr} & 0 & 0 \\ 0 & pL_{md} & 0 & R_{dr}+pL_{dr} & pL_{md} \\ 0 & pL_{md} & 0 & pL_{md} & R_{fr}+pL_{fr} \end{bmatrix} \times \begin{bmatrix} i_{qs} \\ i_{ds} \\ i_{qr} \\ i_{dr} \\ i_{fr} \end{bmatrix} \quad [6.1]$$

where R_s = stator resistance, L_q = q-axis stator self inductance, L_d = d-axis stator self-inductance, L_{mq} = q-axis magnetizing inductance, L_{md} = d-axis magnetizing inductance, R_{qr} = q-axis rotor resistance, R_{dr} = d-axis rotor resistance, R_{fr} = field resistance, L_{qr} = q-axis rotor self inductance, L_{dr} = d-axis rotor self inductance, L_{fr} = field self inductance, and p = d/dt.

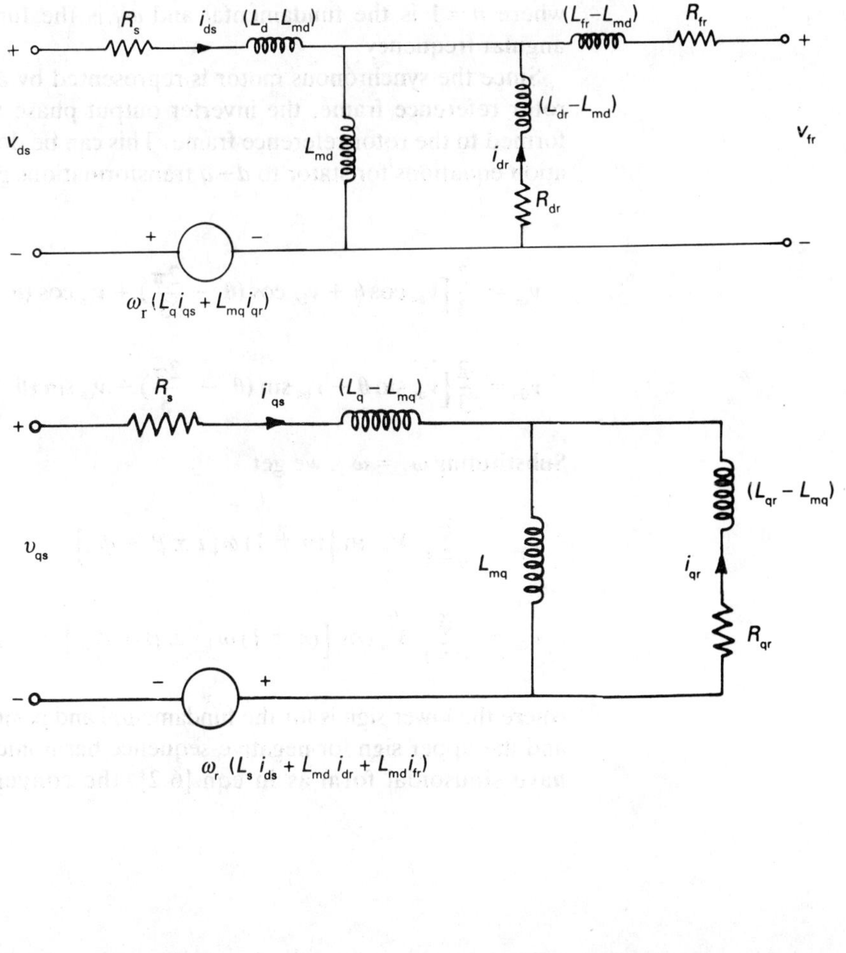

Figure 6.3 *d*- and *q*-axis equivalent circuits of synchronous motor.

All the parameters are per-phase and the rotor quantities are referred to the stator. The q-axis and d-axis rotor circuits are damper windings; hence, their terminal voltages v_{qr} and v_{dr} are constrained to zero. The field is excited by means of a d.c. voltage without any ripple content. The equivalent circuit in the rotor reference frame satisfying eqn [6.1] is shown in Fig. 6.3.

6.3.2 *Performance of the Inverter Motor System*

The Fourier series of the balanced, three-phase output line-to-neutral voltages of the inverter (or input phase voltages to the stator of the motor) have the form

$$\left.\begin{aligned} v_{as} &= \sum_{n=1}^{\infty} V_n \sin\,(n\omega_1 t + \phi_n) \\ v_{bs} &= \sum_{n=1}^{\infty} V_n \sin\,[n(\omega_1 t - 2\pi/3) + \phi_n] \\ v_{cs} &= \sum_{n=1}^{\infty} V_n \sin\,[n(\omega_1 t + 2\pi/3) + \phi_n] \end{aligned}\right\} \quad [6.2]$$

where $n = 1$ is the fundamental and ω_1 is the fundamental synchronous angular frequency.

Since the synchronous motor is represented by a set of equations in the rotor reference frame, the inverter output phase voltages must be transformed to the rotor reference frame. This can be done using the transformation equations for stator to $d-q$ transformations given below.

$$v_{qs} = \frac{2}{3}\left[v_{as}\cos\theta + v_{bs}\cos\left(\theta - \frac{2\pi}{3}\right) + v_{cs}\cos\left(\theta + \frac{2\pi}{3}\right)\right] \quad [6.3]$$

$$v_{ds} = \frac{2}{3}\left[v_{as}\sin\theta + v_{bs}\sin\left(\theta - \frac{2\pi}{3}\right) + v_{cs}\sin\left(\theta + \frac{2\pi}{3}\right)\right] \quad [6.4]$$

Substituting $\omega_r = \omega_1$, we get

$$v_{qs} = \sum_{n=1}^{\infty} V_n \sin\left[(n \pm 1)\,\omega_1 t \pm \beta + \phi_n\right] \quad [6.5]$$

$$v_{ds} = \sum_{n=1}^{\infty} V_n \cos\left[(n \pm 1)\,\omega_1 t \pm \beta + \phi_n\right] \quad [6.6]$$

where the lower sign is for the fundamental and positive-sequence harmonics and the upper sign for negative-sequence harmonics. If the phase voltages have sinusoidal form as in eqn [6.2], the conventional torque angle δ

is equal to $\beta+\pi/2$. If the phase voltages have cosine form, then the load angle β equals the torque angle δ. The torque angle is negative for motoring.

The voltage-current relations of the synchronous machine given in eqn [6.1] are expressed in matrix notation as

$$[V] = [Z]\,[I] \qquad [6.7]$$

Hence, the currents are found by inverting the impedance matrix Z such that

$$[I] = [Z^{-1}]\,[V] \qquad [6.8]$$

Equation [6.8] must be solved for the fundamental and each harmonic current.

The fundamental voltage vector is given by

$$[V] = \begin{bmatrix} V_1 \sin[-\beta + \phi_1] \\ V_1 \cos[-\beta + \phi_1] \\ 0 \\ 0 \\ V_F \end{bmatrix} \qquad [6.9]$$

which indicates that all the voltages are d.c. quantities. Equation [6.8] is solved for fundamental currents after replacing all time derivatives in $[Z^{-1}]$ by zero.

The harmonic voltage vector can be written as

$$[V] = \begin{bmatrix} V_n \cos[\pm\beta + \phi_n - \frac{\pi}{2}] + j\,V_n \sin[\pm\beta + \phi_n - \frac{\pi}{2}] \\ \pm V_n \cos[\pm\beta + \phi_n] \pm j\,V_n \sin[\pm\beta + \phi_n] \\ 0 + j0 \\ 0 + j0 \\ 0 + j0 \end{bmatrix}$$

$$n \neq 1 \qquad [6.10]$$

where the voltages from eqns [6.5] and [6.6] have been expressed in complex rectangular phasor form. The p operator in $[Z^{-1}]$ is

$$p = j(n \pm 1)\,\omega_1 \quad [6.11]$$

Solving eqn [6.5] for harmonic currents gives currents (in the rotor reference frame) of the form

$$i_n = I_n \cos\left[(n \pm 1)\,\omega_1 t + \gamma_n\right],\ n \neq 1 \quad [6.12]$$

where only the real part has been retained and the suppressed $(n \pm 1)\,\omega_1 t$ has been replaced.

It may be noted that the currents obtained are in the rotor reference frame. In order to get the machine currents in the stator reference frame (so as to obtain actual stator currents), the *d*-axis and *q*-axis stator currents must be transformed into the stator axes using the following transformation equations:

$$i_{as} = i_{qs} \cos\theta + i_{ds} \sin\theta \quad [6.13]$$

$$i_{bs} = i_{qs} \cos\left(\theta - \frac{2\pi}{3}\right) + i_{ds} \sin\left(\theta - \frac{2\pi}{3}\right) \quad [6.14]$$

$$i_{cs} = i_{qs} \cos\left(\theta + \frac{2\pi}{3}\right) + i_{ds} \sin\left(\theta + \frac{2\pi}{3}\right) \quad [6.15]$$

The stator a-phase current is found to be of the form

$$\begin{aligned} I_a = {} & \sqrt{I_{qs_1}^2 + I_{ds_1}^2}\ \sin\left[\omega_1 t + \beta + \tan^{-1}(I_{qs_1}/I_{ds_1})\right] \\ & + \sum_{n=2}^{\infty} \left[\frac{1}{2}\sqrt{P^2 + Q^2}\ \sin\left\{(n+1 \pm 1)\,\omega_1 t + \beta + \tan^{-1}(P/Q)\right\}\right. \\ & \left. + \frac{1}{2}\sqrt{R^2 + S^2}\ \sin\left\{(n-1 \pm 1)\,\omega_1 t - \beta + \tan^{-1}(R/S)\right\}\right] \end{aligned} \quad [6.16]$$

where

$$\left.\begin{aligned} P &= I_{qs_n} \cos\gamma_{qs_n} + I_{ds_n} \sin\gamma_{ds_n} \\ Q &= -I_{qs_n} \sin\gamma_{qs_n} + I_{ds_n} \cos\gamma_{ds_n} \\ R &= I_{qs_n} \cos\gamma_{qs_n} - I_{ds_n} \sin\gamma_{ds_n} \\ S &= -I_{qs_n} \sin\gamma_{qs_n} + I_{ds_n} \cos\gamma_{ds_n} \end{aligned}\right| \quad n \neq 1$$

It can be seen from eqn [6.16] that each single-harmonic stator voltage causes a harmonic stator current with two frequency components—one having the same frequency as that of the stator voltage and the other having a different frequency from that of the stator voltage. The latter current component is due to the asymmetry between the *d*-axis and *q*-axis equivalent circuits.

The instantaneous electromagnetic torque is given by

$$T_e = \frac{3}{2}\frac{P}{2}[(L_d\, i_{ds} + L_{md}\, i_{dr} + L_{md}\, i_{fr})\, i_{qs} - (L_q\, i_{qs} + L_{mq}\, i_{qr})\, i_{ds}] \qquad [6.17]$$

The average torque produced by the fundamental currents is found to be

$$T_{av_1} = \frac{3}{2}\frac{P}{2}[(L_{md} - L_{mq})\, I_{qs_1}\, I_{ds_1} + L_{md}\, I_{fr_1}\, I_{qs_1}] \qquad [6.18]$$

The average torque produced by the harmonic currents is given by

$$\begin{aligned} T_{av} = \sum_{n=2}^{\infty} \frac{3}{4}\frac{P}{2} \{ & L_{md}\, [I_{ds_n}\, I_{qs_n} \cos(\gamma_{ds_n} - \gamma_{qs_n}) \\ & + I_{dr_n}\, I_{qs_n} \cos(\gamma_{dr_n} - \gamma_{qs_n}) \\ & + I_{fr_n}\, I_{qs_n} \cos(\gamma_{fr_n} - \gamma_{qs_n}) \\ & - L_{mq}\, [I_{qs_n}\, I_{ds_n} \cos(\gamma_{qs_n} - \gamma_{ds_n}) \\ & + I_{qr_n}\, I_{qs_n} \cos(\gamma_{qr_n} - \gamma_{qs_n})]\} \end{aligned} \qquad [6.19]$$

The inverter link-current I_{dc} is calculated by equating power input to and output from the inverter as

$$I_{dc} = \frac{3}{2\, V_{dc}}\, (v_{qs}\, i_{qs} + v_{ds}\, i_{ds}) \qquad [6.20]$$

If I_{dc} is positive, the machine is motoring and if it is negative, the machine is generating. The I^2R losses are calculated from the *d-q* equivalent circuit. The actual I^2R losses are 1.5 times the I^2R losses obtained for the *d-q* circuit, since the transformation employed is not power-invariant.

Figures 6.4 and 6.5 show the steady-state waveforms of phase voltage, phase current and electromagnetic torque of a salient-pole synchronous motor, fed from a six-step square-wave inverter, operating at 0.8 lagging and leading power factor respectively. The frequency of the fundamental of the inverter output voltage is the rated frequency of the motor in both cases.

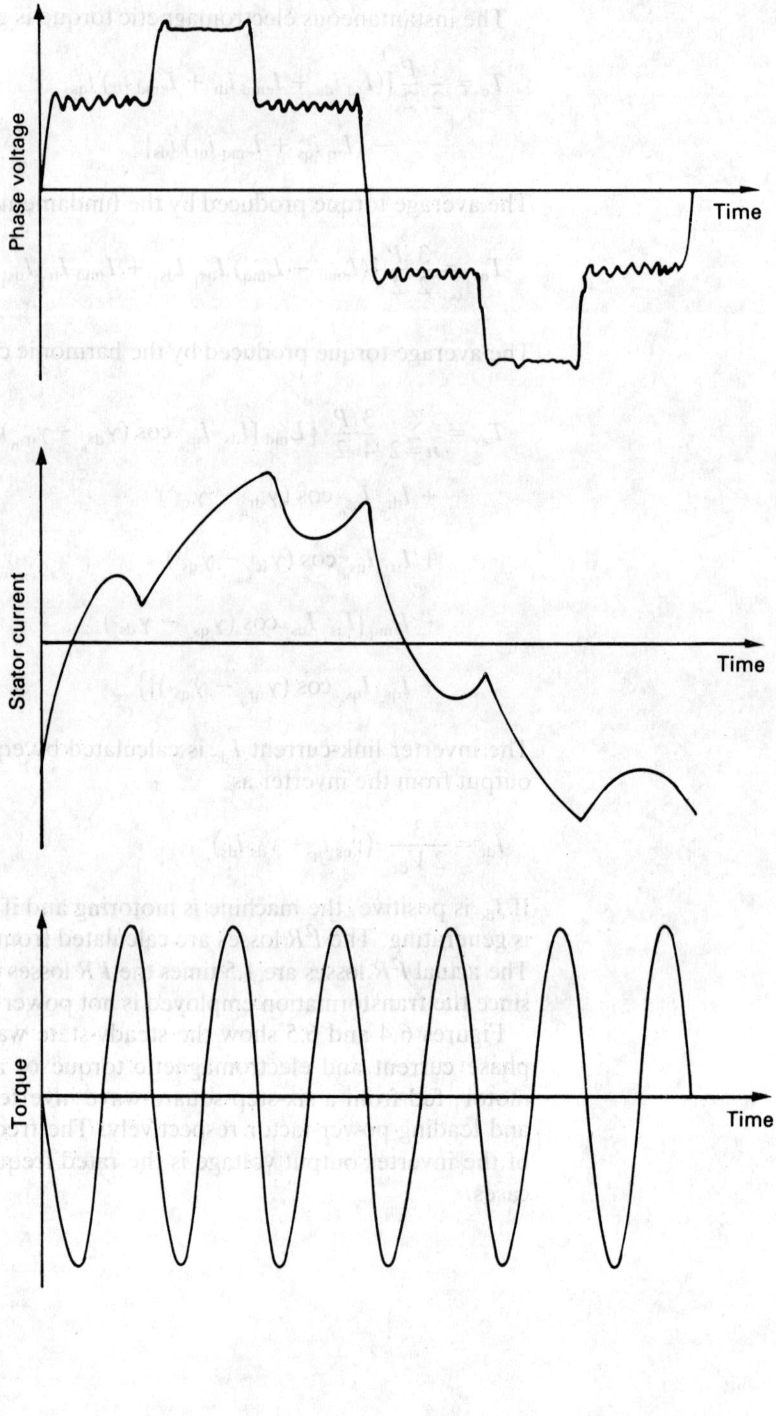

Figure 6.4 Waveforms of stator phase voltage, phase current and motor torque for lagging power factor operation of motor fed from 6-step voltage source.

Figure 6.5 Waveforms of stator phase voltage, phase current and motor torque for leading power factor operation of motor fed from 6-step voltage source.

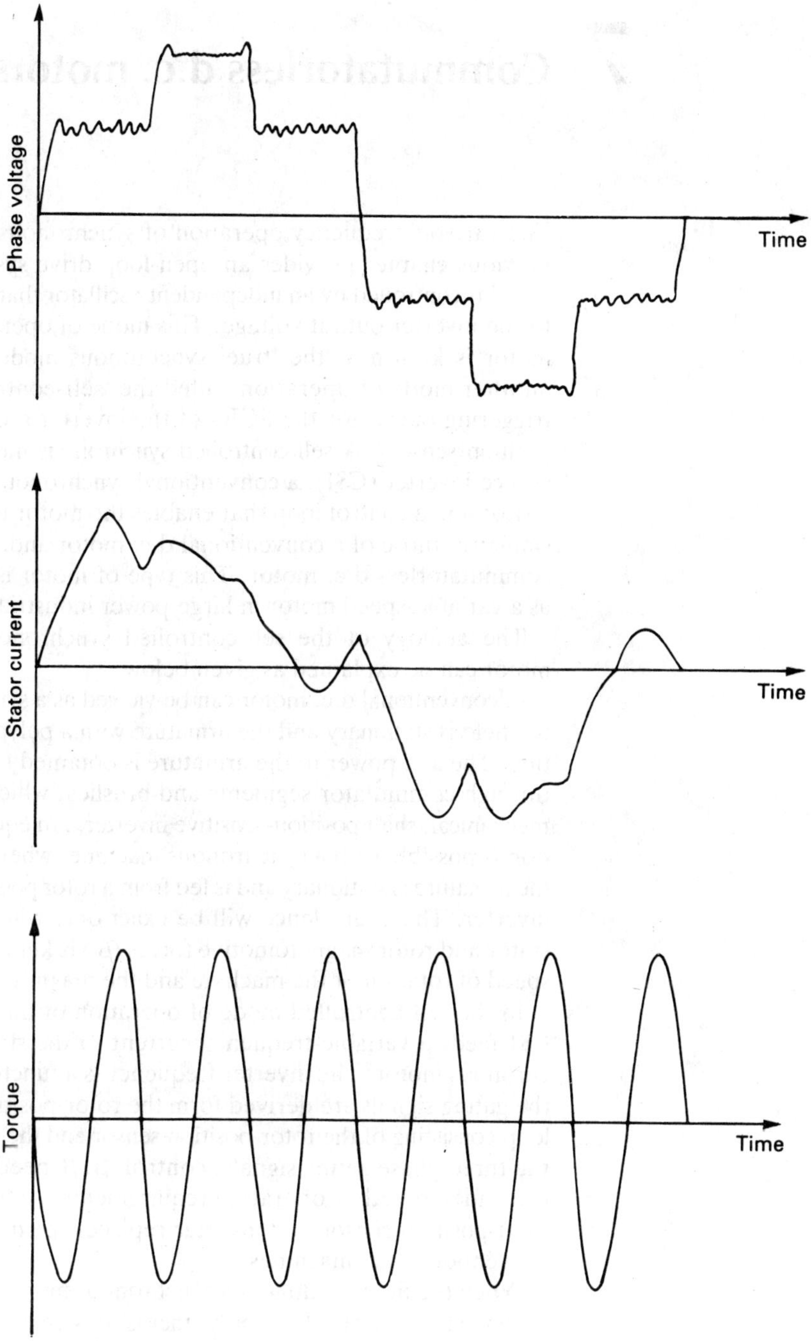

7 Commutatorless d.c. motors

The variable-frequency operation of synchronous motors discussed in the previous chapter provides an open-loop drive system in which the motor speed is controlled by an independent oscillator that gives various frequencies to the inverter output voltage. This mode of operation of the synchronous motor is known as the 'true' synchronous mode. However, there exists another mode of operation called the 'self-controlled' mode, that is the triggering pulses for the SCRs of the inverter are derived from the shaft-position sensors. A self-controlled synchronous motor consists of a current-source inverter (CSI), a conventional synchronous motor, a rotor-position sensor and a control loop that enables the motor to produce characteristics similar to those of a conventional d.c. motor and, hence, is often termed a commutatorless d.c. motor. This type of motor is being used increasingly as a variable-speed motor in large-power industrial applications.

The analogy of the self-controlled synchronous motor with the d.c. motor can be explained as given below.

A conventional d.c. motor can be viewed as a synchronous motor in which the field is stationary and the armature with a polyphase a.c. winding is rotating. The a.c. power to the armature is obtained from the input d.c. supply through commutator segments and brushes, which can be thought of as a mechanical, shaft position-sensitive inverter. An equivalent d.c. motor operation is possible with a synchronous machine, where the field is rotating but the armature is stationary and is fed from a rotor position-controlled electronic inverter. The equivalence will be exact only when the angle between the stator and rotor magnetomotive forces (β) is kept at 90°, irrespective of the speed of rotation of the machine and the magnitude of armature current.

In the self-controlled mode of operation of the synchronous motor, the CSI feeds a variable-frequency current to the stator windings of the synchronous motor. The inverter frequency is a function of motor speed, since the gating signals are derived form the rotor-position sensor. The feedback loop consisting of the rotor-position sensor and the logic unit, which provides the three-phase gating signals, controls β. β need not be equal to 90° and is decided by other operating requirements. Actually, the combination of shaft-position sensor and inverter replaces the mechanical commutator of conventional d.c. machines.

When the field winding of a synchronous motor is overexcited, it draws a leading current from the supply, that is, it is able to supply the commutating reactive power required by the inverter. Above a certain speed of rotation of the motor, when there is adequate e.m.f. induced in the armature, natural commutation of the inverter SCRs can be obtained. In fact, a gating signal originating from the position sensor turns on a corresponding SCR in a specified sequence so that the armature induced voltage appears as a reverse bias across the previously conducting SCR and turns it off. Natural commutation considerably simplifies the inverter circuit by dispensing with the commutation devices such as inductors, capacitors and auxiliary SCRs. However, this type of commutation is not possible at low speeds where the induced armature e.m.f. is insufficient to commutate the inverter SCRs. Therefore, some method must be employed to start the machine and run it at low speeds. Yet another disadvantage of natural commutation is the absolute necessity of leading power-factor operation of the motor which in turn demands a motor of larger power rating with reduced capacity utilization. Actually, an angle of 90° between the stator and rotor m.m.f.s, which will enable the torque developed by the motor to be a maximum for specified mangnitudes of armature and field currents (as in the case of a conventional d.c. motor), can be obtained only when the field excitation is such that the motor draws a lagging current from the supply.

The shaft-position sensor, employed for synchronizing the converter triggering pulses to the rotor position, tends to reduce the system ruggedness and to limit control possibilities. However, it is possible to use the motor terminal voltages as synchronizing signals, thus eliminating the shaft-position detector.

7.1 Basic Commutatorless d.c. Motor

Figure 7.1 shows the schematic diagram for a separately-excited, naturally commutated, commutatorless d.c. motor. The star-connected stator winding

Figure 7.1 Schematic diagram of a commutatorless d.c. motor.

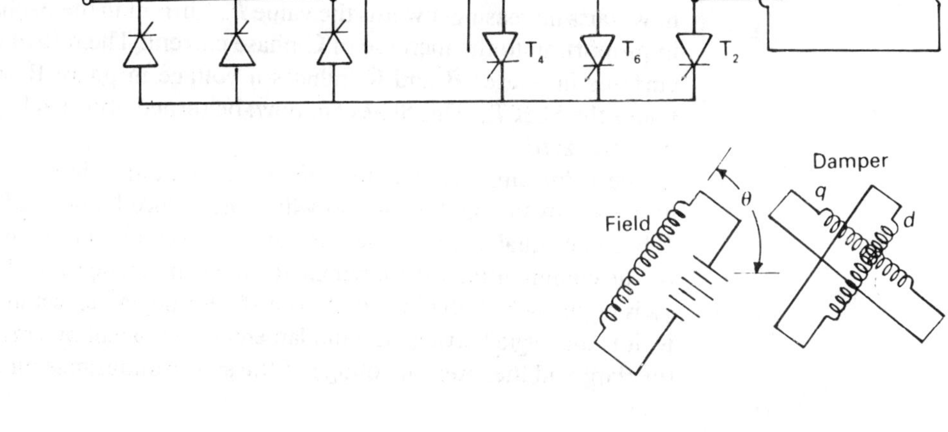

of a salient-pole synchronous machine is fed from a load-commutated CSI. The *ripple-free* unidirectional current input to the inverter is obtained from a six-pulse, phase-controlled rectifier, operating from the normal three-phase a.c. supply, through a smoothing inductor. Natural commutation of the inverter is made possible by the induced e.m.f. of the synchronous machine. Neither the auxiliary commutation devices, which may be required for starting the motor nor the logic, which provides gating signals for the SCRs for every 120 electrical degrees are shown.

7.2 Modes of Operation

When the CSI fed synchronous motor is operating in the steady state, inverter SCRs T_1 to T_6 trigger in sequence, one every 60 electrical degrees of operation, causing the stator m.m.f. to advance 60° with each switching event. Hence, a complete steady-state solution can be obtained by analyzing the electromagnetic processes of any interval of 60° duration. Two distinct modes of operation occur within each 60° interval. The part of the interval during which only two stator phases carry current is known as the conduction interval or mode of operation and that during which switching of the line current from one stator phase to another stator phase occurs is termed the commutation interval.

Typical waveforms of stator phase induced e.m.f.s and phase currents are illustrated in Fig. 7.2. The 60° interval chosen for the purpose of analysis described below begins when SCR T_5 turns off and ends when SCR T_6 turns off. During the conduction mode, SCRs T_1 and T_6 are 'on' and the d.c. link current flows from phase A to phase B. The commutation mode starts when SCR T_2 is gated 'on'. The SCRs are assumed to be ideal switches and the C-phase induced e.m.f. at the instant of triggering 'on' of SCR T_2 is positive with respect to the negative side of the rectifier output; the SCR T_2 starts conducting instantaneously and forces the B-phase and C-phase voltages to be equal. The C-phase current, which is the commutating current i_k in this particular 60° interval, now starts increasing towards the value I_d. Current in the B-phase decreases in proportion to the increase of C-phase current. The rate of change of the currents in phases B and C induces a voltage in phase B which reverse-biases the SCR T_6. This SCR can, now, be turned off when B-phase current becomes zero.

The rotor angle at the start of the commutation interval is defined as $\theta = -\gamma_0$, by taking the angle at which the induced e.m.f.s of phases B and C become equal as zero. The duration of the commutation interval is given by the commutation overlap angle μ in electrical degrees. The firing angle γ_0 is equivalent to the internal power-factor angle neglecting overlap, that is, it is the angle between the fundamental component of current, neglecting overlap, and the internal voltage of the synchronous machine.

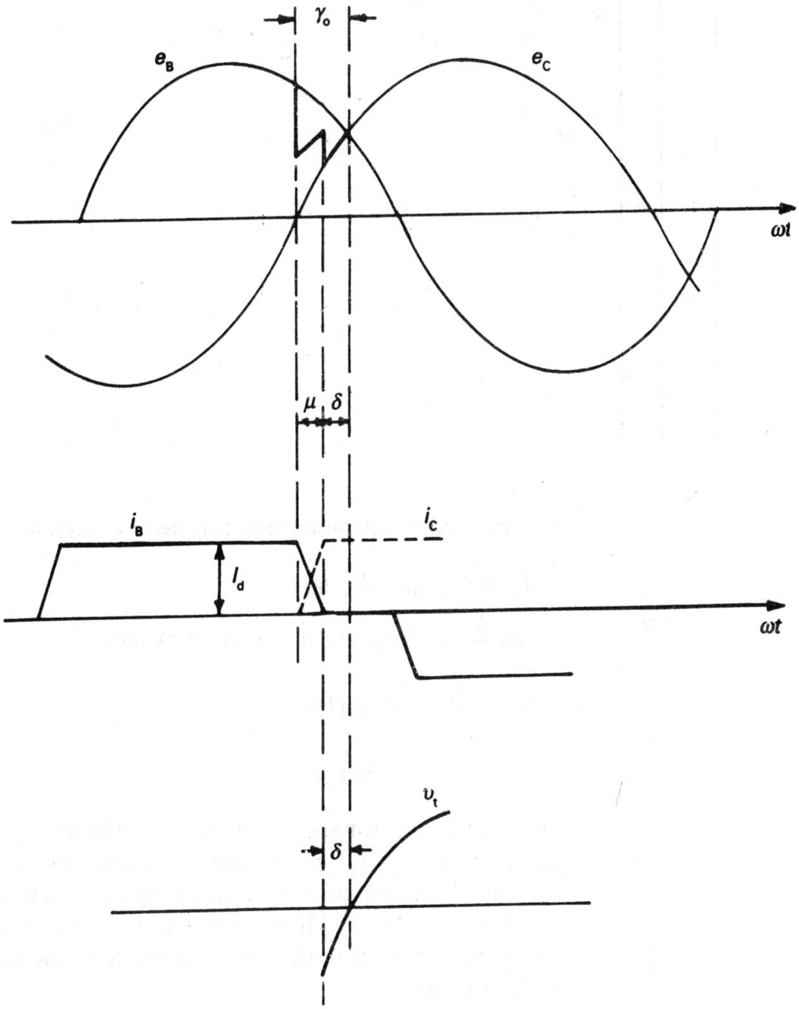

Figure 7.2 Waveforms of stator phase induced e.m.f.s. and phase currents.

By our definition, the conduction interval ranges from $-(\gamma_0 + 60° - \mu)$ to $-\gamma_0$ and the commutation interval from $-\gamma_0$ to $-(\gamma_0 - \mu)$.

7.3 Steady-State Analysis

Apart from the assumptions stated in Chapter 6 with respect to the synchronous machine and switching elements, the d.c. link current is assumed to be constant, that is free from ripple.

The analysis[33] is done using the circuit equations of the synchronous machine expressed in the rotor reference frame. In matrix form and per-unit quantities, they become

$$\begin{bmatrix} v_{qs} \\ v_{ds} \\ 0 \\ 0 \\ V_{fr} \end{bmatrix} = \begin{bmatrix} R_s + \frac{p}{\omega_b} x_q & \frac{\omega_r}{\omega_b} x_d & \frac{p}{\omega_b} x_{mq} & \frac{\omega_r}{\omega_b} x_{md} & \frac{\omega_r}{\omega_b} x_{md} \\ -\frac{\omega_r}{\omega_b} x_q & R_s + \frac{p}{\omega_b} x_q & -\frac{\omega_r}{\omega_b} x_{mq} & \frac{p}{\omega_b} x_{md} & \frac{p}{\omega_b} x_{md} \\ \frac{p}{\omega_b} x_{mq} & 0 & R_{qr} + \frac{p}{\omega_b} x_{qr} & 0 & 0 \\ 0 & \frac{p}{\omega_b} x_{md} & 0 & R_{dr} + \frac{p}{\omega_b} x_{dr} & \frac{p}{\omega_b} x_{md} \\ 0 & \frac{p}{\omega_b} x_{md} & 0 & \frac{p}{\omega_b} x_{md} & R_{fr} + \frac{p}{\omega_b} x_{fr} \end{bmatrix} \times \begin{bmatrix} i_{qs} \\ i_{ds} \\ i_{qr} \\ i_{dr} \\ i_{fr} \end{bmatrix} \qquad [7.1]$$

The per-unit electromagnetic torque is written as

$$T_e = \psi_{ds} i_{qs} - \psi_{qs} i_{ds} \qquad [7.2]$$

where ψ_{ds} and ψ_{qs} are stator flux-linkages.

$$\psi_{ds} = x_d i_{ds} + x_{md} (i_{dr} + i_{fr}) \qquad [7.3]$$

$$\psi_{qs} = x_q i_{qs} + x_{mq} i_{qr} \qquad [7.4]$$

At a constant rotor speed, the state of the motor is determined wholly by the currents i_{qs}, i_{ds}, i_{qr}, i_{dr} and i_{fr}. However, with a constant d.c. link current, the stator currents contain only one independent variable, the circulating current i_k, and that is non-zero only during the commutation interval. The stator currents in the rotor reference frame can be expressed in terms of I_d and i_k as

$$I_d (\cos\theta - 1/\sqrt{3} \sin\theta) + 2/\sqrt{3}\, i_k \sin\theta \qquad [7.5]$$

$$i_{ds} = I_d (1/\sqrt{3} \cos\theta + \sin\theta) - 2/\sqrt{3}\, i_k \cos\theta \qquad [7.6]$$

All electromagnetic variables calculated in the solution as well as the field voltage are normalized to a d.c. link current of 1.0 p.u. for the sake of convenience in calculation. Steady-state operating points, which have the same values of γ_0 and μ but different values of I_d, can be determined simply by multiplying all voltages and currents in the normalized solution by a constant scale factor.

Since the circulating current i_k is non-zero only during the commutation interval, the state equations must be of somewhat different forms during the two modes.

7.3.1 State Equations During Conduction Mode

During conduction mode the circulating current i_k is zero. This constraint is satisfied by the dummy state equation

$$(1 + \frac{p}{\omega_b})\, i_k = 0 \qquad [7.7]$$

The rotor circuit equations, namely the bottom three rows of eqn [7.1], after substituting $i_k = 0$ in eqns [7.5] and [7.6], contain terms proportional to $\cos\theta$ and $\sin\theta$ which are due to the constant d.c. link current being referred to the moving rotor. Since the rotor speed and the initial rotor position are known, it is easy to generate $\cos\theta$ and $\sin\theta$ as auxiliary state variables y_1 and y_2 by solving the auxiliary equation

$$\begin{bmatrix} \frac{p}{\omega_r} & 1 \\ -1 & \frac{p}{\omega_r} \end{bmatrix} \begin{bmatrix} y_1 \\ y_2 \end{bmatrix} = \begin{bmatrix} 0 \\ 0 \end{bmatrix} \qquad [7.8]$$

The functions y_1 and y_2 are added to the currents to form an augmented state vector

$$\bar{x} = [\, i_{qr}, i_{dr}, i_{fr}, y_1, y_2 \,]^t \qquad [7.9]$$

The three rotor circuit equations, the dummy state eqn [7.7] and the auxiliary state eqn [7.9] can be expressed in matrix form as

$$\begin{bmatrix} R_{qr} + \frac{p}{\omega_b} x_{qr} & 0 & 0 & 0 & -\frac{1}{\sqrt{3}}\frac{\omega_r}{\omega_b} x_{mq} & -\frac{\omega_r}{\omega_b} x_{mq} \\ 0 & R_{dr} + \frac{p}{\omega_b} x_{dr} & \frac{p}{\omega_b} x_{md} & 0 & \frac{\omega_r}{\omega_b} x_{md} & -\frac{1}{\sqrt{3}}\frac{\omega_r}{\omega_b} x_{md} \\ 0 & \frac{p}{\omega_b} x_{md} & R_{fr} + \frac{p}{\omega_b} x_{fr} & 0 & \frac{\omega_r}{\omega_b} x_{md} & -\frac{1}{\sqrt{3}}\frac{\omega_r}{\omega_b} x_{md} \\ 0 & 0 & 0 & 1 + \frac{p}{\omega_b} & 0 & 0 \\ 0 & 0 & 0 & 0 & \frac{p}{\omega_r} & 1 \\ 0 & 0 & 0 & 0 & -1 & \frac{p}{\omega_r} \end{bmatrix} \times \begin{bmatrix} i_{qr} \\ i_{dr} \\ i_{fr} \\ i_k \\ y_1 \\ y_2 \end{bmatrix} = \begin{bmatrix} 0 \\ 0 \\ V_{fr} \\ 0 \\ 0 \\ 0 \end{bmatrix} \qquad [7.10]$$

By suitable manipulation of eqn [7.10], the state equations can be put into a standard form

$$\dot{x} = A\,\bar{x} + B\,\bar{u} \qquad [7.11]$$

where $\bar{u}$ is the input vector given by

$$\bar{u} = [\,V_{fr}, I_{dc}\,]^t \qquad [7.12]$$

which, by our assumptions, consists of constant elements. It must be noted that during the conduction mode, the system matrix A and the input coefficient B are constants, that is the system is time-variant.

7.3.2 *State Equations During Commutation Mode*

Since during the commutation interval the circulating current i_k is non-zero, the dummy state eqn [7.7] is no longer valid. The suitable state equation for this mode is one that takes into account the short-circuit between phases B and C. Transformation of the stator voltage expressions to a stationary reference frame gives

$$0 = \frac{1}{\sqrt{3}}(v_C - v_B)$$

$$= \frac{R_s}{\sqrt{3}}(I_d - 2i_k) - \frac{1}{\sqrt{3}}[x_d + x_q + (x_d - x_q)\cos 2\theta\,]\frac{p}{\omega_b}\,i_k$$

$$- x_{mq}\sin\theta\,\frac{p}{\omega_b}\,i_{qr} + x_{md}\cos\theta\,\frac{p}{\omega_b}\,(i_{dr} + i_{fr})$$

$$+ \frac{2\,\omega_r}{\sqrt{3}\omega_b}(x_d - x_q)\sin 2\theta \cdot i_k$$

$$- \frac{\omega_r}{\omega_b}\,x_{mq}\cos\theta \cdot i_{qr} - \frac{\omega_r}{\omega_b}\,x_{md}\sin\theta \cdot (i_{dr} + i_{fr})$$

$$+ \frac{\omega_r}{\omega_b}(x_d - x_q)\,(\cos 2\theta - \frac{1}{\sqrt{3}}\sin 2\theta\,) \qquad [7.13]$$

The last term in eqn [7.13], in its present form, would appear as a time-varying input to the system. To eliminate this difficulty, the trigonometric terms are split into the equivalent form

$$\left(\cos 2\theta - \frac{1}{\sqrt{3}} \sin 2\theta \right)$$

$$= \left[\cos\theta - \left(1 + \frac{1}{\sqrt{3}}\right) \sin\theta \right] \cos\theta + \left[\left(1 - \frac{1}{\sqrt{3}}\right) \cos\theta - \sin\theta \right] \sin\theta \qquad [7.14]$$

In the above form the double-frequency terms appear explicitly in terms of the auxiliary state variables with time-varying coefficients.

The state equations corresponding to commutation mode can be expressed in matrix form as in eqn [7.15] on page 152.

By suitable matrix manipulation, eqn [7.15] can also be put into the standard form

$$\dot{\bar{x}} = A' \bar{x} + B' \bar{u} \qquad [7.16]$$

During the commutation interval, the system matrix A' and the input coefficient matrix B' are time-varying, since they are functions of the rotor angle.

7.3.3 *Determination of Initial Conditions*

The symmetry of steady-state operation enables us to determine the boundary conditions for the steady-state operating point in a closed form, without resorting to any iterative calculations. At first, a relation is found between the initial values and the final values of the state variables at the end of the 60° interval. The symmetry conditions are, then, applied to solve for the initial values of the rotor currents i_{qr}, i_{dr}, i_{fr} and for the field voltage V_{fr}.

The state of any linear time-invariant system with constant inputs of the form $\dot{\bar{x}} = A\bar{x} + B\bar{u}$ at time t_1 is related to the initial state by

$$\bar{x}(t_1) = e^{AT_1}\,\bar{x}(0) + \lambda\,(t_1, 0)\,B\,\bar{u} \qquad [7.17]$$

where e^{AT_1} is the state transition matrix and

$$\lambda\,(t_1, 0) = \int_0^{t_1} e^{At}\,dt \qquad [7.18]$$

$$
\begin{bmatrix}
R_{qr} + \frac{p}{\omega_b} x_{qr} & 0 & 0 & \frac{2}{\sqrt{3}} x_{mq} \left(\cos\theta \cdot \frac{\omega_r}{\omega_b} + \sin\theta \cdot \frac{p}{\omega_b}\right) & -\frac{1}{\sqrt{3}} \frac{\omega_r}{\omega_b} x_{mq} & -\frac{\omega_r}{\omega_b} x_{mq} \\
0 & R_{dr} + \frac{p}{\omega_b} x_{dr} & \frac{p}{\omega_b} x_{md} & \frac{2}{\sqrt{3}} x_{md} \left(\sin\theta \cdot \frac{\omega_r}{\omega_b} - \cos\theta \cdot \frac{p}{\omega_b}\right) & \frac{\omega_r}{\omega_b} x_{md} & -\frac{1}{\sqrt{3}} \frac{\omega_r}{\omega_b} x_{md} \\
0 & \frac{p}{\omega_b} x_{md} & R_{fr} + \frac{p}{\omega_b} x_{fr} & \frac{2}{\sqrt{3}} x_{md} \left(\sin\theta \cdot \frac{\omega_r}{\omega_b} - \cos\theta \cdot \frac{p}{\omega_b}\right) & \frac{\omega_r}{\omega_b} x_{md} & -\frac{1}{\sqrt{3}} \frac{\omega_r}{\omega_b} x_{md} \\
-x_{mq} \left(\sin\theta \frac{p}{\omega_b} + \cos\theta \frac{\omega_r}{\omega_b}\right) & x_{md} \left(\cos\theta \cdot \frac{p}{\omega_b} - \sin\theta \cdot \frac{\omega_r}{\omega_b}\right) & x_{md} \left(\cos\theta \cdot \frac{p}{\omega_b} - \sin\theta \cdot \frac{\omega_r}{\omega_b}\right) & \frac{1}{\sqrt{3}} \left[\{x_d + x_q + (x_d - x_q)\cos 2\theta\} \frac{p}{\omega_b} + 2 \frac{\omega_r}{\omega_b} (x_d - x_q) \sin 2\theta - 2R_s\right] & \frac{\omega_r}{\omega_b} (x_d - x_q) \left[\cos\theta - \left(1 + \frac{1}{\sqrt{3}}\right) \sin\theta\right] & \frac{\omega_r}{\omega_b} (x_d - x_q) \left[-\sin\theta + \left(1 - \frac{1}{\sqrt{3}}\right) \cos\theta\right] \\
0 & 0 & 0 & 0 & \frac{p}{\omega_r} & 1 \\
0 & 0 & 0 & 0 & -1 & \frac{p}{\omega_r}
\end{bmatrix}
\times
\begin{bmatrix} i_{qr} \\ i_{dr} \\ i_{fr} \\ i_k \\ y_1 \\ y_2 \end{bmatrix}
=
\begin{bmatrix} 0 \\ 0 \\ V_{fr} \\ -\frac{R_s}{\sqrt{3}} I_d \\ 0 \\ 0 \end{bmatrix}
\qquad [7.15]
$$

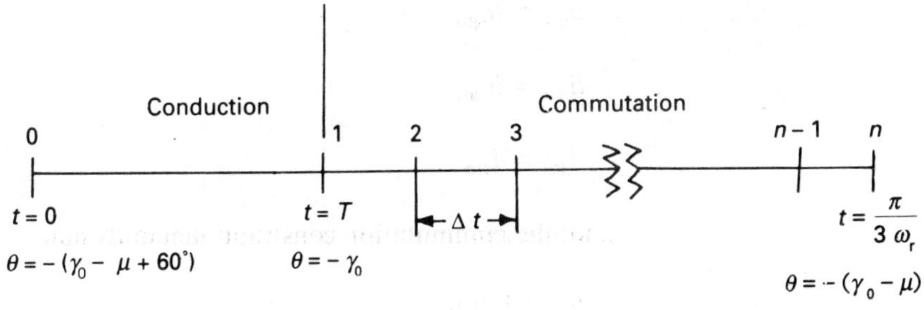

Figure 7.3 Division of 60° interval under study.

Let the 60° interval under study be divided as shown in Fig. 7.3. If the initial state is denoted as $\bar{x}_0$, the state at the mode of transition, where $t = T$, can be expressed as

$$\bar{x}_1 = e^{A_0 T}\, \bar{x}_0 + \lambda_0\, B_0\, \bar{u}_0 \qquad [7.19]$$

where the subscript 0 of the matrices indicates that they were calculated for the zeroth increment in Fig. 7.3.

During the commutation interval, the system is time-varying and the final value of the state variables cannot be easily found. However, sufficiently accurate values can be obtained by dividing the commutation interval into small increments and assuming the system to be time-variant over each increment. The value of the state vector at the end of any increment is related to the value at the end of the previous increment by

$$\bar{x}_n = e^{A_{n-1}\Delta t}\, \bar{x}_{n-1} + \lambda_{n-1}\, B_{n-1}\, \bar{u} \qquad [7.20]$$

where the state transition matrix and its integral are evaluated at the mid-point of each increment. Successive use of eqn [7.20] gives a relation for the final state, at the end of the 60° interval, in terms of the initial state

$$\bar{x}_n = D\, \bar{x}_0 + C_{n-1}\, \bar{u} \qquad [7.21]$$

where

$$D = e^{A_{n-1}\Delta t}\, e^{A_{n-2}\Delta t} \ldots e^{A_1 \Delta t}\, e^{A_0 T} \qquad [7.22]$$

and C_{n-1} is given recursively by

$$C_{n-1} = e^{A_{n-1}\Delta t}\, C_{n-2} + \lambda_{n-1}\, B_{n-1} \qquad [7.23]$$

$$C_0 = \lambda_0\, B_0 \qquad [7.24]$$

The top four rows of eqn [7.21] are used to solve for the unknown currents and the voltage applied to the field. Symmetry of steady-state operation implies that

$$i_{qrn} = i_{qro} \qquad [7.25]$$

$$i_{drn} = i_{dro} \qquad [7.26]$$

$$i_{frn} = i_{fro} \qquad [7.27]$$

and the commutation constraint demands that

$$i_{kn} = 1 \text{ p.u.} \qquad [7.28]$$

These expressions are substituted into the top four rows of eqn [7.21] to obtain four equations in i_{qr}, i_{dr}, i_{fr} and V_{fr}. These four equations can be solved by linear algebra techniques.

7.3.4 *Determination of Steady-State Performance*

After the determination of initial conditions, it is easy and straight forward to integrate the state equations to evaluate the state at convenient time intervals. If the time interval is chosen to be the same as the increment for calculation of the initial condition, the state transition matrices can be stored and used again, thus saving some computation time.

The waveforms for the completecycle can be easily plotted from the waveforms obtained over the 60° region analysed. While rotor currents, flux-linkages and electromagnetic torque repeat simply every 60°, the stator phase voltage, current and flux-linkages possess half-wave and three-phase symmetry.

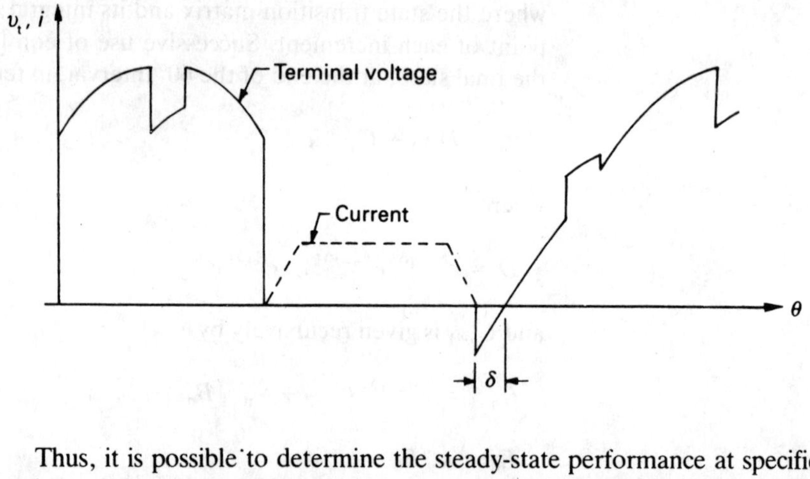

Figure 7.4 Waveforms of motor terminal voltage and phase current.

Thus, it is possible to determine the steady-state performance at specified values of motor speed, d.c. link current and field voltage for assumed values of γ_0 and μ. Figure 7.4 shows typical waveforms of motor terminal voltage and phase current. δ denotes the commutation margin angle which indicates how long the concerned inverter SCR is reverse-biased before it must support

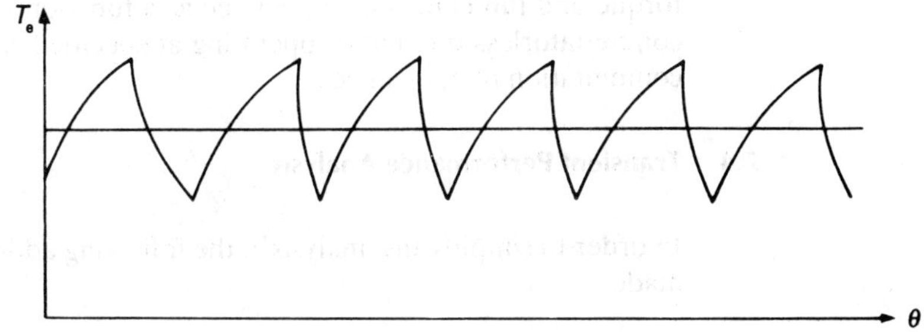

Figure 7.5 Variation of torque with rotor position.

forward voltage. Figure 7.5 illustrates the variation of electromagnetic torque with rotor position for a complete cycle. The sixth harmonic ripple component caused inevitably by sequential switching of inverter SCRs is clearly seen. However, this method of determination of the performance for assumed values of γ_0 and μ is quite inconvenient, since the latter, namely the commutation overlap angle itself is a variable dependent on the field current, d.c. link current, firing angle and the inductance of the stator phases. Hence, instead of the variable μ, a safe value of the commutation margin angle δ, required for successful commutation of inverter SCRs, which is independent of the above factors, can be chosen as a parameter. In fact, $\delta \geq \dfrac{180\ \omega\ t_{off}}{\pi}$, where t_{off} is the turn-off time of the concerned SCR and ω the angular frequency corresponding to the speed of operation of the motor. Thus, for a given ω_r and I_d (which roughly indicates the SCR to be used and thereby gives an idea of t_{off}), a reasonable value of δ can be fixed. Then, for various values of firing angle γ_0, an iterative technique has to be used to find the value of μ (which defines a steady-state operating point) that yields the desired value of the commutationmargin angle δ. Once the values of γ_0 and μ, which give the assumed fixed value of δ are known, it is possible to get the average value of the electromagnetic torque developed by the motor at specified values of ω_r, I_d and V_{fr}, using the method described earlier. Figure 7.6 shows typical steady-state performance curves of average

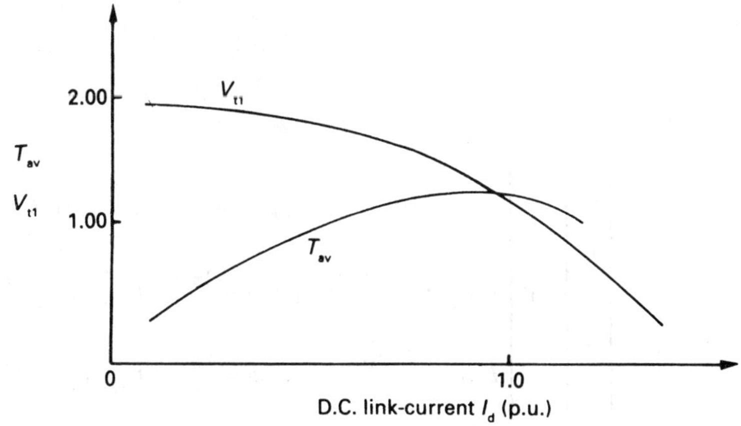

Figure 7.6 Variation of average torque and fundamental motor terminal voltage with d.c. link-current.

torque and fundamental a.c. voltage as a function of d.c. link current of a commutatorless d.c. motor operating at specified speed, field current and commutation margin angle.

7.4 Transient Performance Analysis

In order to simplify the analysis[34], the following additional assumptions are made.

(i) The mechanical and electrical transient responses are slow compared with the time between two successive commutations.
(ii) The leading angle of commutation of SCRs and the angle of overlap of armature currents which are essentially time-discrete quantities could be regarded as continuous quantities.
(iii) The inverter d.c. side voltage and the developed motor torque do not contain any ripple and could be denoted by their average values.
(iv) The field current also is free from ripple.
(v) The armature current is of trapezoidal waveform.

7.4.1 *Derivation of Equations*

The voltage equation for the stator phases of the synchronous motor can be expressed as

$$\begin{bmatrix} v_A \\ v_B \\ v_C \end{bmatrix} = \begin{bmatrix} R_s + p(l + L + L_0 \cos 2\theta) & p(\frac{-L}{2} + L_0 \cos \overline{2\theta - \frac{2\pi}{3}}) & p(\frac{-L}{2} + L_0 \cos \overline{2\theta + \frac{2\pi}{3}}) \\ p(-\frac{L}{2} + L_0 \cos \overline{2\theta - \frac{2\pi}{3}}) & R_s + p(l + L + L_0 \cos \overline{2\theta + \frac{2\pi}{3}}) & p(\frac{-L}{2} + L_0 \cos 2\theta) \\ p(\frac{-L}{2} + L_0 \cos \overline{2\theta + \frac{2\pi}{3}}) & p(\frac{-L}{2} + L_0 \cos 2\theta) & R_s + p(l + L + L_0 \cos \overline{2\theta - \frac{2\pi}{3}}) \end{bmatrix}$$

$$\begin{bmatrix} i_A \\ i_B \\ i_C \end{bmatrix} + p \begin{bmatrix} L_{af} \cos\theta & L_{add} \cos\theta & -L_{aqd} \sin\theta \\ L_{af} \cos\overline{\theta - \frac{2\pi}{3}} & L_{add} \cos\overline{\theta - \frac{2\pi}{3}} & -L_{aqd} \sin\overline{\theta - \frac{2\pi}{3}} \\ L_{af} \cos\overline{\theta + \frac{2\pi}{3}} & L_{add} \cos\overline{\theta + \frac{2\pi}{3}} & -L_{aqd} \sin\overline{\theta + \frac{2\pi}{3}} \end{bmatrix} \begin{bmatrix} i_{fr} \\ i_{dr} \\ i_{qr} \end{bmatrix} \quad [7.29]$$

where l, L and L_0 denote the leakage inductance, mean effective inductance and maximum value of effective inductance due to saliency; and L_{af}, L_{add} and L_{aqd} represent the maximum value of mutual inductance between one stator phase and field winding, d-axis damper winding and q-axis damper winding respectively, all values being per-phase.
Now, the magnetic flux-linkages of the d-axis damper winding and q-axis damper winding due to armature currents and damper currents themselves (they do not include the flux-linkages due to flux produced by the field winding) are given as

$$\begin{bmatrix} \psi_{ddo} \\ \\ \psi_{qdo} \end{bmatrix} = \begin{bmatrix} L_{add}\left(\cos\theta \cdot i_A + \cos\overline{\theta - \frac{2\pi}{3}} \cdot i_B + \cos\overline{\theta + \frac{2\pi}{3}} \cdot i_C\right) + L_{dr} i_{dr} \\ \\ -L_{aqd}\left(\sin\theta \cdot i_A + \sin\overline{\theta - \frac{2\pi}{3}} \cdot i_B + \sin\overline{\theta + \frac{2\pi}{3}} \cdot i_C\right) + L_{qr} i_{qr} \end{bmatrix} \quad [7.30]$$

From eqn [7.30], we can get expressions for the damper currents i_{dr} and i_{qr} in terms of ψ_{ddo}, ψ_{qdo} and armature phase currents. By substituting those expressions in eqn [7.29], v_A can be written as

$$\begin{aligned} v_A = {} & [\,R_s + p\,(L''_d + L''_q)/2\,]\, i_A \\ & + (L''_d - L''_q)/3 \cdot p\left(\cos 2\theta \cdot i_A + \cos\overline{2\theta + \frac{2\pi}{3}} \cdot i_B + \cos 2\theta + \frac{2\pi}{3} \cdot i_C\right) \\ & + p\left(L_{af}\cos\theta \cdot i_{fr} + \frac{L_{add}}{L_{dr}} \cdot \cos\theta \,.\, \psi_{ddo} - \frac{L_{aqd}}{L_{qr}} \cdot \sin\theta \cdot \psi_{qdo}\right) \end{aligned} \quad [7.31]$$

where L''_d and L''_q denote the direct-axis and quadrature-axis subtransient inductances respectively. They are related to the direct- and quadrature-axis synchronous inductances L_d and L_q as given below.
$L''_d = \sigma_d \,.\, L_d$, where σ_d is known as the direct-axis leakage coefficient and is equal to $(1 - 3L^2_{add}/2L_{dr}\, L_d)$ and $L_d = [\,1 + 3(L + L_0)/2]$.
Similarly,

$$L''_q = \sigma_q\, L_q$$

where

$$\sigma_q = (1 - 3L^2_{aqd}/2L_{qr}\, L_q)$$

and

$$L_q = [\,1 + 3(L - L_0)/2]$$

v_B and v_C can also be written in a form similar to eqn [7.31]. For machines with damper windings, L''_d is approximately equal to L''_q and, therefore, the voltage equations become

$$\begin{bmatrix} v_A \\ v_B \\ v_C \end{bmatrix} = (R_s + L''_s p) \begin{bmatrix} i_A \\ i_B \\ i_C \end{bmatrix} + \begin{bmatrix} e_A \\ e_B \\ e_C \end{bmatrix} \qquad [7.32]$$

where $L''_s = (L''_d + L''_q)/2$ and e_A, e_B, e_C are the electromotive forces induced in the armature windings and are given by

$$\begin{bmatrix} e_A \\ e_B \\ e_C \end{bmatrix} = \begin{bmatrix} -\sin\theta & \cos\theta \\ -\sin(\theta - 2\pi/3) & \cos(\theta - 2\pi/3) \\ -\sin(\theta - 4\pi/3) & \cos(\theta - 4\pi/3) \end{bmatrix} \begin{bmatrix} A \\ B \end{bmatrix}$$

$$= \sqrt{2}\, V_i \begin{bmatrix} \sin(\theta - \pi - \alpha) \\ \sin(\theta + \pi/3 - \alpha) \\ \sin(\theta - \pi/3 - \alpha) \end{bmatrix} \qquad [7.33]$$

where

$$\begin{bmatrix} A \\ B \end{bmatrix} = \omega_e \begin{bmatrix} L_{af} i_{fr} + K_d \psi_{ddo} \\ -K_q \psi_{qdo} \end{bmatrix} + p \begin{bmatrix} K_q \psi_{qdo} \\ L_{af} i_{fr} + K_d \psi_{ddo} \end{bmatrix} \qquad [7.34]$$

in which

$$\omega_e = \frac{d\theta}{dt}, \quad K_d = \frac{L_{add}}{L_{dr}}, \quad K_q = \frac{L_{aqd}}{L_{qr}}$$

and

$$V_i = (A^2 + B^2)^{1/2}/\sqrt{2}\,; \quad \tan\alpha = B/A \qquad [7.35]$$

Under steady state, the *d*-axis and *q*-axis damper resistances can be ignored. Since the damper windings are closed windings, from the constant flux-linkage theorem it follows that the flux linkages ψ_{ddo} and ψ_{qdo} are constant with respect to time during steady state. This means that the damper-winding currents flow in such a way as to nullify the fluxes created by the higher harmonic components of the armature currents. Therefore, ψ_{ddo} and ψ_{qdo} are determined only by the fundamental components of the armature currents.

The fundamental component of the A-phase armature current assumed to be trapezoidal in nature is given as

$$i_{A_1} = \sqrt{2}\, I_1 \sin(\theta - \pi - \alpha + \gamma - u/2) \qquad [7.36]$$

where

$$\begin{aligned} I_1 &= (\sqrt{6}/\pi) \sin(u/2)/(u/2) \cdot I_d \\ &\simeq (\sqrt{6}/\pi) \cdot I_d \end{aligned} \qquad [7.37]$$

By substituting eqn [7.36] as well as the expressions for the fundamental components of the B-phase and C-phase armature currents i_{B1} and i_{C1} (obtained by phase-shifting eqn [7.36] by time-angles of $2\pi/3$ and $4\pi/3$ respectively) in eqn [7.30] and omitting the higher harmonic terms, we get

$$\begin{bmatrix} \psi_{ddo1} \\ \psi_{qdo1} \end{bmatrix} = \frac{3}{2}\sqrt{2}\, I_1 \begin{bmatrix} L_{add} \sin(-\alpha + \gamma - u/2) \\ L_{aqd} \cos(-\alpha + \gamma - u/2) \end{bmatrix} \qquad [7.38]$$

The equivalent circuit for the motor fed from a CSI viewed from the d.c. source is shown in Fig. 7.7. The voltage equation of this circuit can be written as

Figure 7.7 Equivalent circuit.

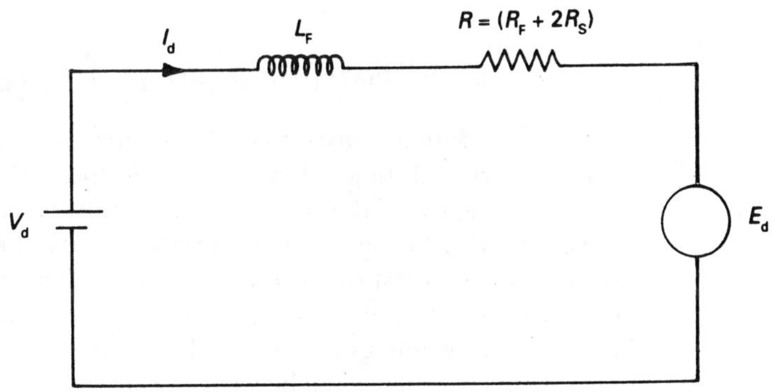

$$V_d = (R + L_F p) I_d + E_d \qquad [7.39]$$

where $R = (R_F + 2R_s)$ and E_d is the mean value of the voltage e_d that appears on the d.c. side of the inverter, which can be expressed in the form

$$E_d = E_{do} \cos\gamma + E_u \qquad [7.40]$$

where E_u represents the voltage drop due to overlap of armature currents and is given by

$$E_u = 3\,\omega_e L_s'' I_d/\pi \qquad [7.41]$$

$$= E_{do}(\cos\overline{\gamma - u} - \cos\gamma)/2 \qquad [7.42]$$

and

$$E_{do} = 3\sqrt{6}\,V_i/\pi \qquad [7.43]$$

Now, the average motor torque can be calculated from the instantaneous torque which is obtained by differentiating the stored magnetic coenergy in the machine

$$W'_{fld} = \frac{1}{2}[i]_t\,[M(\theta)]\,[i]$$

with respect to the mechanical angle of rotation θ,
where $[i]$ is the current matrix and
$[M(\theta)]$ is the inductance matrix.
Eliminating the damper winding currents i_D and i_Q from the expression for the instantaneous torque by using eqn [7.30] and simplifying it, we get the following expression for the average torque:

$$T_{av} = 3\sqrt{2}/2\, I_l\, \psi_g \cos\delta \qquad [7.44]$$

where

$$\psi_g = [(L_{af}\, i_{fr} + K_d\, \psi_{ddo})^2 + (K_q\, \psi_{qdo})^2]^{1/2} \qquad [7.45]$$

and

$$\delta = -\alpha + \gamma + \tan^{-1}[-K_q\,\psi_{qdo}/(L_{af}\, i_{fr} + K_d\,\psi_{ddo})] - u/2 \qquad [7.46]$$

However, *during transient conditions* the flux-linkages of the damper windings vary with time. Hence, the resistances of the damper windings, which were neglected during steady state, must be taken into account.
The total flux-linkages of the *d*-axis and *q*-axis damper windings during transient state consist of those due to the fundamental components of the armature currents as well as the flux-linkages due to the transient currents in the damper windings and the field current. Thus, the total flux-linkages of the damper windings can be written as

$$\psi_{dd} = \psi_{ddo} + L_{md}\, i_{fr} = \psi_{ddo1} + L_{dr}\, i_{dr} + L_{md}\, i_{fr} \qquad [7.47]$$

$$\psi_{qd} = \psi_{qdo1} + L_{qr}\, i_{qr} \qquad [7.48]$$

where L_{md} is the mutual inductance between the field and the *d*-axis damper winding.
The voltage equations of the damper windings are therefore expressed as

$$0 = R_{dr}\, i_{dr} + p\,\psi_{dd} \qquad [7.49]$$

and

$$0 = R_{dr}\, i_{qr} + p\,\psi_{qd} \qquad [7.50]$$

where R_{dr} and R_{qr} are the resistances of the d-axis and q-axis damper windings respectively.
The voltage equation of the field winding is given by

$$V_f = R_{fr} i_{fr} + p \psi_f \quad [7.51]$$

where ψ_f, the total flux-linkage of the field winding, can be written as

$$\psi_f = \frac{L_{af}}{L_{add}} \psi_{ddo} + (L_{md} - L_{af} \frac{L_{af}}{L_{add}}) i_{dr} + L_{fr} i_{fr} \quad [7.52]$$

Usually L_{md} is approximately equal to $L_{af} \cdot L_{dr}/L_{add}$. Hence, the second term in the right-hand side of eqn [7.52] can be ignored. Therefore, the voltage equation of the field winding can be written as

$$V_f \simeq (R_f + l_f p) i_{fr} + \frac{L_{af}}{L_{add}} p \psi_{dd} \quad [7.53]$$

where $l_f = (L_{fr} - \dfrac{L_{af} L_{md}}{L_{add}})$ is termed the field leakage inductance.

Hence

$$\Delta V_f = (R_f + l_f p) \Delta i_{fr} + (\frac{L_{af}}{L_{add}}) p \Delta \psi_{dd}, \quad [7.54]$$

Now, let us derive the equations for determining the transients for a change in the input d.c. voltage V_d and load torque T_L.
From Fig. 7.7, we can write

$$(V_d + \Delta V_d) = (L_F p + R)(I_d + \Delta I_d) + (E_d + \Delta E_d)$$

Since I_d = constant and $V_d = R I_d + E_d$ in the steady-state condition, we get

$$\Delta V_d = (L_F p + R) \Delta I_d + \Delta E_d \quad [7.55]$$

From eqns [7.40] to [7.43], we obtain

$$\Delta E_d = (3/\sqrt{6}/\pi) \cos\gamma \cdot \Delta V_i - E_{do} \sin\gamma \cdot \Delta\gamma + \Delta E_\mu \quad [7.56]$$

where

$$\Delta E_\mu = (3/\pi) L_s'' (I_d \Delta \omega_e + \omega_e \Delta I_d) \quad [7.57]$$

$$= \frac{3\sqrt{6}}{2\pi} [\cos(\gamma - \mu) - \cos\gamma] \Delta V_i$$

$$+ (\frac{E_{do}}{2}) \{[\sin\gamma - \sin(\gamma - \mu)] \Delta\gamma + \sin(\gamma - \mu) \Delta\mu\} \quad [7.58]$$

The equation of motion of the drive system is given by

$$T_{av} = (Jp + B)\,\Omega + T_L \qquad [7.59]$$

where Ω_m denotes the angular speed of rotation in mechanical radians per second.
Hence

$$\Delta\ T_L = \Delta\ T_{av} - (Jp + B)\,\Delta\,\Omega \qquad [7.60]$$

where

$$\Delta\ T_{av} = \frac{3\sqrt{2}}{2}\left[I_1\ \cos\delta\ \Delta\ \psi_g + I_1\psi_g \cdot \Delta(\cos\delta) + \psi_g \cos\delta \cdot \Delta\ I_1\right] \qquad [7.61]$$

Equations [7.54], [7.55] and [7.61] can be used to find the transient response for sudden changes in field voltage, input d.c. voltage and load torque.

8 Switched-reluctance motors

The switched-reluctance motor is a simple and robust machine which is finding applications over a wide power and speed range. It requires only unipolar or unidirectional currents and this enables operating it with only one switching device in series per phase, instead of two in series in each phase leg of an a.c. or brushless d.c. drive. The converter circuits for driving the switched-reluctance motor use fewer semiconductor devices than their a.c. counterparts and they have only one forward voltage drop in series per phase, so that the power losses may, in principle, be lower than in conventional inverters. Other factors being equal, both these factors should allow a reduction in the physical size of the converter and an increase in its reliability. In terms of cost, therefore, the switched-reluctance motor drive system is significantly cheaper than equivalent a.c. motor-based variable-speed drive systems. It is also cheaper than the d.c. motor-based drive systems, a major portion of whose cost goes towards the cost of the d.c. motor.

Switched-reluctance motor drive systems are fully reversible, regenerative and provide very flexible speed/torque characteristics merely through appropriate timing of switching angles, giving full four-quadrant operation with no additional converter components.

The switched-reluctance drive has additional advantages compared with the conventional variable-speed a.c or d.c. drives, including commutatorless d.c. motor drives.

- Shoot-through faults in converter circuits are impossible, since there is always a motor winding in series with each main power switching device.
- There is a greater degree of independence between the phases than is possible in conventional a.c. or d.c. drives. A fault in one phase, whether in the motor or in the converter, generally affects only that phase; the other phases can continue to operate independently. In a.c. drives, a fault in one phase can disable two phases.
- The switched-reluctance motor has zero short-circuit current and zero open-circuit voltage, so that the secondary effects, such as overvoltages or overheating, of faults in either the motor or the converter tend to be mild.
- Last but not the least, they have the much sought- after operational advantages of being 'commutatorless' or 'brushless' designs.

Switched-reluctance motors with power capabilities from 4 kW to 22 kW are now commercially available for variable-speed applications. Substantial improvements in power ratings are expected in future.

8.1 Construction and Basis of Operation

The switched-reluctance motor is simple in construction, consisting of a salient-pole structure, made of laminations, on both the stator and the rotor. Concentrated windings are located on each stator pole and no windings of any kind are on the rotor. The number of stator and rotor poles are different. The motor excitation is often provided to series-connected windings located on diametrically opposite stator poles, termed a-phase. In general, there is no fixed relationship between the number of poles and number of phases. In any case, the basic power-supply requirement remains d.c.

Figure 8.1 shows the elements of a four-phase switched-reluctance motor with only one phase excited. The excitation of windings kept around diametrically opposite stator poles, when the rotor poles are nearby, creates a torque tending to align the stator and rotor poles. When the number of stator and rotor poles differ, the sequential switching of excitation from one set of stator poles to the next, that is from one phase to the next, in synchronism with the rotor position, results in a nearly constant torque. The synchronization of the switching 'on' of excitation with the rotor position can be achieved with simple rotor-position feedback using suitable position transducers. If control is exercised over the rotor positions at which switching is effected and also over the magnitude of the current, considerable flexibility of operating characteristics is available in both motoring and regenerating modes.

Figure 8.1 Elements of a 4-phase switched-reluctance motor.

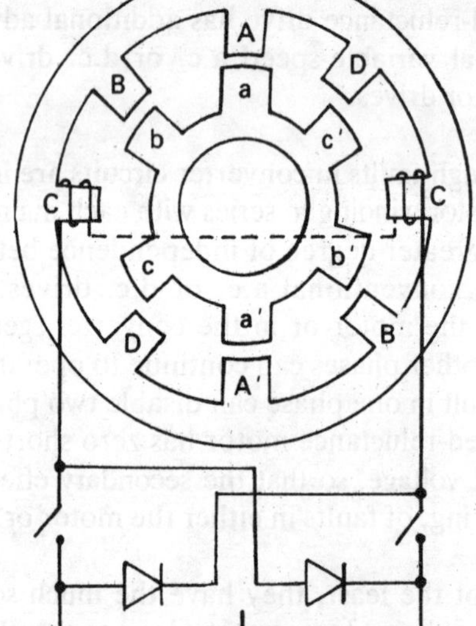

Figure 8.2 shows the basic elements of a switched-reluctance motor drive system.

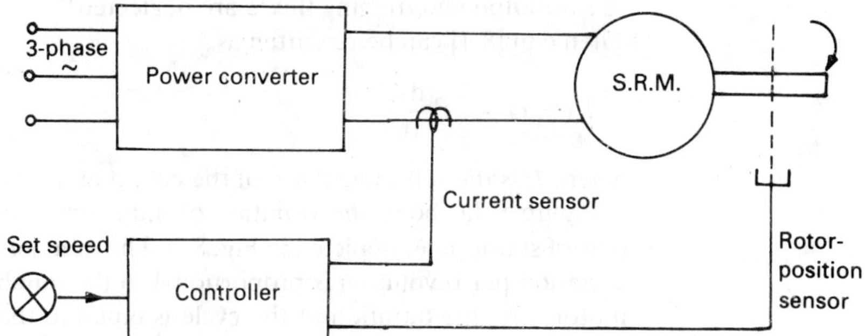

Figure 8.2 Basic elements of a switched-reluctance drive system.

8.2 Principle of Torque Production

In switched-reluctance motors, the torque is developed by the tendency of the rotor to align itself with the pair of stator poles whose windings have been excited so as to maximize the inductance of the excited coils. It may be noted that the torque is independent of the direction of current flow, so that unidirectional currents can be used.

The expression for torque, which takes into account the presence of magnetic nonlinearities, is given as

$$T(\theta, i) = \frac{\partial W'_{\text{fld}}(\theta, i)}{\partial \theta} \tag{8.1}$$

where θ is the angle corresponding to the rotor position as shown in Fig. 8.3

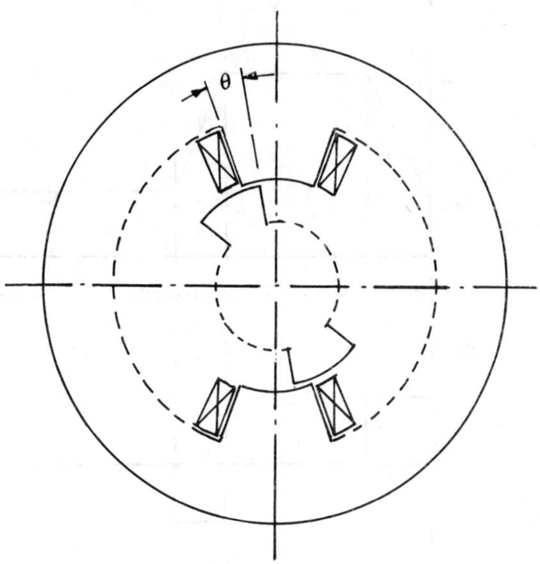

Figure 8.3 Sketch indicating the angle corresponding to the rotor position.

and i is the current in the exciting coil. Although the operation of the switched-reluctance motor depends very much on nonlinear magnetic parameters, it is helpful to consider first a simple model in which the effects of saturation and fringing fluxes are neglected[35].
Then eqn [8.1] can be rewritten as

$$T(\theta, i) = \frac{1}{2} i^2 \frac{dL}{d\theta} \quad [8.2]$$

where L is the self-inductance of the circuit at any value of θ.

Figure 8.4a shows the variation of inductance with rotor position for a pair of stator poles depicted in Fig. 8.3. The number of cycles of inductance variation per revolution is proportional to the number of pole-pairs of the motor, and the duration of the cycle is equal to the rotor pole-pitch. The corresponding variation of torque with rotor position, calculated using eqn [8.2], for constant exciting current is shown in Fig. 8.4b. It can be easily seen that the torque can be controlled to give a resultant which is positive (for motor action) or negative (for generator action) simply by switching the current in the exciting coil on and off at suitable instants during the inductance cycle. In fact, an average motoring torque is produced by timing current pulses in each phase so as to coincide predominantly with the increasing inductance period. If the switching is delayed such that the current pulses coincide predominantly with negative $dL/d\theta$, negative torque is created and regeneration takes place. It may be noted that regeneration is achieved without the aid of any additional circuit elements. A rotor-position transducer, of course, is essential for determining the switching instants for different phases.

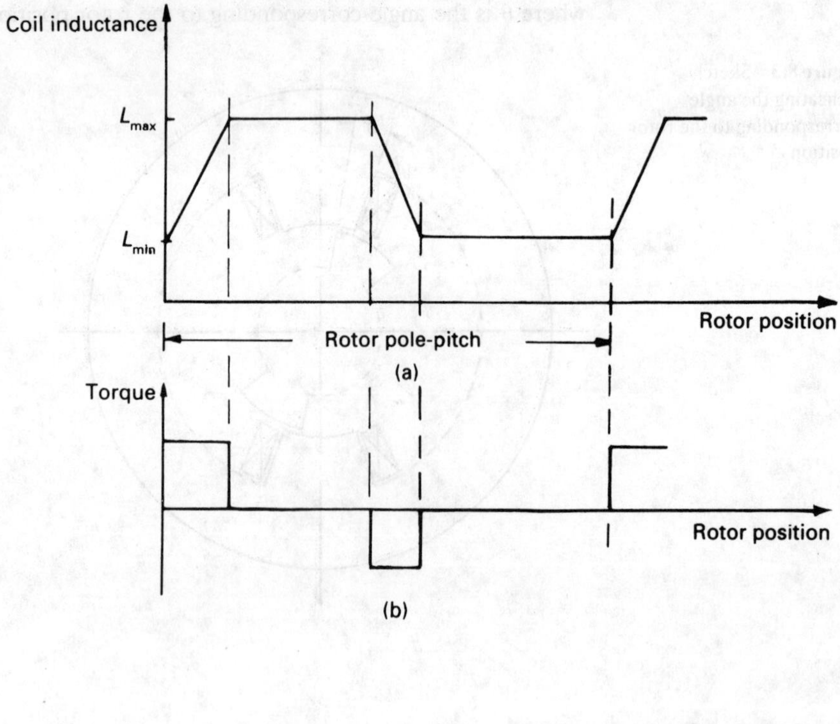

Figure 8.4(a) Variation of inductance with rotor position;
(b) Variation of torque with rotor position for constant exciting current.

8.3 Switching Circuits

Different circuit configurations[36] are available for the converter for a switched-reluctance motor drive, all of them having two essential elements — a controlled switch or switches to connect the direct voltage source to the exciting winding to build up current and an alternative path for the current to take when the switch is turned off. The latter is often provided by a diode or diodes such that the winding experiences a reverse voltage to reduce the current. Figure 8.5 shows the alternatives for one phase of a switched-reluctance motor power converter.

Figure 8.5a shows a circuit that is similar to the conventional six-step

Figure 8.5 Three alternatives for the power converter for the motor.

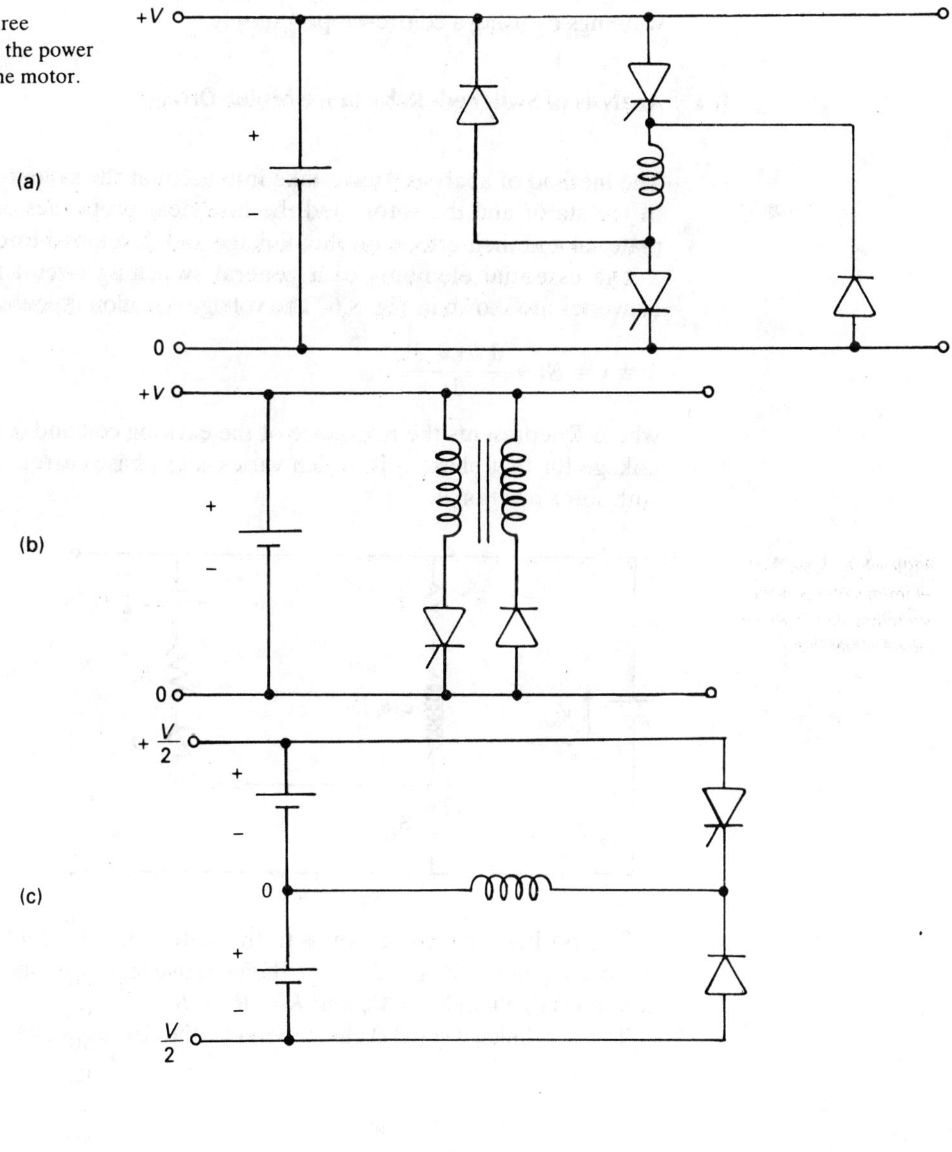

inverter, except that the motor windings are in series with the phase switches. The upper and lower switches (SCRs) turn on and off together and have voltage and current ratings that are practically the same as those of equivalent a.c. inverter drives.

Amongst the circuits that have been proposed to achieve unipolar operation with only one switch per phase, the most simple one shown in Fig. 8.5b uses bifilar motor windings. The bifilar winding is undesirable because the coupling between the primary and secondary windings is always imperfect and this leads to voltage spikes during current turn-off. In addition, the utilization of copper in the motor is less than in a comparable monofilar design and the number of connections between the motor and the converter is doubled.

Figure 8.5c shows a single-switch circuit that avoids the use of bifilar windings by using a centre-tapped supply.

8.4 Analysis of Switched- Reluctance Motor Drives

The method of analysis[37] must take into account the salient-pole geometry of the stator and the rotor, and the nonlinear properties of the magnetic material and their effects on flux-linkage and developed torque.

The essential elements of a general switching circuit for the power converter are shown in Fig. 8.6. The voltage equation describing the circuit is

$$\pm v = Ri + \frac{d\psi(\theta, i)}{dt} \tag{8.3}$$

where R represents the resistance of the exciting coil and $\psi(\theta, i)$ the flux-linkage for that phase coil, which varies with phase current i and cyclically with rotor position θ.

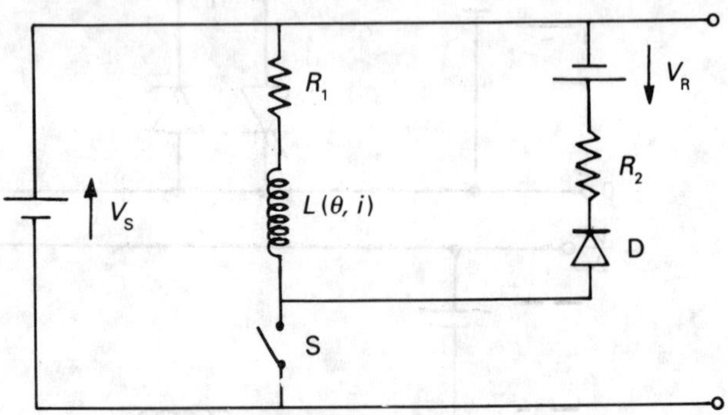

Figure 8.6 Essential elements of a general switching circuit for the power converter.

The positive sign corresponds to the state when the controlling switch S is closed and $v = V_s$ and $R = R_1$; the negative sign corresponds to the state when S is open and $v = V_R$ and $R = R_2 + R_1$.

The flux-linkage $\psi(\theta, i)$ can be found either by measurement or magnetic field analysis. A finite-element solution of the magnetic vector potentials over the motor cross-section would enable us to obtain flux-linkage curves as a function of angle θ and winding current i.

Equation [8.3] can be expressed in the form

$$\frac{d\,\psi(\theta, i)}{dt} = \pm v - Ri \qquad [8.4]$$

The solution of eqn [8.4] to obtain current waveforms and, then, torque, requires the representation of the magnetic behaviour of the motor in the form of a table $i\,(\theta, \psi)$ to enable the value of i to be updated after each step of numerical integration of the equations (after each integration step, to find a new value of ψ, it is necessary to find the corresponding value of current, which is substituted in the right-hand side of eqn [8.4]). The table $i\,(\theta, \psi)$, with a sufficient number of equally spaced angles and flux-linkages to ensure sufficiently accurate interpolation, is obtained by inverting the table of values of $\psi\,(\theta, i)$.

The flux-linkage curves of $\psi\,(\theta, i)\,|_{\theta\,=\,\text{const.}}$ can be represented with adequate accuracy and considerable economy of storage by using unequally spaced values of current. A quadratic interpolation method has been found to be very effective in determining intermediate values of ψ(Fig. 8.7). However, the curves $\psi\,(\theta, i)\,|_{i=\text{const.}}$ are not monotonic (being cyclic) so that the quadratic interpolation cannot be simply used. Equally spaced angles have to be used in constructing the table of input data $\psi\,(\theta, i)$.

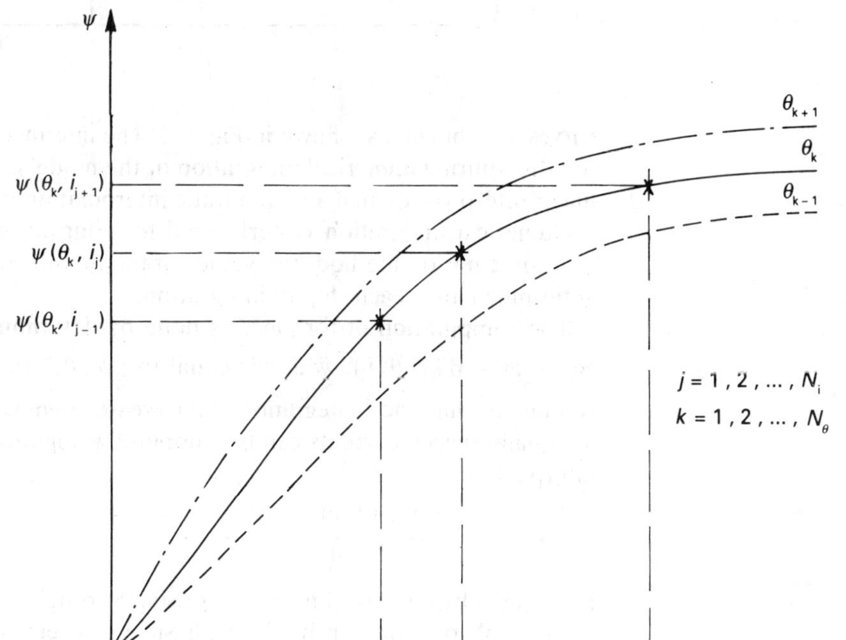

Figure 8.7 Flux-linkage current curves for different values of θ.

The values of $i\ (\psi)$ with constant θ, at equally spaced ψ are determined by using quadratic interpolation through three successive points (Fig. 8.8), because it has been found that zone B of the parabola fits very well with the curves $i\ (\psi)\,|_{\theta\,=\,\text{const.}}$ for relatively large intervals between the currents $i_{(j-1)}$ i_j and $i_{(j+1)}$. Using this method, the table $i\ (\theta, \psi)$ and the corresponding

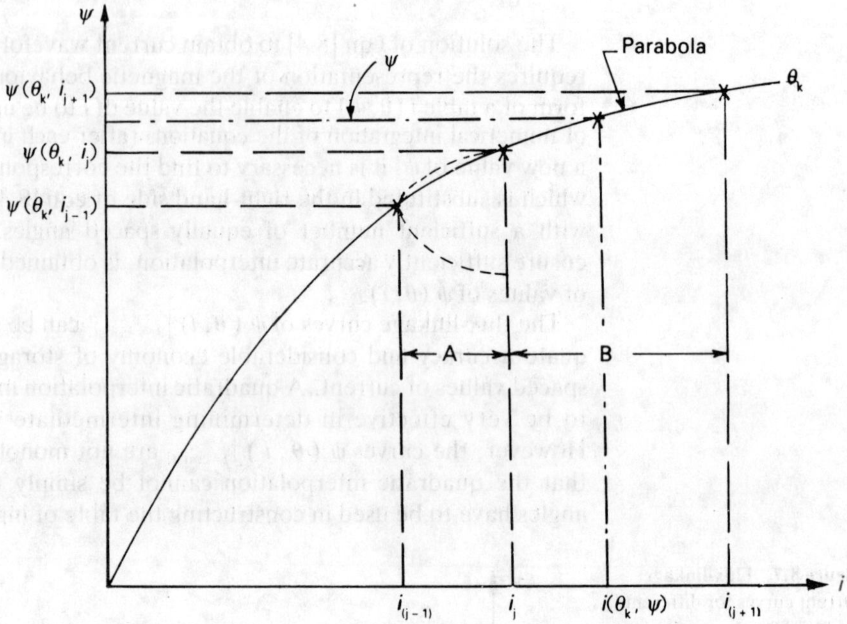

Figure 8.8 Quadratic interpolation to determine the plot of current versus flux-linkage at constant θ.

curves are obtained as shown in Fig. 8.9. The intermediate values of $i\ (\theta, \psi)$ required during numerical integration of the model equations are found by linear interpolation in θ and quadratic interpolation in ψ.

Numerical integration is performed by using the Runge-Kutta fourth-order intégration method, the values of the flux-linkage and current being determined after each step of integration.

The computation of torque T is done by determining first the table of coenergies $W'_{\text{fld}}\ (\theta, i)$, which is equal to $\int_0^i \psi\ (\theta, i)\ \text{d}i\ |_{\theta\,=\,\text{const.}}$ This again is found by numerical integration. An increased number of values of $\psi\ (\theta, i)$ at equally spaced currents can be computed using the method of quadratic interpolation.

$$T\,(\theta, i) = \frac{\partial W'_{\text{fld}}\ (\theta, i)\ |_{i\,=\,\text{const.}}}{\partial \theta}$$

is obtained by numerical techniques using Stirling's formula.

The table of $T\ (\theta,\ i)$ is used for transient problems, with the intermediate values of $T\ (\theta,\ i)$ being found by linear interpolation in θ and quadratic interpolation in i. The steady-state average torque per complete cycle of inductance is computed from the closed area in the $\psi - i$ plane described during a complete cycle.

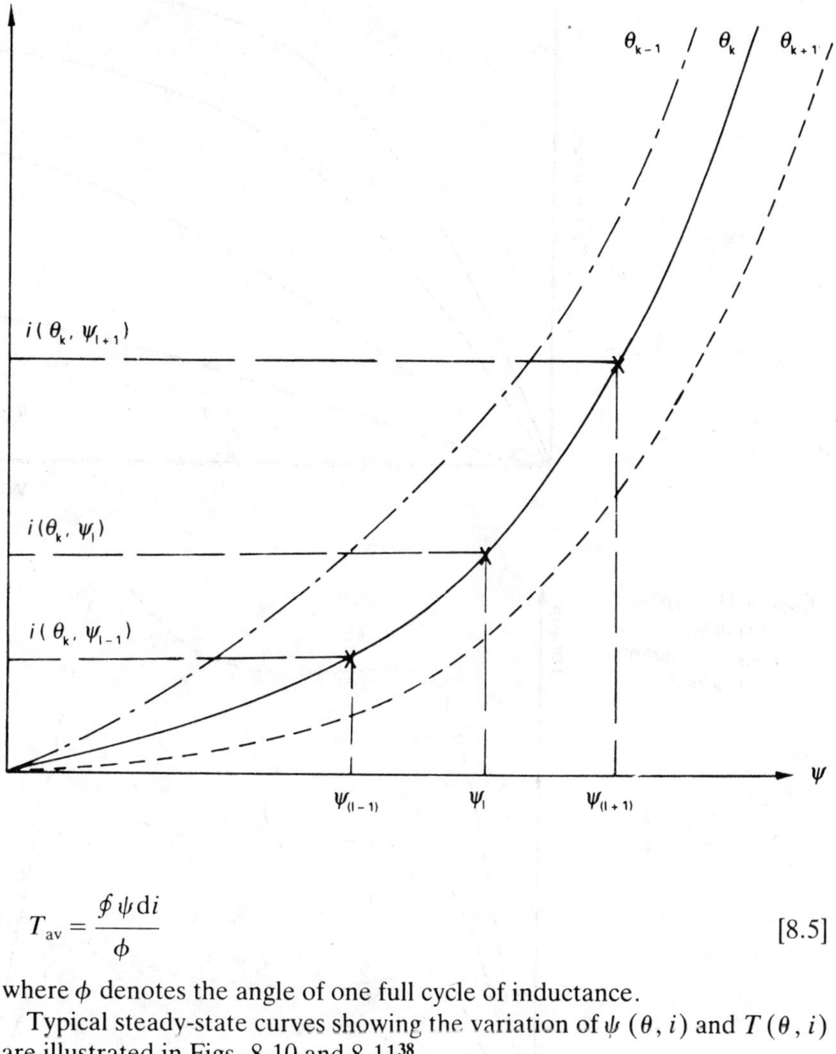

Figure 8.9 Current versus flux-linkage for different values of θ.

$$T_{av} = \frac{\oint \psi \mathrm{d}i}{\phi} \tag{8.5}$$

where ϕ denotes the angle of one full cycle of inductance.

Typical steady-state curves showing the variation of $\psi(\theta, i)$ and $T(\theta, i)$ are illustrated in Figs. 8.10 and 8.11[38].

In order to determine the performance curves under any transient condition, the digital solution of eqn [8.4] must be obtained taking into account the mechanical motion of the motion represented by the equations

$$\frac{\mathrm{d}\theta}{\mathrm{d}t} = \Omega \tag{8.6}$$

and

$$\frac{\mathrm{d}\Omega}{\mathrm{d}t} = \frac{1}{J}[T(\theta, i) - T_L] \tag{8.7}$$

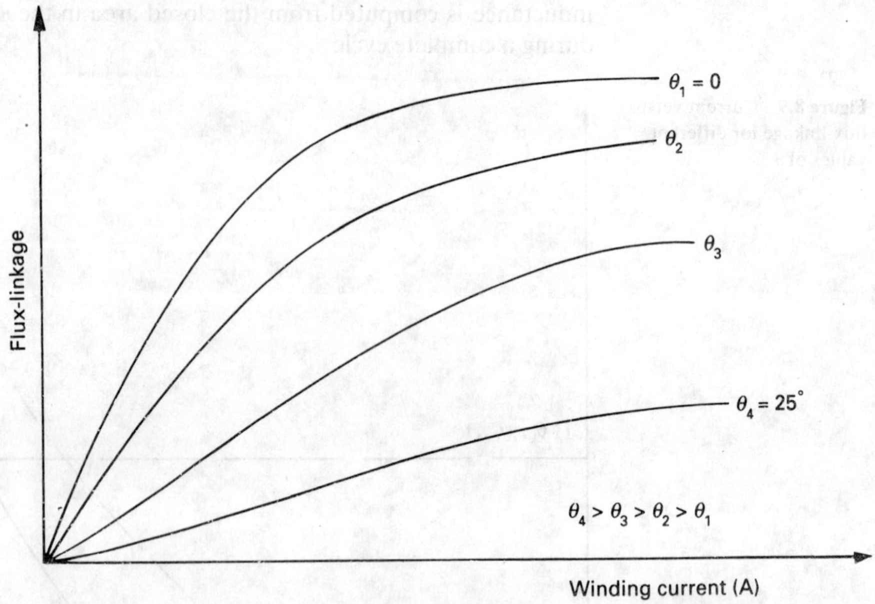

Figure 8.10 Typical variation of flux-linkage with current for various values of θ.

Figure 8.11 Typical variation of torque with rotor angle for different values of current.

References

1. Kusko, A. *Solid State d.c. Motor Drives*, M.I.T. Press, Massachusetts, 1969.
2. Fransua, A. and Magureanu, R. *Electrical Machines and Drive Systems*, Technical Press, Oxford, 1984.
3. Mehta, P. and Mukhopadhyay, S. Modes of operation of converter-controlled d.c. drives, *Proc. IEE*, **121**, (3), 179–184, March 1974.
4. Anjaneyulu, P.B., Bhat, P.S., Prabhu, S.S., Dubey, G.K. and Ghosh, R. Calculation of filter inductance for converter-controlled d.c. separately-excited motor, *Jou. of Institution of Engineers* (*India*), **65**, Pt. EL4, 105–111, February 1985.
5. Revankar, G.N. and Sabnis, D.S. Analysis of dual-converter system, *IEEE Trans. on Indl. Elect. and Contr. Instr.*, **IECI-22**, 55–61, February 1975.
6. Robinson, C.E. Redesign of d.c. motors for applications with thyristor power supplies, *IEEE Trans. on Indl. Appl.*, **IA-4**, 508–514, September/October 1968.
7. Barton, T.H. The Transfer characteristics of a chopper drive, *IEEE Trans. Indl.and Appl.*, **IA-16**, (4), 489–494, July/August 1980.
8. Dubey, G.K. and Shepherd, W. Analysis of d.c. series motor controlled by power pulses, *Proc. IEE*, **122**, 1397–98, December 1975.
9. Franklin, P.W. Theory of the d.c. motor controlled by power pulses, Pt. I — Motor operation, *IEEE Trans. on Pow. Appr. and Systems*, **PAS-91**, 249–255, January 1972.
10. Dubey, G.K. and Shepherd, W. Transient analysis of d.c. motor controlled by power pulses, *Proc. IEE*, **124**, 229–30, January 1977.
11. Dubey, G.K. and Shepherd, W. Transient analysis of d.c. separately-excited motor fed by a chopper with current-limit control, *Jou. of Institution of Engineers* (*India*), **58**, Pt. EL2, 108–112, October 1977.
12. Dubey, G.K. and Shepherd, W. Transient analysis of chopper-fed d.c. series motor, *IEEE Trans. on Indl. Elect. and Contr. Instr.*, **IECI-28**, (2), 146–159, May 1981.
13. Paice, D.A. Induction motor speed control by stator voltage control, *IEEE Trans. on Pow. Appr. and Systems*, **PAS-87**, 585–590, February 1968.
14. Ramamoorthy, M. and Samek, M.F. Steady-state analysis of phase-controlled induction motor with isolated neutral, *IEEE Trans. on Indl. Elect. and Contr. Instr.*, **IECI-23**, (2), 178–184, May 1976.
15. Nath, G. and Berg, G.J. Transient analysis of three-phase SCR-controlled induction motors, *IEEE Trans. on Indl. Appl.*, **IA-17**, (2), 133–142, March/April 1981.

16. Murphy, J.M.D. *Thyristor Control of A.C. Motors*, Pergamon Press, Oxford, 1973.
17. Bose, B.K. Adjustable speed A.C. Drives — A Technology status review, *Proc. IEEE*, 70 (2) 116–135, February 1982.
18. Sloninn, M.A. and Biringer, P.P. Harmonics of cycloconverter voltage wave-form, *IEEE Trans. on Indl. Elect. and Contr. Instr.*, **IECI-27**, (2), 53–56, May 1980.
19. Jones, C.V. *The Unified Theory of Electrical Machines*, Butterworth, London, 1967.
20. Jordan, H.E. Analysis of induction machines in dynamic systems, *IEEE Trans. on Pow. Appr. and systems*, **PAS-84**, (11), 1085–1088, November. 1965.
21. Kovacs, K.P. and Racz, I. *Transient Behaviour of A.C. Machines* (Original in Hungarian), Russian translation: *Perehodyne Processy V Mascsinakh Peremenovo Toka*, Gosenergoizdat, Moscow, 1963.
22. Kovacs, P.K. *Transient Phenomena in Electrical Machines*, Akademiai Kiado, Budapest, 1984.
23. Vas, P. *Vector control of A.C. machines*, Clarendon Press, Oxford, 1990.
24. Blaschke, F. The principle of field-orientation as applied to the new TRANSVEKTOR closed-loop control system for rotating field machines, *Siemens Review*, **39**, (5), 217–220, 1972.
25. Gabriel, R., Leonhard, W. and Nordby, C.J. Field-oriented control of a standard A.C. motor using microprocessor, *IEEE Trans. on Indl. Appl.*, **IA-16**, (2), 186–192, March/April 1980.
26. Sen, P.C. and Ma, K.H.J. Rotor chopper-control for induction motor drive: TRC strategy, *IEEE Trans. on Indl. Appl.*, **IA-11**, (1), 43–49, January/February 1975.
27. Joshi, S.D., Pillai, S.K. and Dubey, G.K. Performance and analysis of induction motor drive using throughpass inverters for slip power recovery, *Jou. of Institution of Engineers (India)*, **63**, Pt. EL5, 220–226, April 1983.
28. Mittle, V.N., Venkatesan, K. and Gupta, S.C. Transients in static slip energy recovery drive, *Jou. of Institution of Engineers (India)*, **59**, Pt. EL3, 134–141, December 1978.
29. Venkatesan, K. Steady-state and stability analysis of a modified Kramer drive, *Jou. of Institution of Engineers (India)*, **59**, Pt. EL4, 234–238, February 1979.
30. Bose, B.K. *Adjustable speed A.C. Drive systems*, IEEE Press, New York, 1981.
31. Slemon, G.R., Dewan, S.B. and Wilson, J.W.A. Synchronous motor drive with current-source inverter, *IEEE Trans. on Indl. Appl.*, **IA-10**, (3), 412–416, May/June 1974.
32. Kaufman, G.A. and Plunkett, A.B. Steady-state performance of voltage-source inverter/synchronous machine drive systems, *IEEE Trans. on Indl. Appl.*, **IA-20**, (4), 753–762, July/August 1984.
33. Colby, R.S., Lipo, T.A. and Novotny, D.W. A state space analysis of LCI-fed synchronous motor drives in the steady state, *IEEE Trans. on Indl. Appl.*, **IA-21**, (4), 1016/1022, July/August 1985.

34. Kataoka, T. and Nishikata, S. Transient performance analysis of self-controlled synchronous motor, *IEEE Trans. on Indl. Appl.*, **IA-17**, (2), 152–159, March/April 1981.
35. Lawrenson, P.J., Stephenson, J.M., Blenkinsop, P.T., Corda, J. and Fulton, N.N. Variable-speed switched-reluctance motors, *Proc. IEE*, **127**, Pt. B, (4), 253–265, July 1980.
36. Ehsani, M., Bass, J.T., Miller, T.J.E. and Steigerwald, R.L. Development of a unipolar converter for variable reluctance motor drives, *IEEE Trans. on Indl. Appl.*, **IA-23**, (3), 545–553, May/June 1987.
37. Stephenson, J.M. and Corda, J. Computation of torque and current in doubly salient reluctance motors from nonlinear magnetization data, *Proc. IEEE*, **126**, (5), 393–396, May 1979.
38. Dawson, G.E., Eastham, A.R. and Mizia, J. Switched-reluctance motor torque characteristics: Finite element analysis and test results, *IEEE Trans. on Indl. Appl.*, **IA-23**, (3), 532–537, May/June 1987.

Index